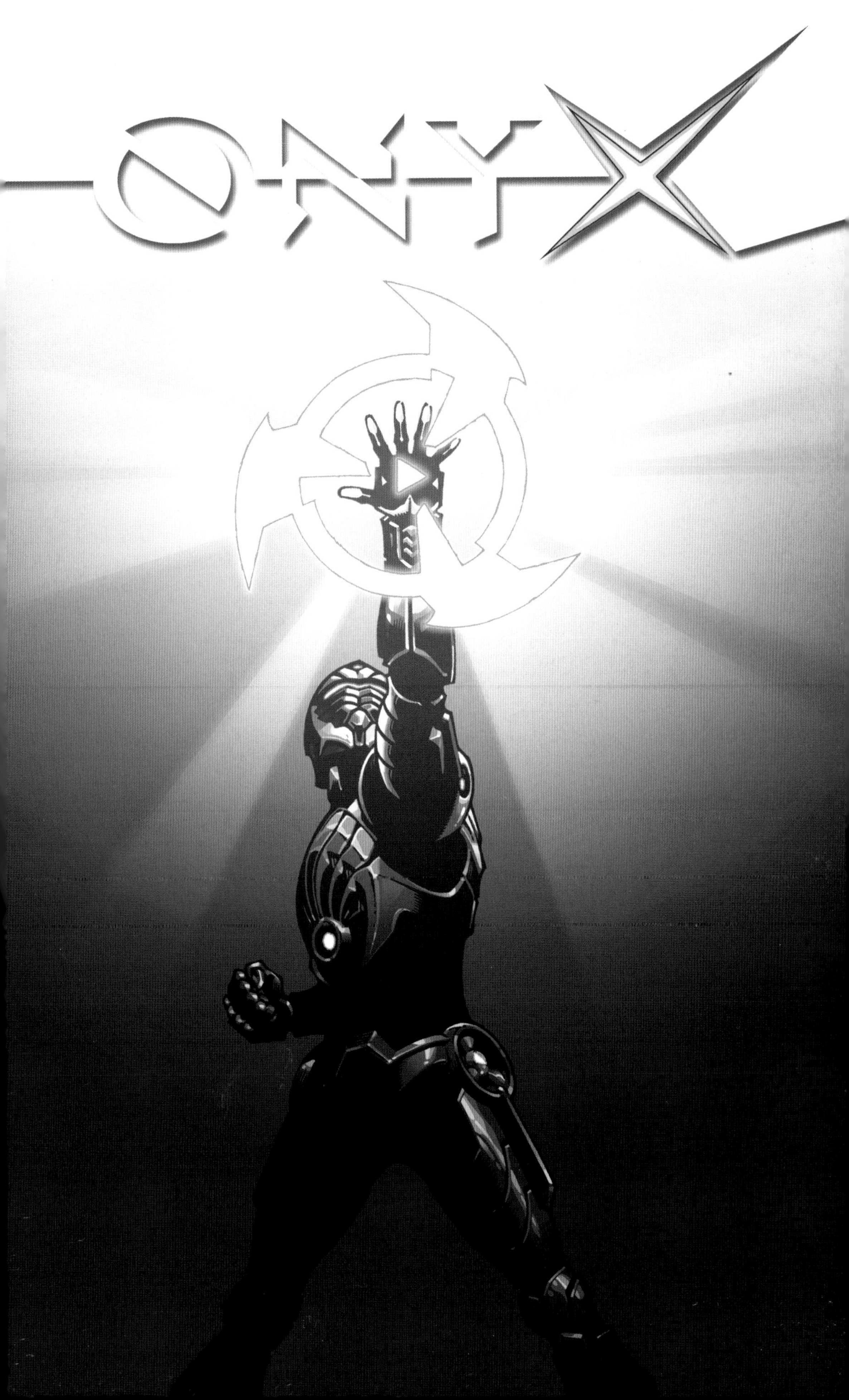
ONYX

978-1-63140-516-7   19 18 17 16   1 2 3 4
For international rights, contact licensing@idwpublishing.com

ONYX. JANUARY 2016. FIRST PRINTING. Onyx © 2016 Chris Ryall, Gabriel Rodriguez, and
Idea and Design Works, LLC. All Rights Reserved. The IDW logo is registered in the U.S.
Patent and Trademark Office. IDW Publishing, a division of Idea and Design Works, LLC.
Editorial offices: 2765 Truxtun Road, San Diego, CA 92106. Any similarities to persons
living or dead are purely coincidental. With the exception of artwork used for review
purposes, none of the contents of this publication may be reprinted without the
permission of Idea and Design Works, LLC. Printed in Korea.
IDW Publishing does not read or accept unsolicited submissions of ideas, stories, or artwork.
Originally published as ONYX issues #1–4.

Become our fan on Facebook facebook.com/idwpublishing
Follow us on Twitter @idwpublishing
Subscribe to us on YouTube youtube.com/idwpublishing
See what's new on Tumblr tumblr.idwpublishing.com
Check us out on Instagram instagram.com/idwpublishing

IDW®
www.idwpublishing.com

ONYX

Storytellers/Creators
CHRIS RYALL &
GABRIEL RODRIGUEZ

Colors
JAY FOTOS

Letters
SHAWN LEE

Cover and Chapter Breaks Art by
GABRIEL RODRIGUEZ

Collection Edits by
JUSTIN EISINGER &
ALONZO SIMON

Collection Design by
CLAUDIA CHONG

Dedicated To
BILL MANTLO & SAL BUSCEMA

ABIGAIL AQUINO

PSI OPS DIVISION
NATIONALITY: FILIPINO
SEX: FEMALE
EYES: BROWN
HAIR: BROWN
AGE: 28

ALIAS: LONER

CICI -

MARINE CORPS
NATIONALITY: AUSTRALIAN
SEX: FEMALE
EYES: GREEN
HAIR: RED
AGE: 27

ALIAS: BOOST

GALINA VOLKOV

AIR FORCE DIVISION
NATIONALITY: RUSSIAN
SEX: FEMALE
EYES: BLUE
HAIR: BLOND
AGE: 30

ALIAS: MAPS

GEN. HAROLD MOUNT

CLASSIFIED OPS DIVISION,
PERSONAL INFO CLASSIFIED

CAST OF CHARACTERS

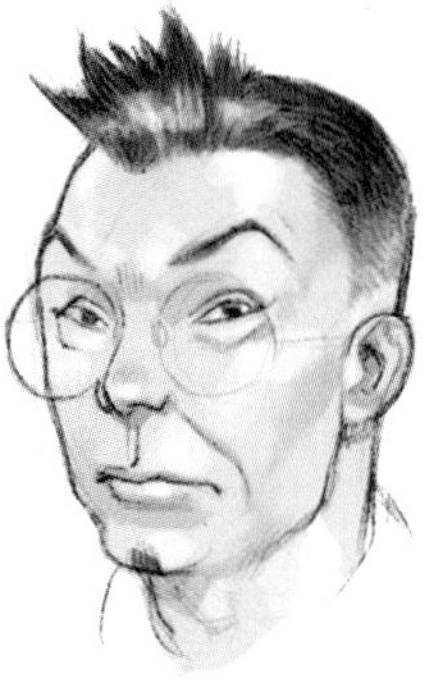

JAMES OSHIRO

STRATEGIC SCIENCE DIVISION
NATIONALITY: JAPANESE
SEX: MALE
EYES: BROWN
HAIR: BLACK
AGE: 34

ALIAS: CASTLE

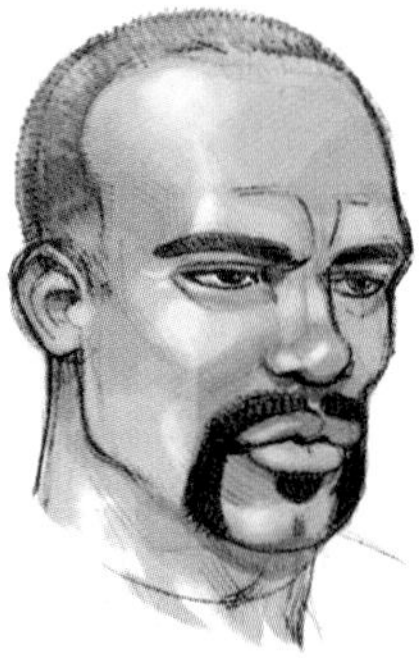

KELVIN SAMPSON

MARINE CORPS,
PERSONAL INFO CLASSIFIED

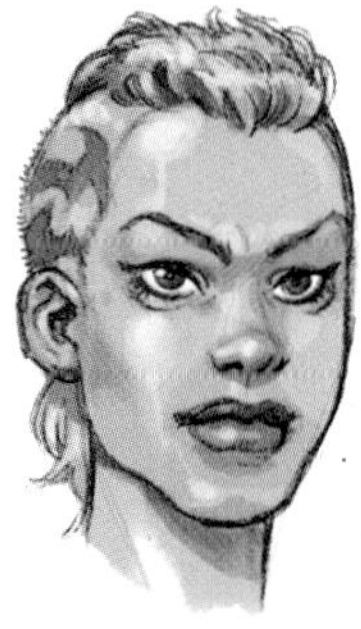

TALLA RUDOLPH

STRATEGIC SCIENCE DIVISION
NATIONALITY: USA
SEX: FEMALE
EYES: PURPLE
HAIR: PURPLE
AGE: 38

ALIAS: COSMO

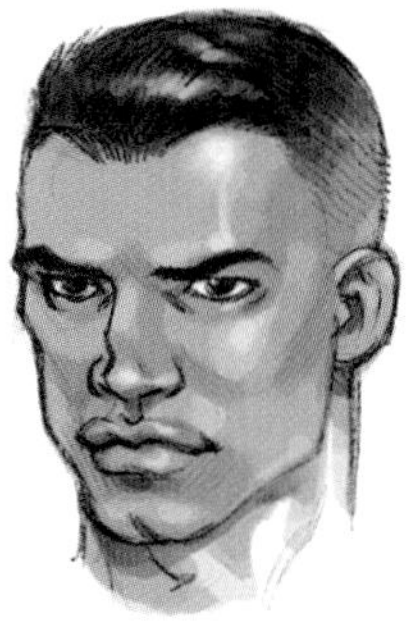

CAPT. YASIEL ARBONA

MARINE CORPS
NATIONALITY: CUBAN
SEX: MALE
EYES: BROWN
HAIR: BROWN
AGE: 38

ALIAS: CAP

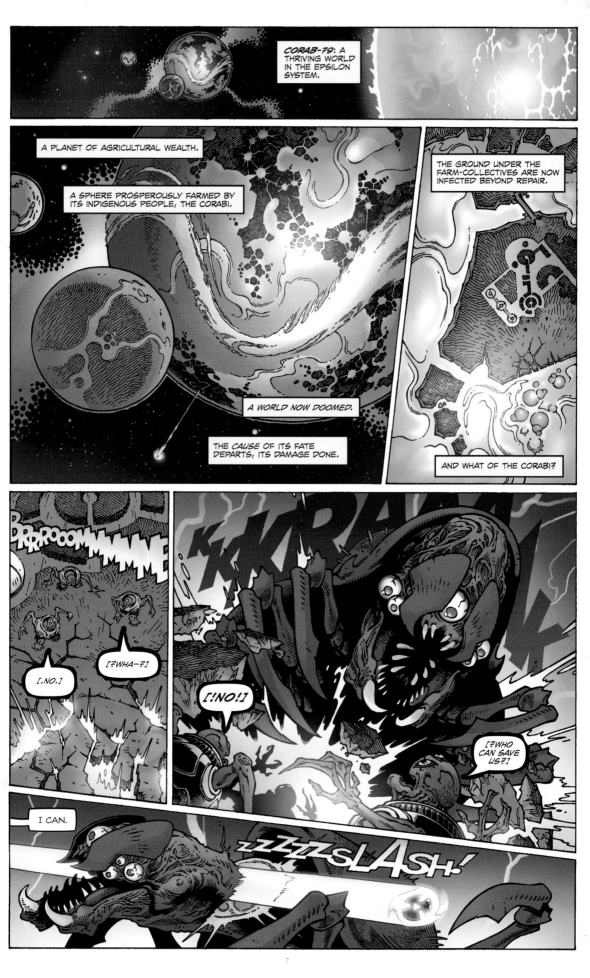

CORAB-79: A THRIVING WORLD IN THE EPSILON SYSTEM.

A PLANET OF AGRICULTURAL WEALTH.

A SPHERE PROSPEROUSLY FARMED BY ITS INDIGENOUS PEOPLE, THE CORABI.

A WORLD NOW DOOMED.

THE CAUSE OF ITS FATE DEPARTS, ITS DAMAGE DONE.

THE GROUND UNDER THE FARM-COLLECTIVES ARE NOW INFECTED BEYOND REPAIR.

AND WHAT OF THE CORABI?

BRRROOOMMMME

KKKRAAA

[.NO.]

[?WHA-?]

[!NO!]

[?WHO CAN SAVE US?]

I CAN.

ZZZSLASH!

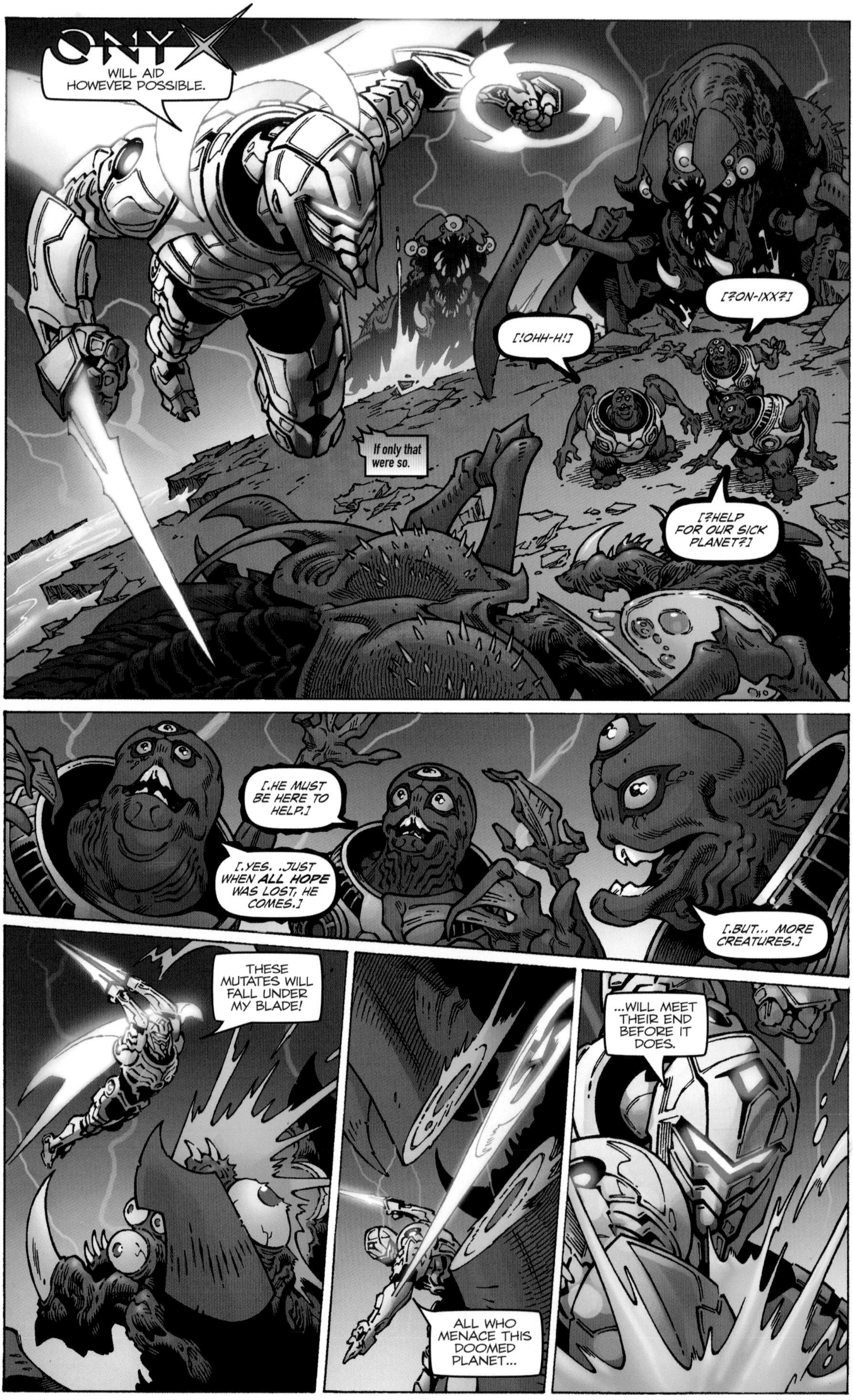
ONYX
WILL AID HOWEVER POSSIBLE.
If only that were so.
[!OHH-H!]
[?ON-IXX?]
[?HELP FOR OUR SICK PLANET?]
[.HE MUST BE HERE TO HELP.]
[.YES. .JUST WHEN ALL HOPE WAS LOST, HE COMES.]
[.BUT... MORE CREATURES.]
THESE MUTATES WILL FALL UNDER MY BLADE!
ALL WHO MENACE THIS DOOMED PLANET...
...WILL MEET THEIR END BEFORE IT DOES.

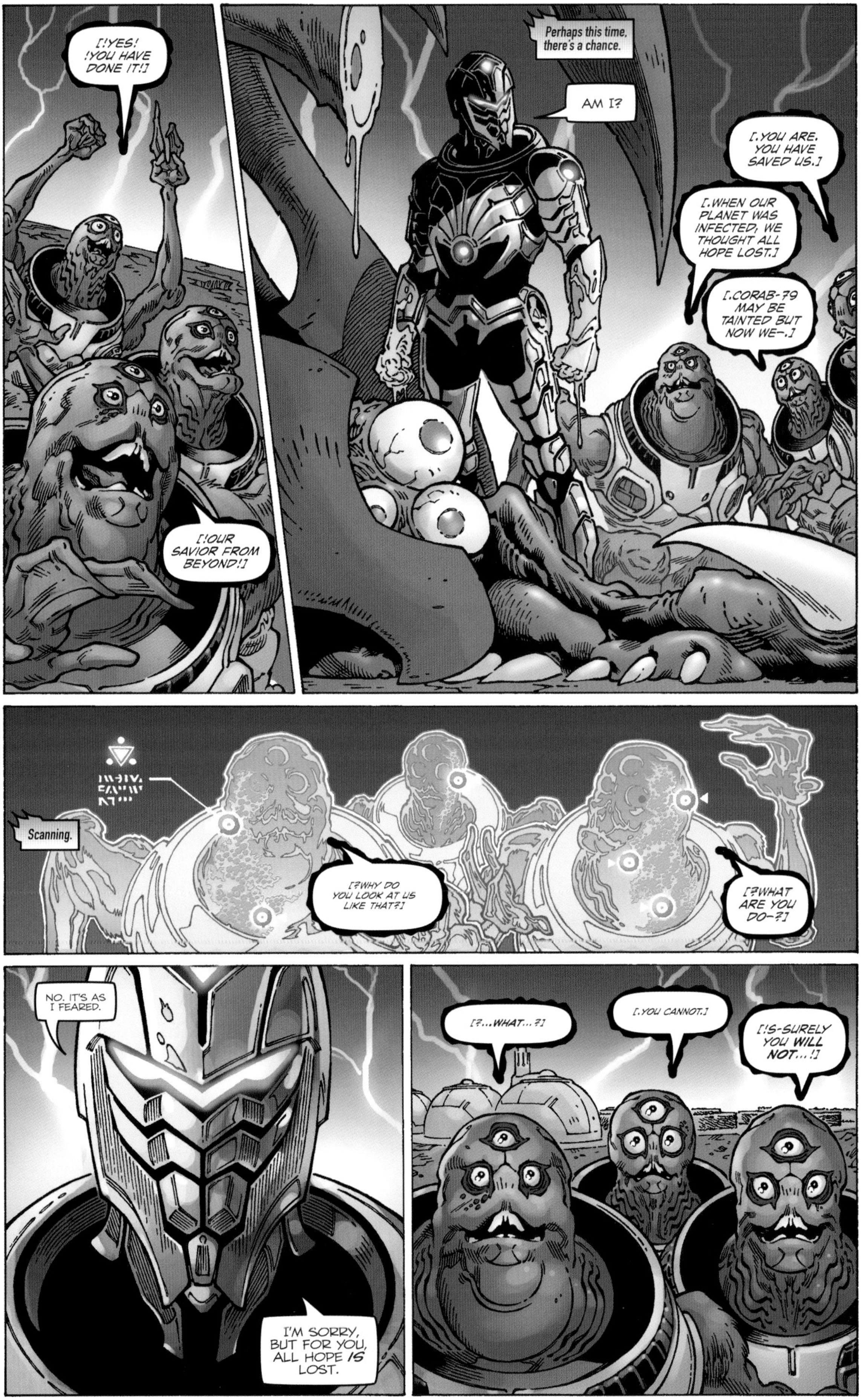
[!YES! !YOU HAVE DONE IT!]
[!OUR SAVIOR FROM BEYOND!]
Perhaps this time, there's a chance.
AM I?
[.YOU ARE. YOU HAVE SAVED US.]
[.WHEN OUR PLANET WAS INFECTED, WE THOUGHT ALL HOPE LOST.]
[.CORAB-79 MAY BE TAINTED BUT NOW WE--.]
Scanning.
[?WHY DO YOU LOOK AT US LIKE THAT?]
[?WHAT ARE YOU DO-?]
NO. IT'S AS I FEARED.
I'M SORRY, BUT FOR YOU, ALL HOPE *IS* LOST.
[?...WHAT...?]
[.YOU CANNOT.]
[!S-SURELY YOU **WILL NOT**...!]

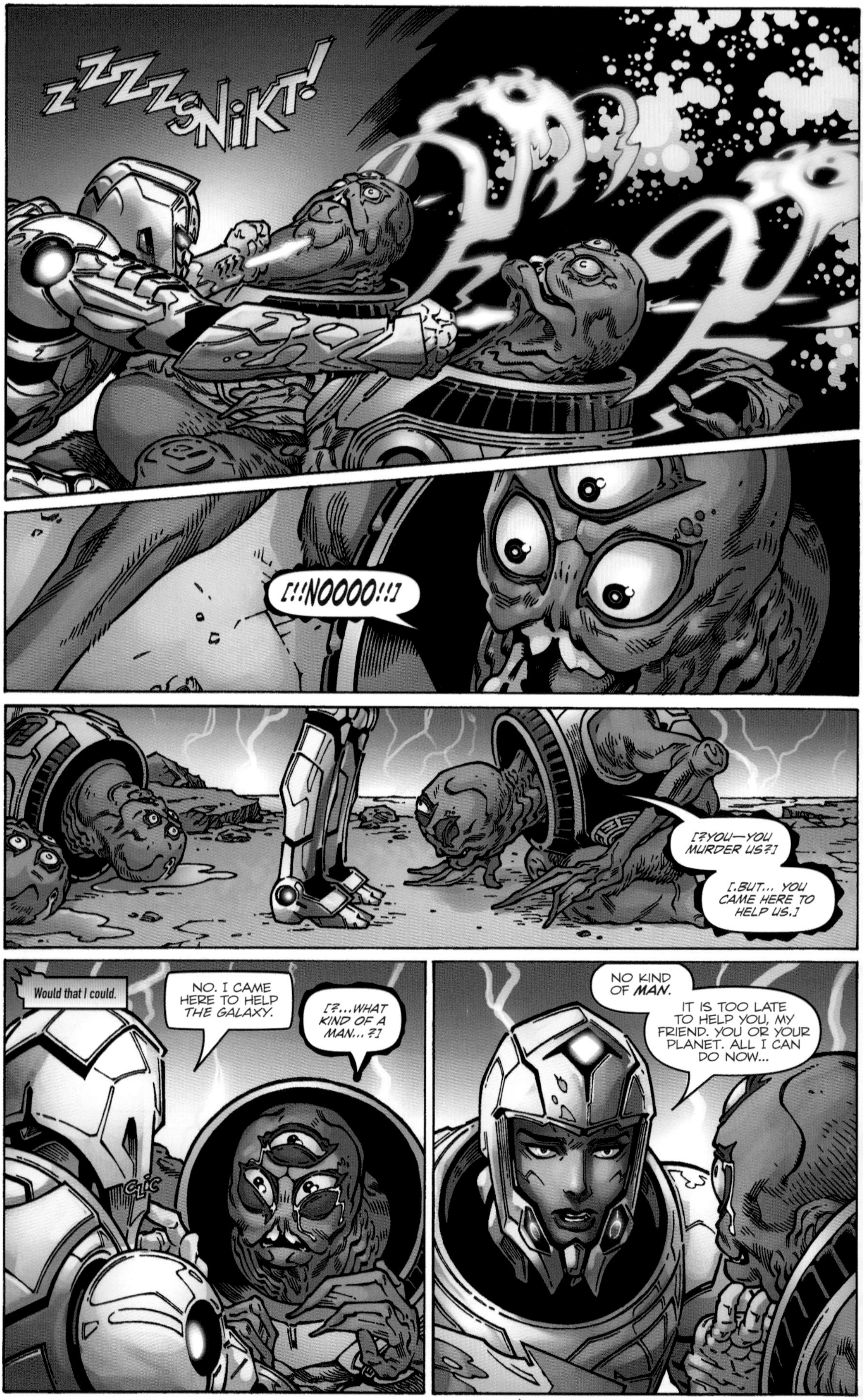
ZZZZZSNIKT!
[!!NOOOO!!]
[?YOU—YOU MURDER US?]
[.BUT... YOU CAME HERE TO HELP US.]
Would that I could.
NO. I CAME HERE TO HELP THE GALAXY.
[?...WHAT KIND OF A MAN...?]
CLIC
NO KIND OF MAN.
IT IS TOO LATE TO HELP YOU, MY FRIEND. YOU OR YOUR PLANET. ALL I CAN DO NOW...

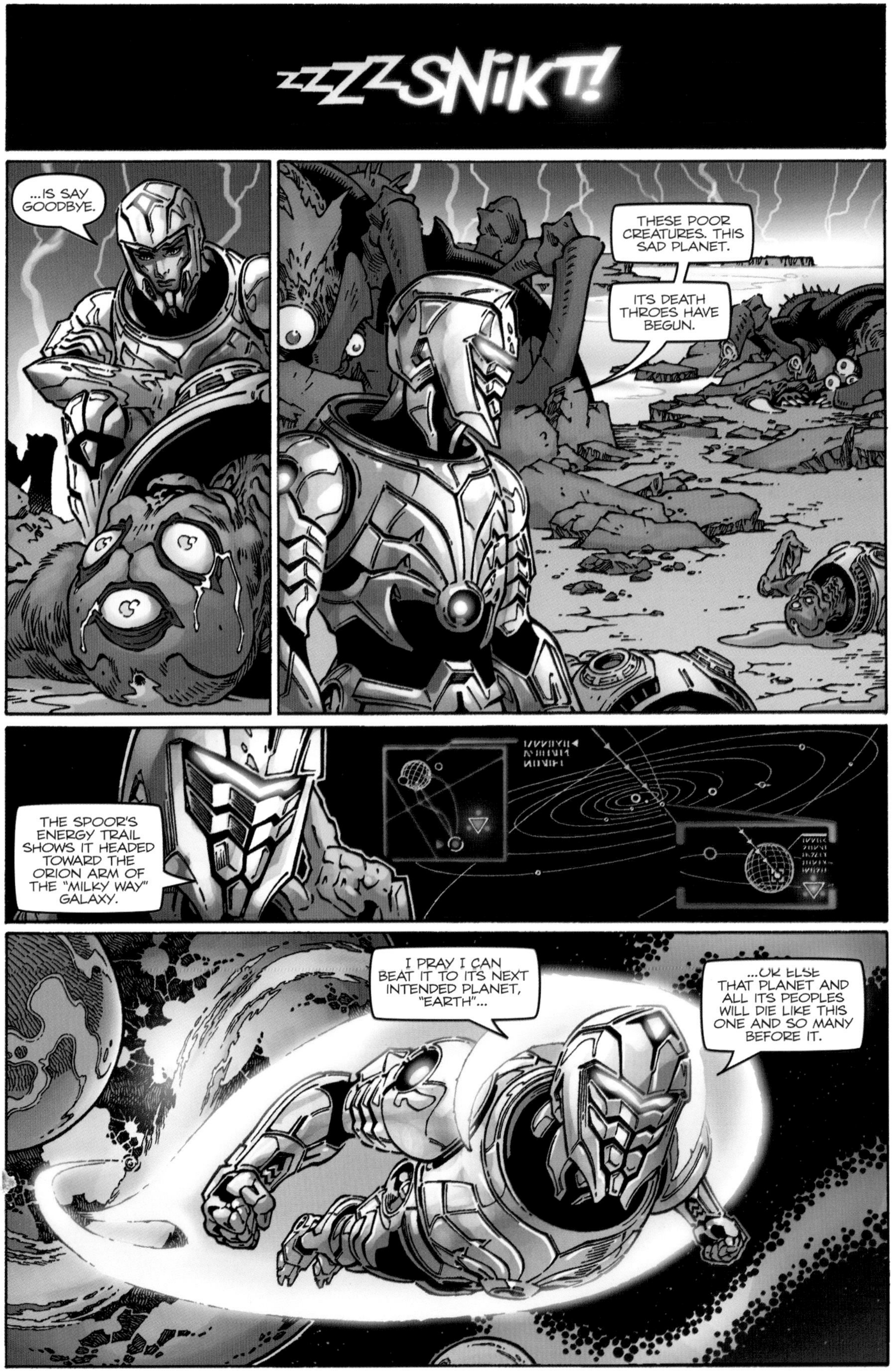
ZZZZSNIKT!
...IS SAY GOODBYE.
THESE POOR CREATURES. THIS SAD PLANET.
ITS DEATH THROES HAVE BEGUN.
THE SPOOR'S ENERGY TRAIL SHOWS IT HEADED TOWARD THE ORION ARM OF THE "MILKY WAY" GALAXY.
I PRAY I CAN BEAT IT TO ITS NEXT INTENDED PLANET, "EARTH"...
...OR ELSE THAT PLANET AND ALL ITS PEOPLES WILL DIE LIKE THIS ONE AND SO MANY BEFORE IT.

1

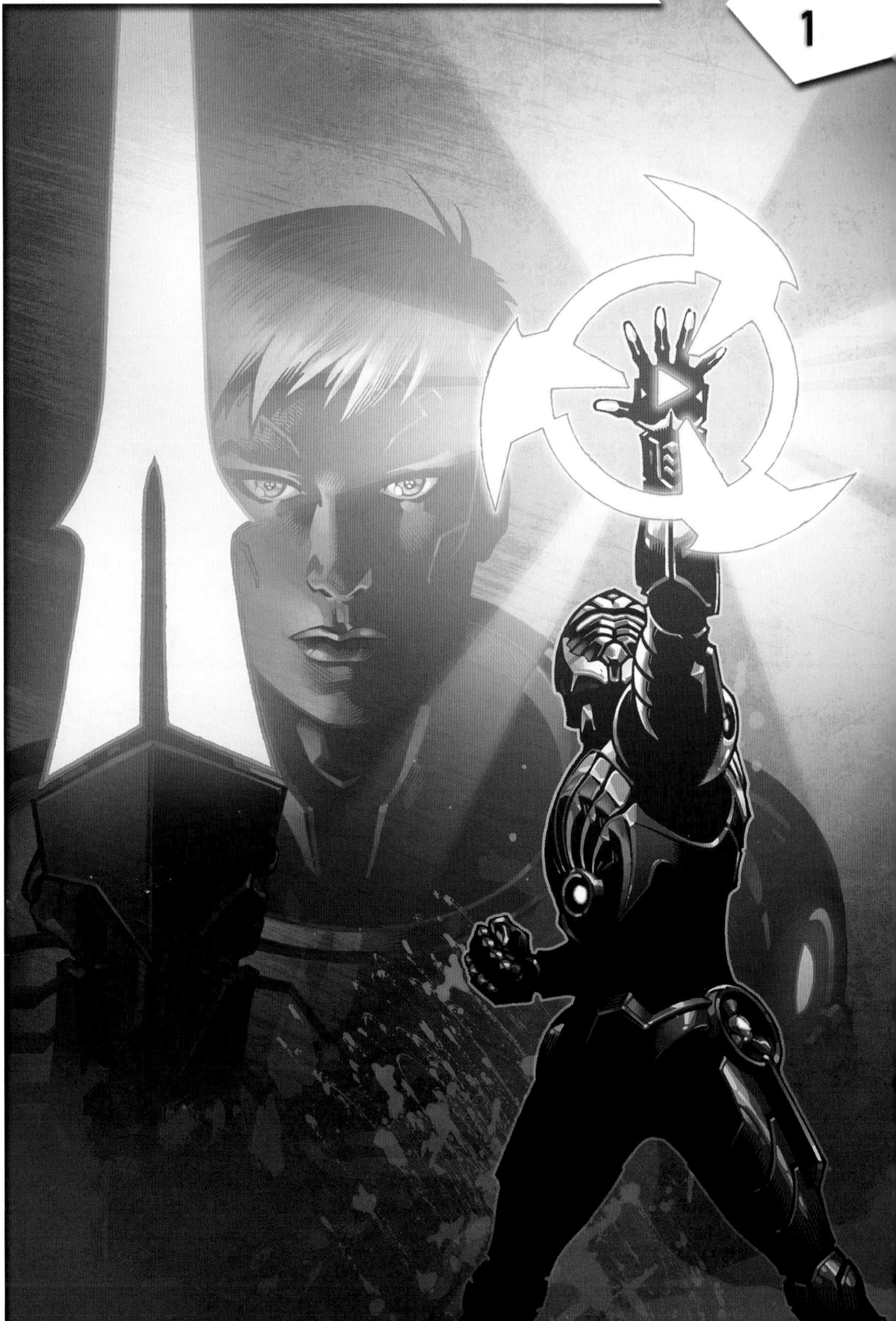

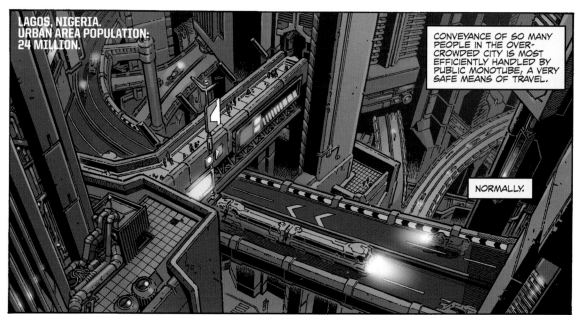

LAGOS, NIGERIA.
URBAN AREA POPULATION:
24 MILLION.

CONVEYANCE OF SO MANY PEOPLE IN THE OVER-CROWDED CITY IS MOST EFFICIENTLY HANDLED BY PUBLIC MONOTUBE, A VERY SAFE MEANS OF TRAVEL.

NORMALLY.

MOM? WHAT IS *THAT*—

HOLY SH—

"THE CITY CENTER METRO-TUBE WAS IMPACTED AT 15:34, SIR."

"THE METEOR THEN KEPT MOVING. ONLY—THIS IS VERY ODD—IT THEN MOVED... *UPWARD.*"

WHAT, DID IT *BOUNCE?* BECAUSE OTHERWISE, IMMUTABLE LAWS OF PHYSICS SAY THAT'S IMPOSSIBLE.

NO ARGUMENT HERE. BUT IT HAPPENED.

IT DID GREAT DAMAGE ON ITS DESCENT, YES. 183 LIVES LOST.

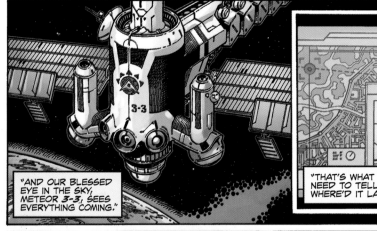

BUT THINGS GOT WORSE AS IT MOVED ON.

"MOST WORRISOME, SOMEHOW THE *EYE* NEVER SAW IT COMING."

"AND OUR BLESSED EYE IN THE SKY, METEOR *3-3,* SEES EVERYTHING COMING."

THE ROCK BLEW RIGHT BY IT, UNNOTICED.

IT TRACKS EVERY ERRANT SPACE ROCK... BUT NOT THIS ONE. *WHY?*

"THAT'S WHAT YOU ALL NEED TO TELL ME. WHERE'D IT LAND?"

I ASSUME IT *DID* EVENTUALLY LAND?

SIR...! A SECOND BOGIE— SMALLER—JUST IMPACTED NEAR THE FIRST.

CLEAR OF THE CITY, IN THE JUNGLE.

WELL, THAT IS NOT AT ALL GOOD.

"OUR... *CONCERNS*... IN THAT AREA NEED TO BE PROTECTED.

"I WANT PROBES IN THE AIR, AND SCRAMBLE TEAMS *ZAIN* AND *AVIN.* NOW!"

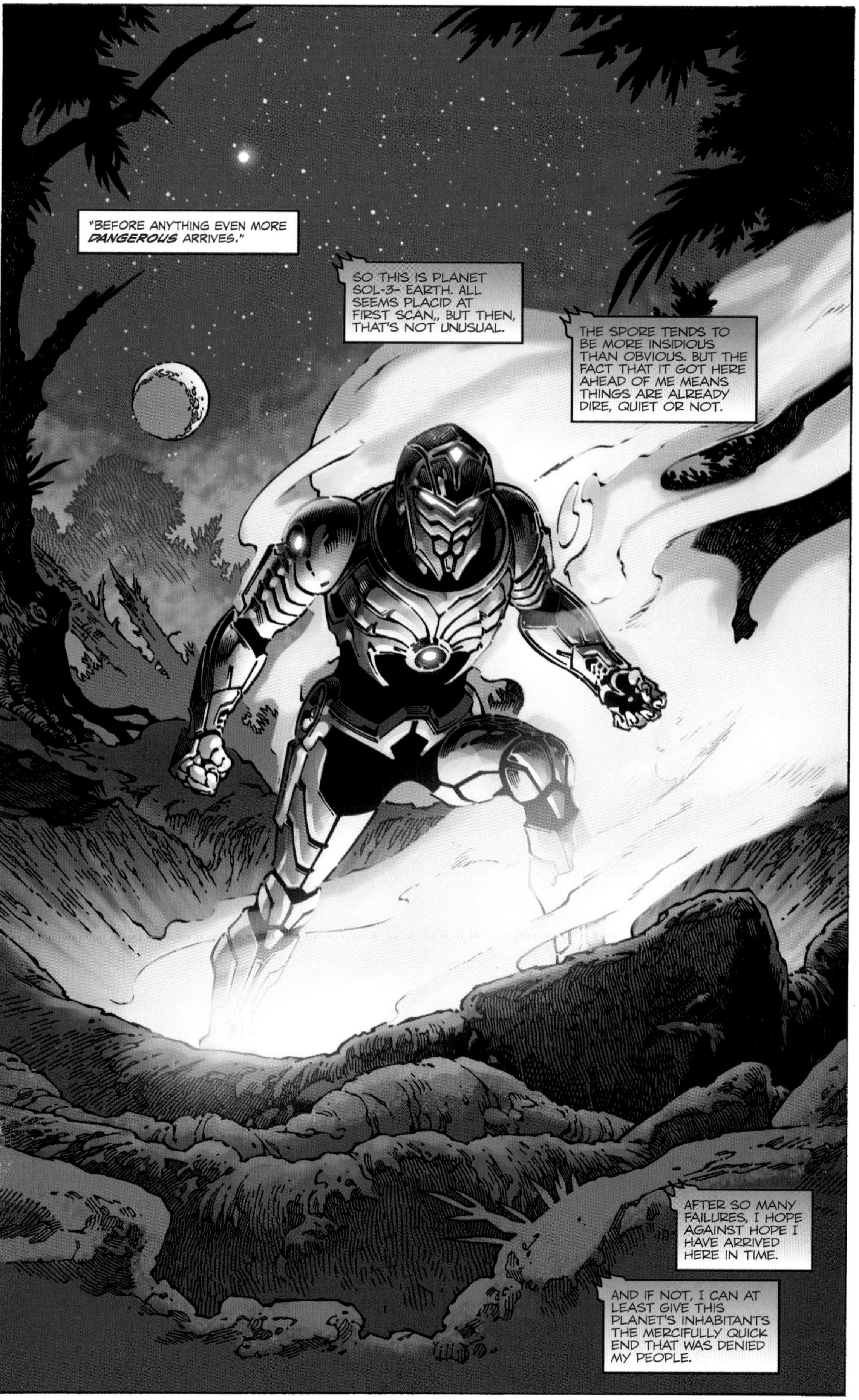
"BEFORE ANYTHING EVEN MORE *DANGEROUS* ARRIVES."
SO THIS IS PLANET SOL-3- EARTH. ALL SEEMS PLACID AT FIRST SCAN,, BUT THEN, THAT'S NOT UNUSUAL.
THE SPORE TENDS TO BE MORE INSIDIOUS THAN OBVIOUS. BUT THE FACT THAT IT GOT HERE AHEAD OF ME MEANS THINGS ARE ALREADY DIRE, QUIET OR NOT.
AFTER SO MANY FAILURES, I HOPE AGAINST HOPE I HAVE ARRIVED HERE IN TIME.
AND IF NOT, I CAN AT LEAST GIVE THIS PLANET'S INHABITANTS THE MERCIFULLY QUICK END THAT WAS DENIED MY PEOPLE.

THE INTERNATIONAL GLOBAL DEFENSE ARMY TEAM AVIN. TEAM ZAIN HASN'T BEEN HEARD FROM IN 12 HOURS.

ANY WORD ON ZAIN YET?

NEGATIVE, SIR. ALL COMM REMAINS DEAD.

PERHAPS A BETTER WORD CHOICE NEXT TIME, MY FRIEND.

SILENCE DOESN'T MEAN ANYTHING.

I REALLY HOPE IT DOESN'T MEAN ANYTHING.

GEN. HAROLD MOUNT
CLASSIFIED OPS DIVISION

KELVIN SAMPSON
MARINE CORPS DIVISION

GALINA "MAPS" VOLKOV
AIR FORCE; NAVIGATOR

TALIA "COSMO" RUDOLPH
STRATEGIC SCIENCE DIVISION; ASTROPHYSICIST

LONER'S REALLY LIVIN' UP TO HER NAME AGAIN.

OH, LEAVE HER BE. NERVES, MOST LIKELY.

PERHAPS SHE, LIKE ME, IS RELISHING THE THOUGHT OF EXPLORING ACTUAL NATURE.

YASIEL "CAP" ARBONA
MARINE CORPS DIVISION

CICI "BOOST"
MARINE CORPS DIVISION

JAMES "CASTLE" OSHIRO
STRATEGIC SCIENCE DIVISION; BIOLOGIST

LABORATORY MUST BE PROTECTED

I'M NO WARRIOR LIKE THESE OTHERS

NEVER SHOT ANYONE

SO ANTISOCIAL

LIVING FLORA

CONCERNS MUST BE PROTECT

DID I TURN OFF THE STOVE?

BEEN HOURS SINCE TEAM ZAIN

SHOULD' CALLED HIM

WEAPONS AREN'T FOR SHOW

ALWAYS KEEPS TO HERSELF

NOT HARDLY, JAMES.

KEEP IT TOGETHER, ABIGAIL. HOLD IT TOGETHER.

WISH I GOT TO PICK THE TEAM

NOT PART OF THE TEAM

NOT SURE WHO SHE THINKS SHE IS

WHO NEEDS HER

ABIGAIL "LONER" AQUINO
PSI OPS DIVISION

16

TELL ME AGAIN ABOUT THAT METEOR, COSMO...

...YOU OR YOUR TEAM EVER SEEN ITS LIKE BEFORE?

NEVER. INANIMATE ROCKS JUST *CAN'T* MOVE LIKE THAT.

COME ON, STARGAZER. A BAD OL' SPACE ROCK SLIPPED THROUGH AND SMASHED THINGS UP, YES.

BUT IT WAS NOTHING MORE THAN THAT.

YOUR SILENCE MEAN YOU READIN' MY THOUGHTS RIGHT NOW, LONER? BEST NOT.

SHOCK YOUR PURE LITTLE HEART ALL KINDS'A WAYS, TRUST ME ON THAT.

DON'T FLATTER YOURSELF, WITCH.

IF I HAD MY WAY, I'D NEVER READ ONE OF YOUR EMPTY THOUGHTS.

THIS LOUSY TECH HEADBAND USED TO BLOCK IT ALL OUT. BUT STATIC FINDS A WAY.

STUCK-UP PSI-FREAK

KNOWS HOW I FEEL

COAL INTO DIAMONDS

SCREW HER

WHY'D WE GET STUCK

HUNGRY

TURN OFF THE STOVE?

ALL THOSE PEOPLE

KINDA HOT, THOUGH

SO MUCH NOISE...

WHAT

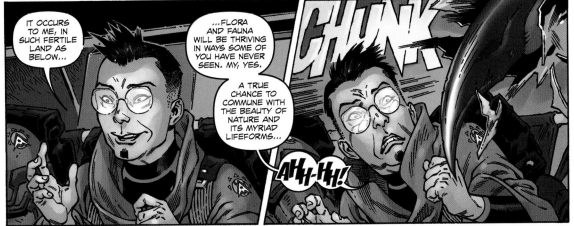

IT OCCURS TO ME, IN SUCH FERTILE LAND AS BELOW...

...FLORA AND FAUNA WILL BE THRIVING IN WAYS SOME OF YOU HAVE NEVER SEEN. MY, YES.

A TRUE CHANCE TO COMMUNE WITH THE BEAUTY OF NATURE AND ITS MYRIAD LIFEFORMS...

CHUNK

AHH-H!

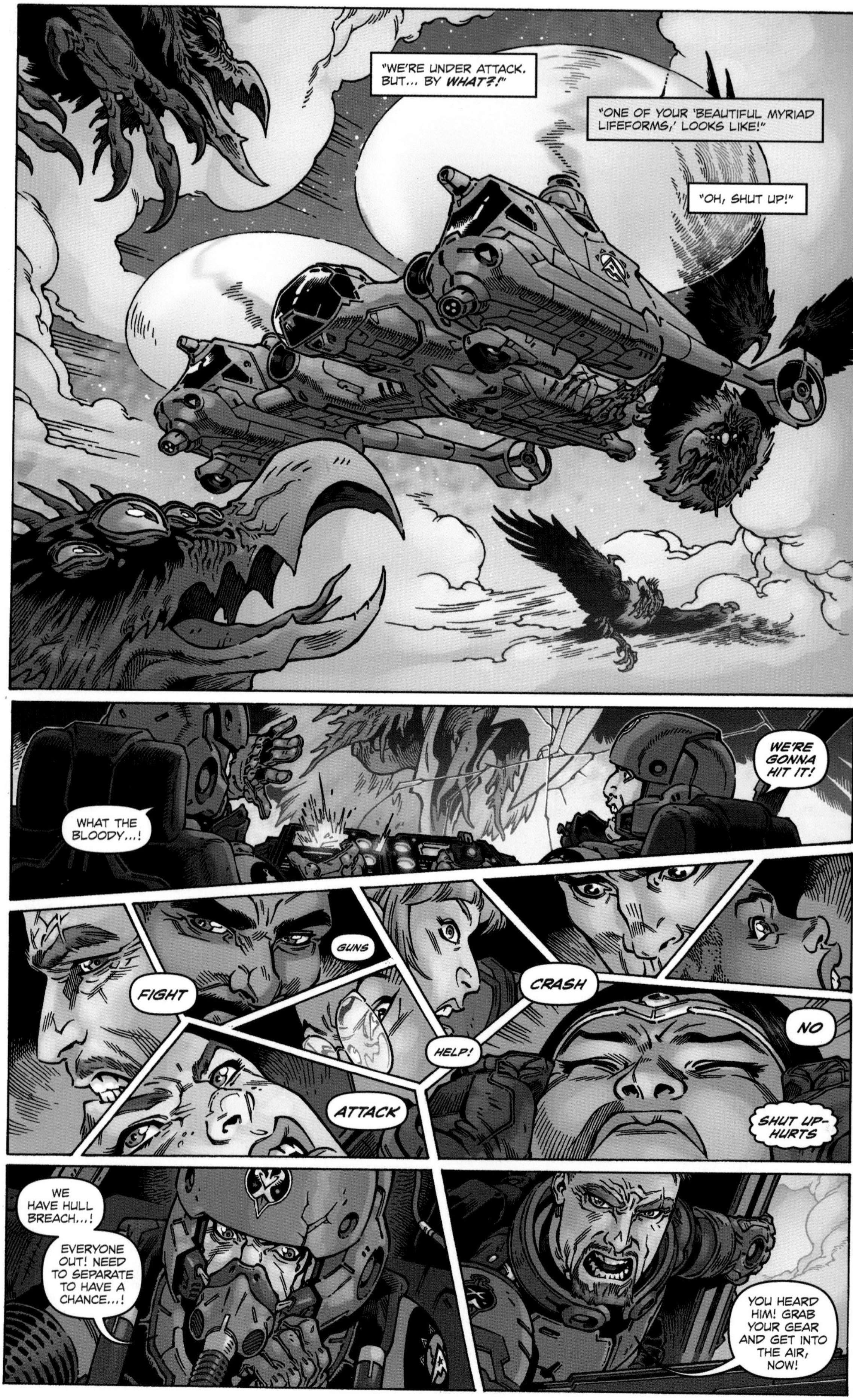
"WE'RE UNDER ATTACK. BUT... BY WHAT?!"
"ONE OF YOUR 'BEAUTIFUL MYRIAD LIFEFORMS,' LOOKS LIKE!"
"OH, SHUT UP!"
WHAT THE BLOODY...!
WE'RE GONNA HIT IT!
FIGHT
GUNS
CRASH
HELP!
ATTACK
NO
SHUT UP-HURTS
WE HAVE HULL BREACH...!
EVERYONE OUT! NEED TO SEPARATE TO HAVE A CHANCE...!
YOU HEARD HIM! GRAB YOUR GEAR AND GET INTO THE AIR, NOW!

NO GUNS UP HERE!

DON'T GO ANTI-GRAV YET, DROP BELOW THE CREATURES!

THEY ARE EVERYWHERE!

ABIGAIL! YOU'RE FALLING AWAY; FIRE YOUR BOOSTERS *NOW*...!

CLIC, CLIC-CLIC

WOULD IF I COULD.

C'MON, DAMN YOU, SPARK! COME ON!

...CAN'T...

JUST NO GOOD...

CLIC, CLIC. CLI-

P-FFFFFF

ZZZFT

AT LEAST IT'LL BE *QUIET* ON THE WAY DOWN...

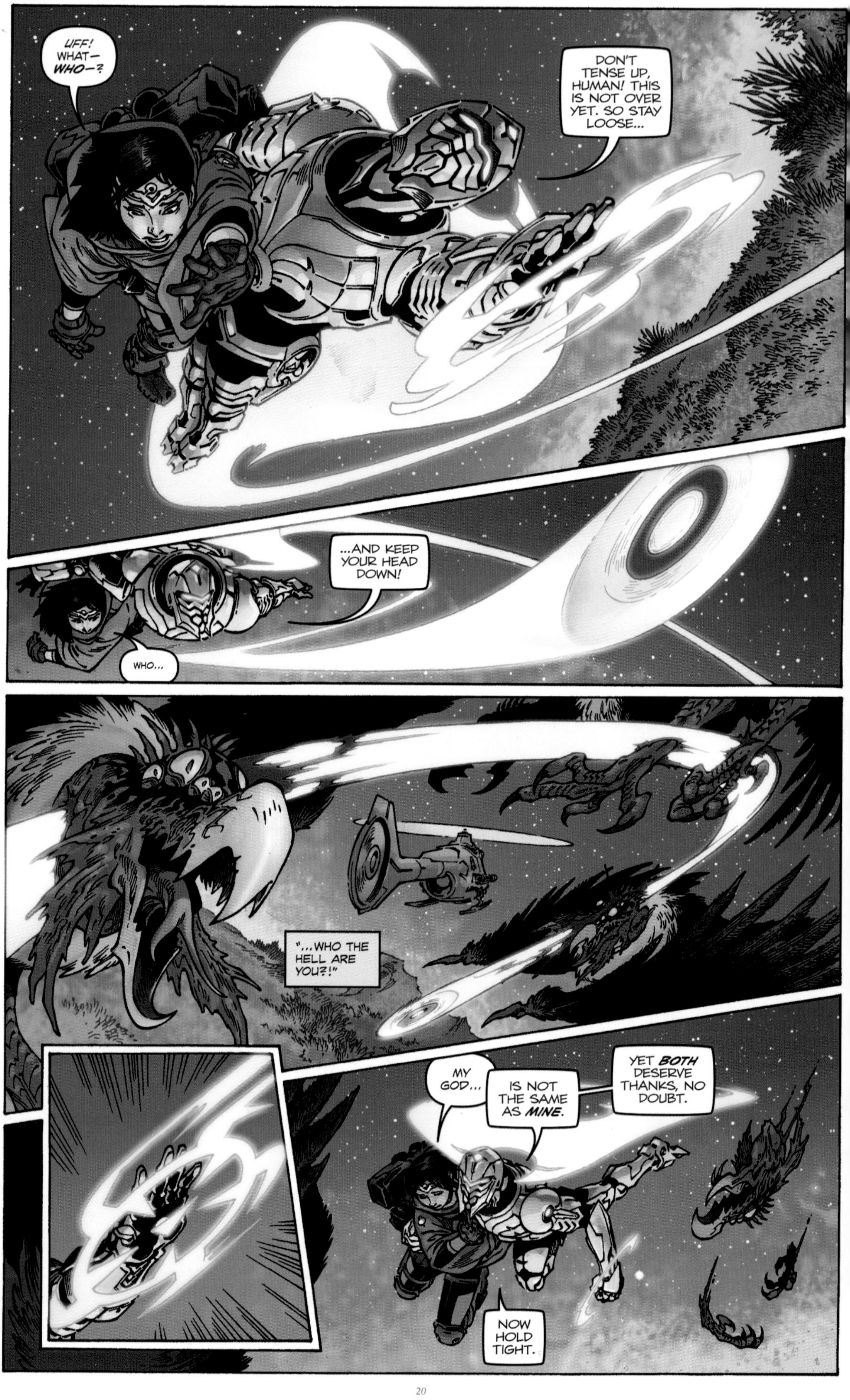
UFF! WHAT— WHO—?
DON'T TENSE UP, HUMAN! THIS IS NOT OVER YET. SO STAY LOOSE...
...AND KEEP YOUR HEAD DOWN!
WHO...
"...WHO THE HELL ARE YOU?!"
MY GOD...
IS NOT THE SAME AS MINE.
YET BOTH DESERVE THANKS, NO DOUBT.
NOW HOLD TIGHT.

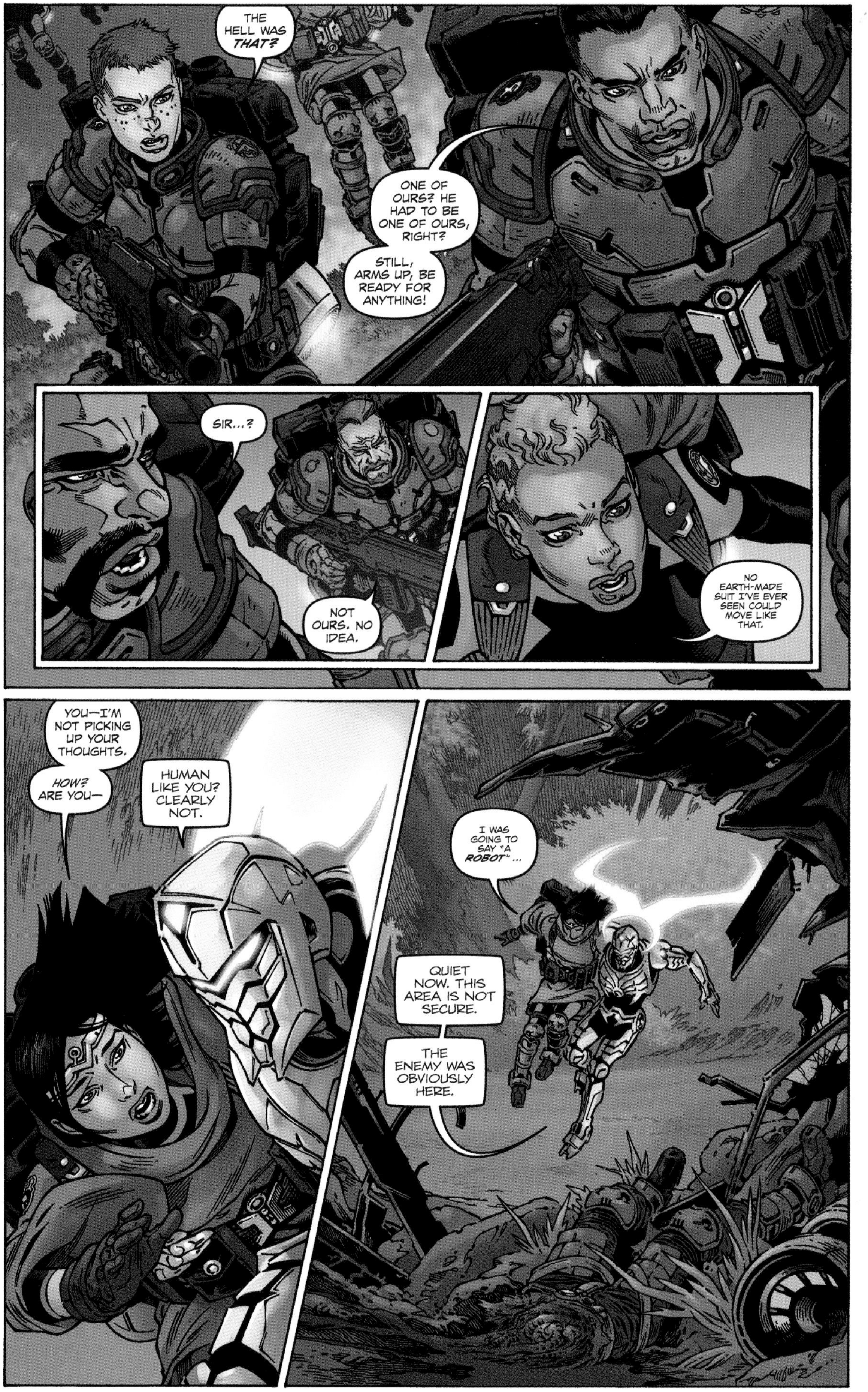
THE HELL WAS *THAT?*
ONE OF OURS? HE HAD TO BE ONE OF OURS, RIGHT?
STILL, ARMS UP, BE READY FOR ANYTHING!
SIR...?
NOT OURS. NO IDEA.
NO EARTH-MADE SUIT I'VE EVER SEEN COULD MOVE LIKE THAT.
YOU—I'M NOT PICKING UP YOUR THOUGHTS.
HOW? ARE YOU—
HUMAN LIKE YOU? CLEARLY NOT.
I WAS GOING TO SAY "A *ROBOT*"...
QUIET NOW. THIS AREA IS NOT SECURE.
THE ENEMY WAS OBVIOUSLY HERE.

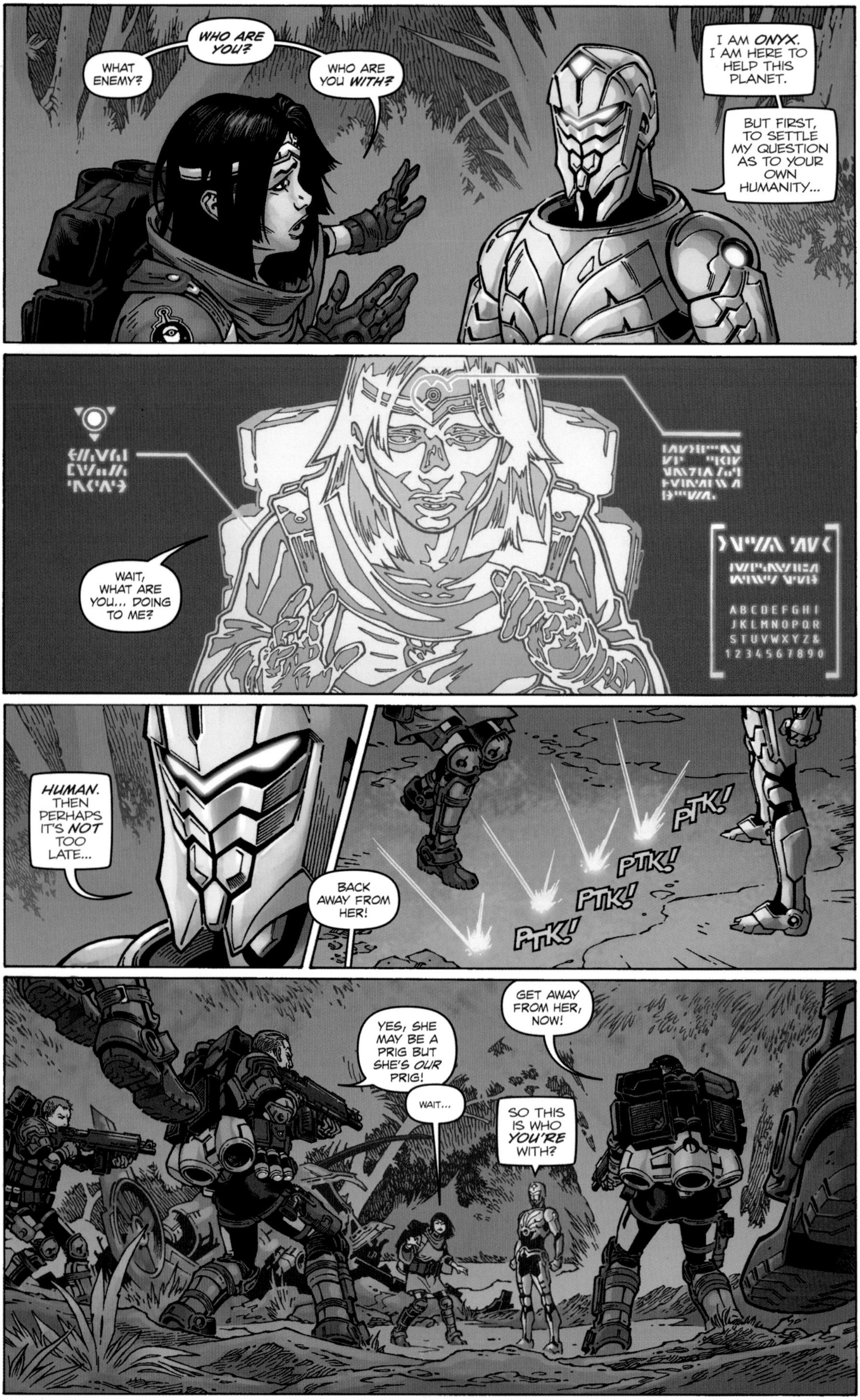
WHAT ENEMY?
WHO ARE YOU?
WHO ARE YOU WITH?
I AM ONYX. I AM HERE TO HELP THIS PLANET.
BUT FIRST, TO SETTLE MY QUESTION AS TO YOUR OWN HUMANITY...
WAIT, WHAT ARE YOU... DOING TO ME?
A B C D E F G H I
J K L M N O P Q R
S T U V W X Y Z &
1 2 3 4 5 6 7 8 9 0
HUMAN. THEN PERHAPS IT'S NOT TOO LATE...
BACK AWAY FROM HER!
PTK!
PTK!
PTK!
PTK!
GET AWAY FROM HER, NOW!
YES, SHE MAY BE A PRIG BUT SHE'S OUR PRIG!
WAIT...
SO THIS IS WHO YOU'RE WITH?

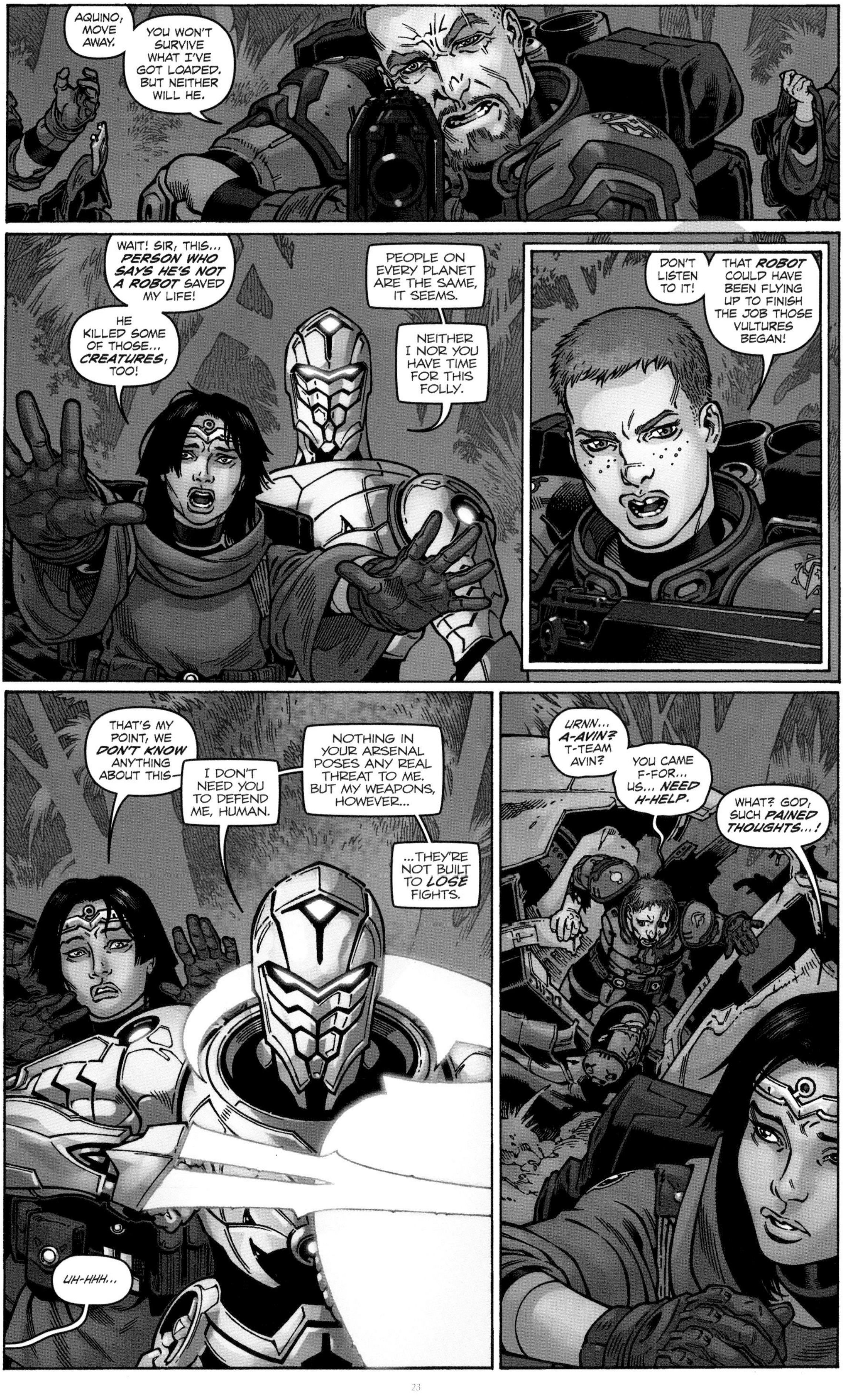

AQUINO, MOVE AWAY.
YOU WON'T SURVIVE WHAT I'VE GOT LOADED. BUT NEITHER WILL HE.
WAIT! SIR, THIS... PERSON WHO SAYS HE'S NOT A ROBOT SAVED MY LIFE!
HE KILLED SOME OF THOSE... CREATURES, TOO!
PEOPLE ON EVERY PLANET ARE THE SAME, IT SEEMS.
NEITHER I NOR YOU HAVE TIME FOR THIS FOLLY.
DON'T LISTEN TO IT!
THAT ROBOT COULD HAVE BEEN FLYING UP TO FINISH THE JOB THOSE VULTURES BEGAN!
THAT'S MY POINT, WE DON'T KNOW ANYTHING ABOUT THIS—
I DON'T NEED YOU TO DEFEND ME, HUMAN.
NOTHING IN YOUR ARSENAL POSES ANY REAL THREAT TO ME. BUT MY WEAPONS, HOWEVER...
...THEY'RE NOT BUILT TO LOSE FIGHTS.
UH-HHH...
URNN... A-AVIN? T-TEAM AVIN?
YOU CAME F-FOR... US... NEED H-HELP.
WHAT? GOD, SUCH PAINED THOUGHTS...!

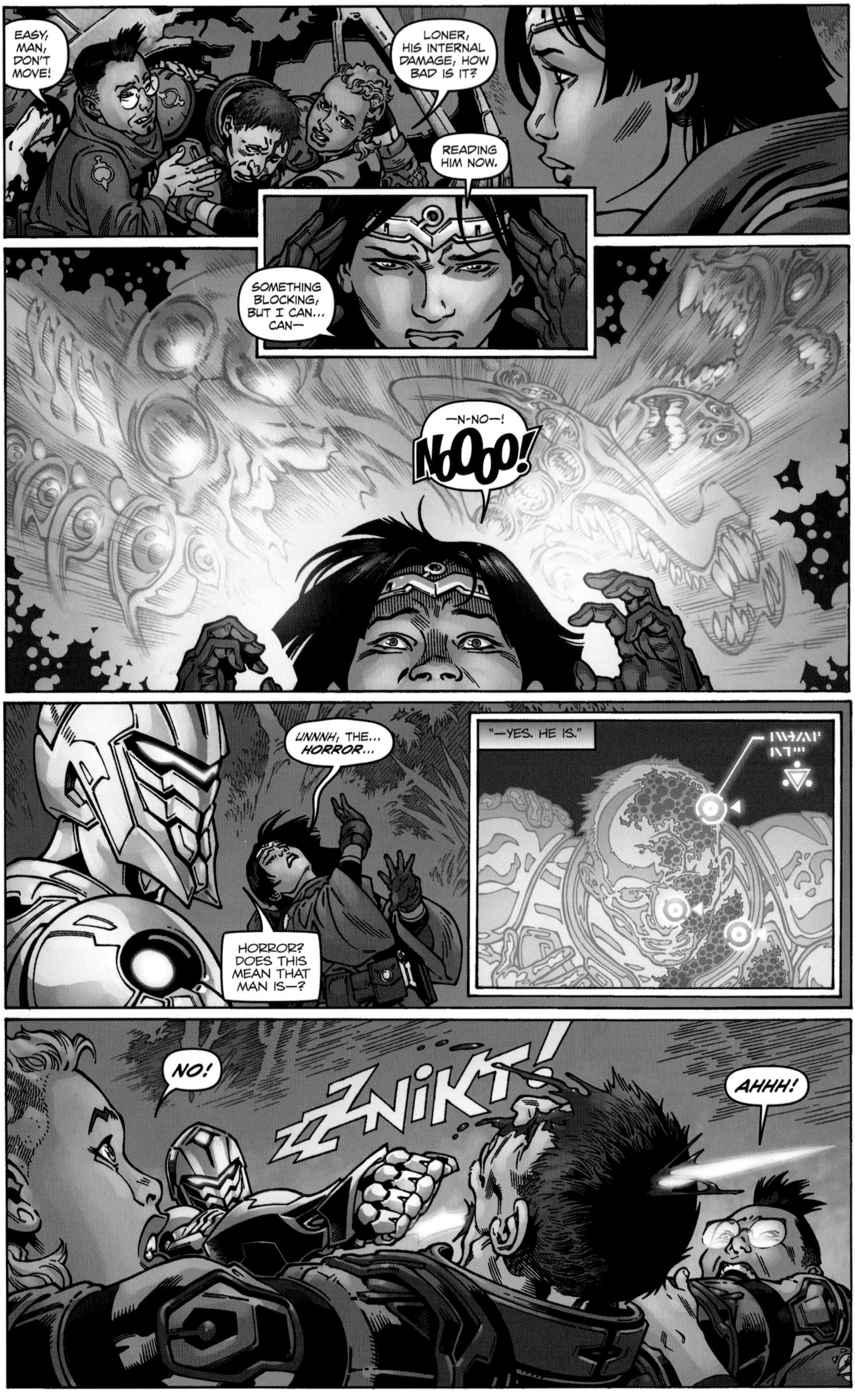
EASY, MAN, DON'T MOVE!
LONER, HIS INTERNAL DAMAGE, HOW BAD IS IT?
READING HIM NOW.
SOMETHING BLOCKING, BUT I CAN... CAN—
—N-NO—!
NOOOO!
UNNNH, THE... HORROR...
HORROR? DOES THIS MEAN THAT MAN IS—?
"—YES. HE IS."
NO!
ZZNIKT!
AHHH!

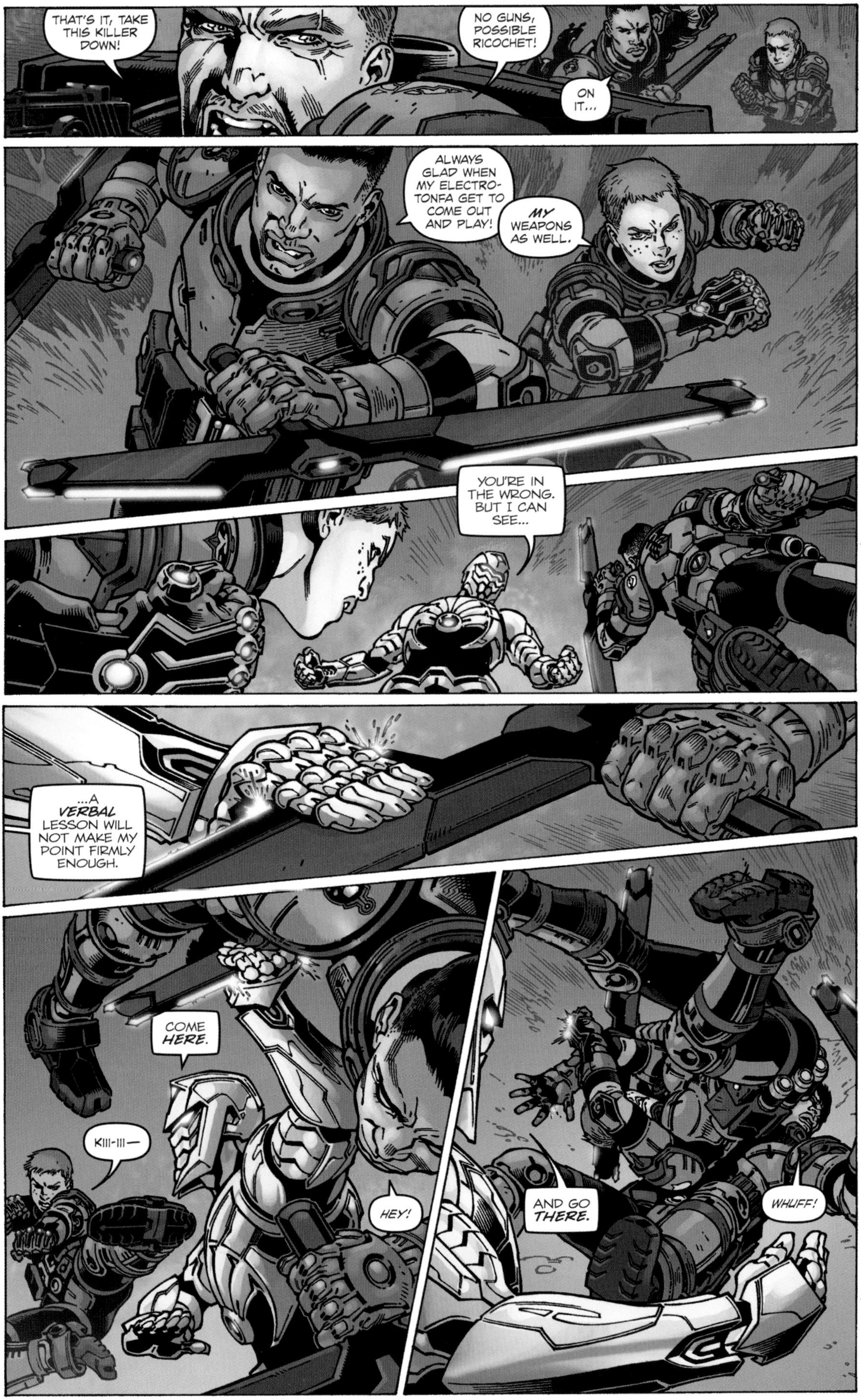
THAT'S IT, TAKE THIS KILLER DOWN!
NO GUNS, POSSIBLE RICOCHET!
ON IT...
ALWAYS GLAD WHEN MY ELECTRO-TONFA GET TO COME OUT AND PLAY!
MY WEAPONS AS WELL.
YOU'RE IN THE WRONG. BUT I CAN SEE...
...A VERBAL LESSON WILL NOT MAKE MY POINT FIRMLY ENOUGH.
COME HERE.
KIII-III—
HEY!
AND GO THERE.
WHUFF!

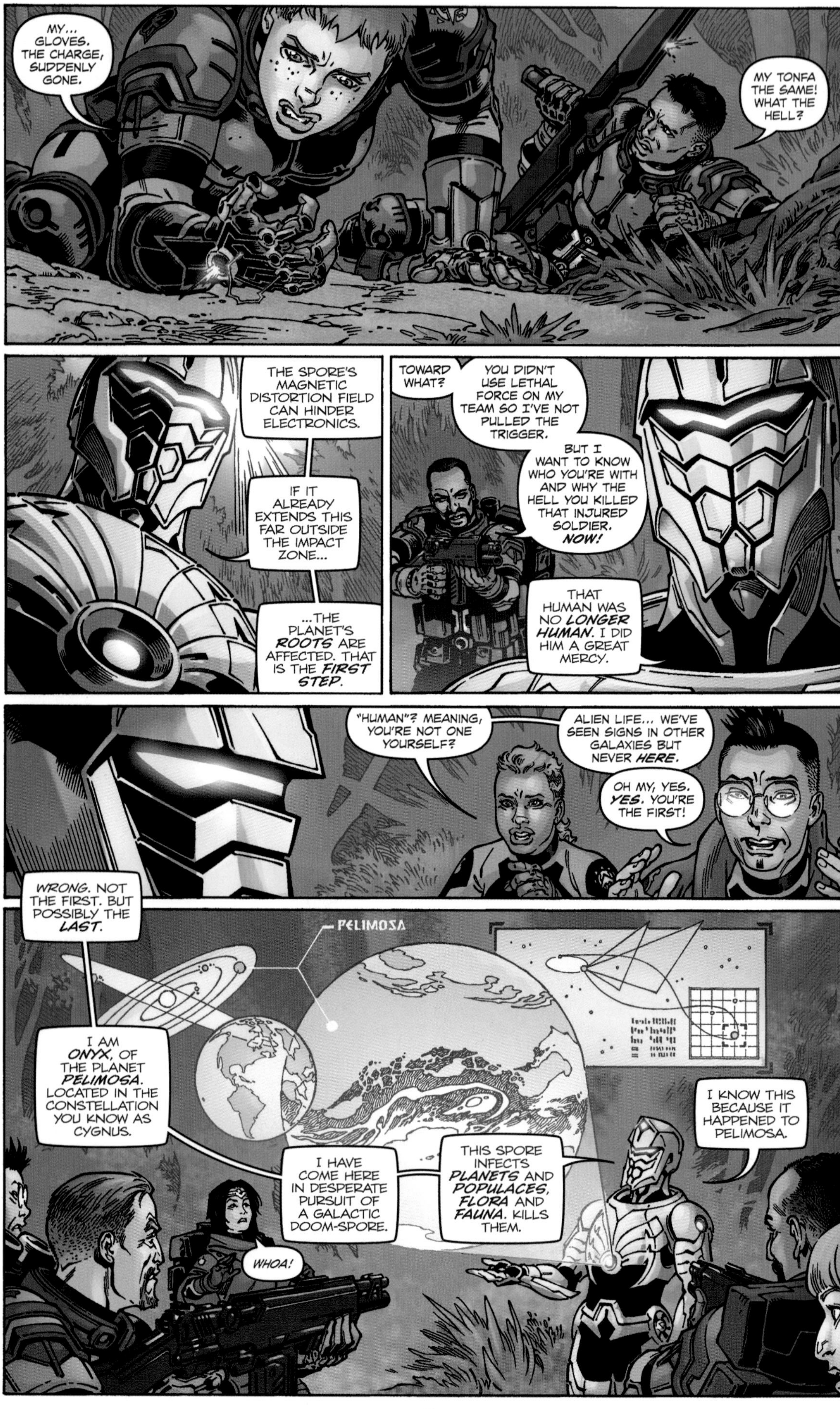

MY... GLOVES. THE CHARGE, SUDDENLY GONE.
MY TONFA THE SAME! WHAT THE HELL?
THE SPORE'S MAGNETIC DISTORTION FIELD CAN HINDER ELECTRONICS.
IF IT ALREADY EXTENDS THIS FAR OUTSIDE THE IMPACT ZONE...
...THE PLANET'S ROOTS ARE AFFECTED. THAT IS THE FIRST STEP.
TOWARD WHAT?
YOU DIDN'T USE LETHAL FORCE ON MY TEAM SO I'VE NOT PULLED THE TRIGGER.
BUT I WANT TO KNOW WHO YOU'RE WITH AND WHY THE HELL YOU KILLED THAT INJURED SOLDIER. NOW!
THAT HUMAN WAS NO LONGER HUMAN. I DID HIM A GREAT MERCY.
"HUMAN"? MEANING, YOU'RE NOT ONE YOURSELF?
ALIEN LIFE... WE'VE SEEN SIGNS IN OTHER GALAXIES BUT NEVER HERE.
OH MY, YES. YES. YOU'RE THE FIRST!
WRONG. NOT THE FIRST. BUT POSSIBLY THE LAST.
PELIMOSA
I AM ONYX, OF THE PLANET PELIMOSA. LOCATED IN THE CONSTELLATION YOU KNOW AS CYGNUS.
I HAVE COME HERE IN DESPERATE PURSUIT OF A GALACTIC DOOM-SPORE.
THIS SPORE INFECTS PLANETS AND POPULACES, FLORA AND FAUNA. KILLS THEM.
I KNOW THIS BECAUSE IT HAPPENED TO PELIMOSA.
WHOA!

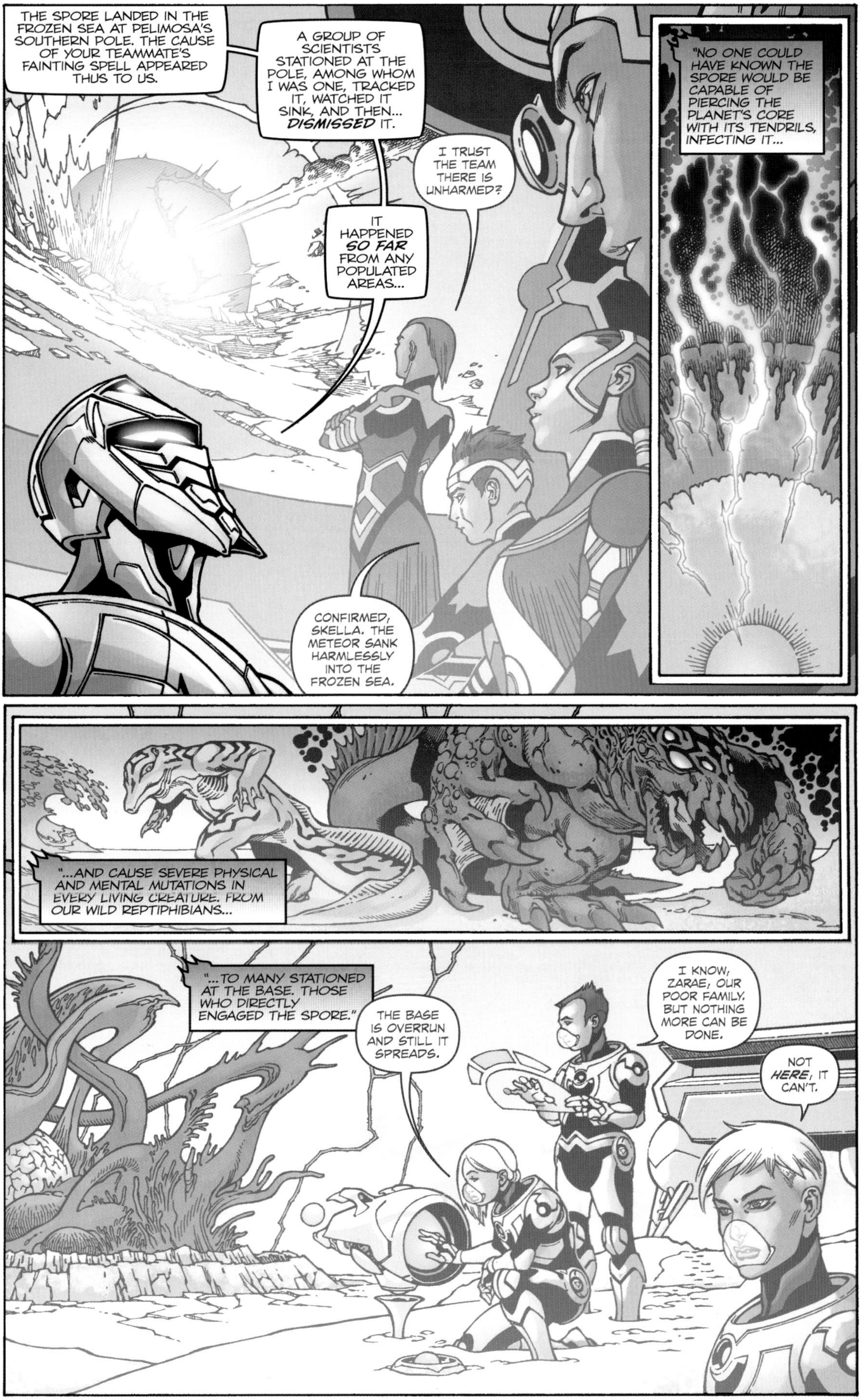
THE SPORE LANDED IN THE FROZEN SEA AT PELIMOSA'S SOUTHERN POLE. THE CAUSE OF YOUR TEAMMATE'S FAINTING SPELL APPEARED THUS TO US.
A GROUP OF SCIENTISTS STATIONED AT THE POLE, AMONG WHOM I WAS ONE, TRACKED IT, WATCHED IT SINK, AND THEN... DISMISSED IT.
I TRUST THE TEAM THERE IS UNHARMED?
IT HAPPENED SO FAR FROM ANY POPULATED AREAS...
CONFIRMED, SKELLA. THE METEOR SANK HARMLESSLY INTO THE FROZEN SEA.
"NO ONE COULD HAVE KNOWN THE SPORE WOULD BE CAPABLE OF PIERCING THE PLANET'S CORE WITH ITS TENDRILS, INFECTING IT...
"...AND CAUSE SEVERE PHYSICAL AND MENTAL MUTATIONS IN EVERY LIVING CREATURE. FROM OUR WILD REPTIPHIBIANS...
"...TO MANY STATIONED AT THE BASE. THOSE WHO DIRECTLY ENGAGED THE SPORE."
THE BASE IS OVERRUN AND STILL IT SPREADS.
I KNOW, ZARAE, OUR POOR FAMILY. BUT NOTHING MORE CAN BE DONE.
NOT HERE, IT CAN'T.

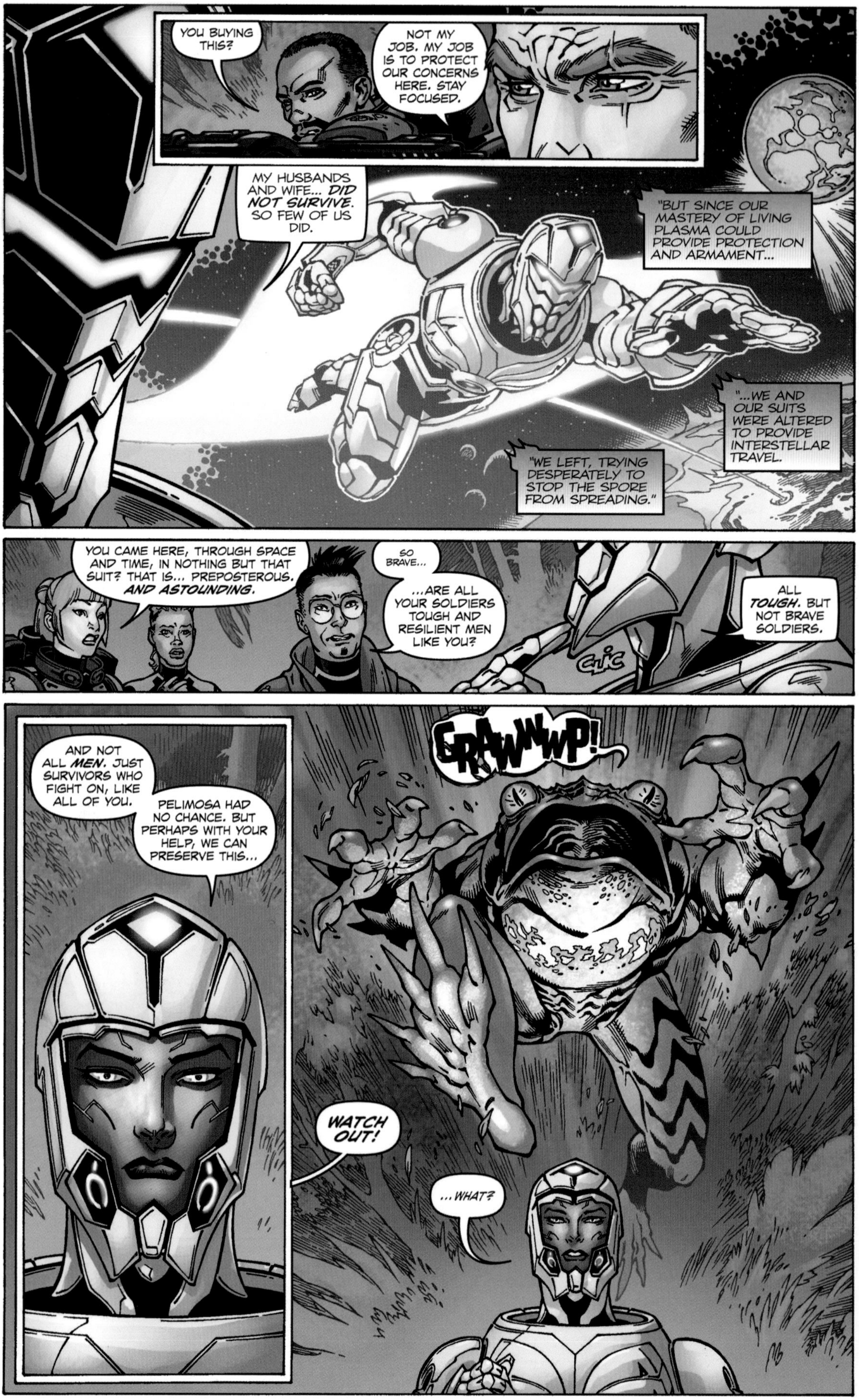

YOU BUYING THIS?
NOT MY JOB. MY JOB IS TO PROTECT OUR CONCERNS HERE. STAY FOCUSED.
MY HUSBANDS AND WIFE... DID NOT SURVIVE. SO FEW OF US DID.
"BUT SINCE OUR MASTERY OF LIVING PLASMA COULD PROVIDE PROTECTION AND ARMAMENT...
"...WE AND OUR SUITS WERE ALTERED TO PROVIDE INTERSTELLAR TRAVEL.
"WE LEFT, TRYING DESPERATELY TO STOP THE SPORE FROM SPREADING."
YOU CAME HERE, THROUGH SPACE AND TIME, IN NOTHING BUT THAT SUIT? THAT IS... PREPOSTEROUS. AND ASTOUNDING.
SO BRAVE...
...ARE ALL YOUR SOLDIERS TOUGH AND RESILIENT MEN LIKE YOU?
CLIC
ALL TOUGH. BUT NOT BRAVE SOLDIERS.
AND NOT ALL MEN. JUST SURVIVORS WHO FIGHT ON, LIKE ALL OF YOU.
PELIMOSA HAD NO CHANCE. BUT PERHAPS WITH YOUR HELP, WE CAN PRESERVE THIS...
GRAWWWP!
WATCH OUT!
...WHAT?

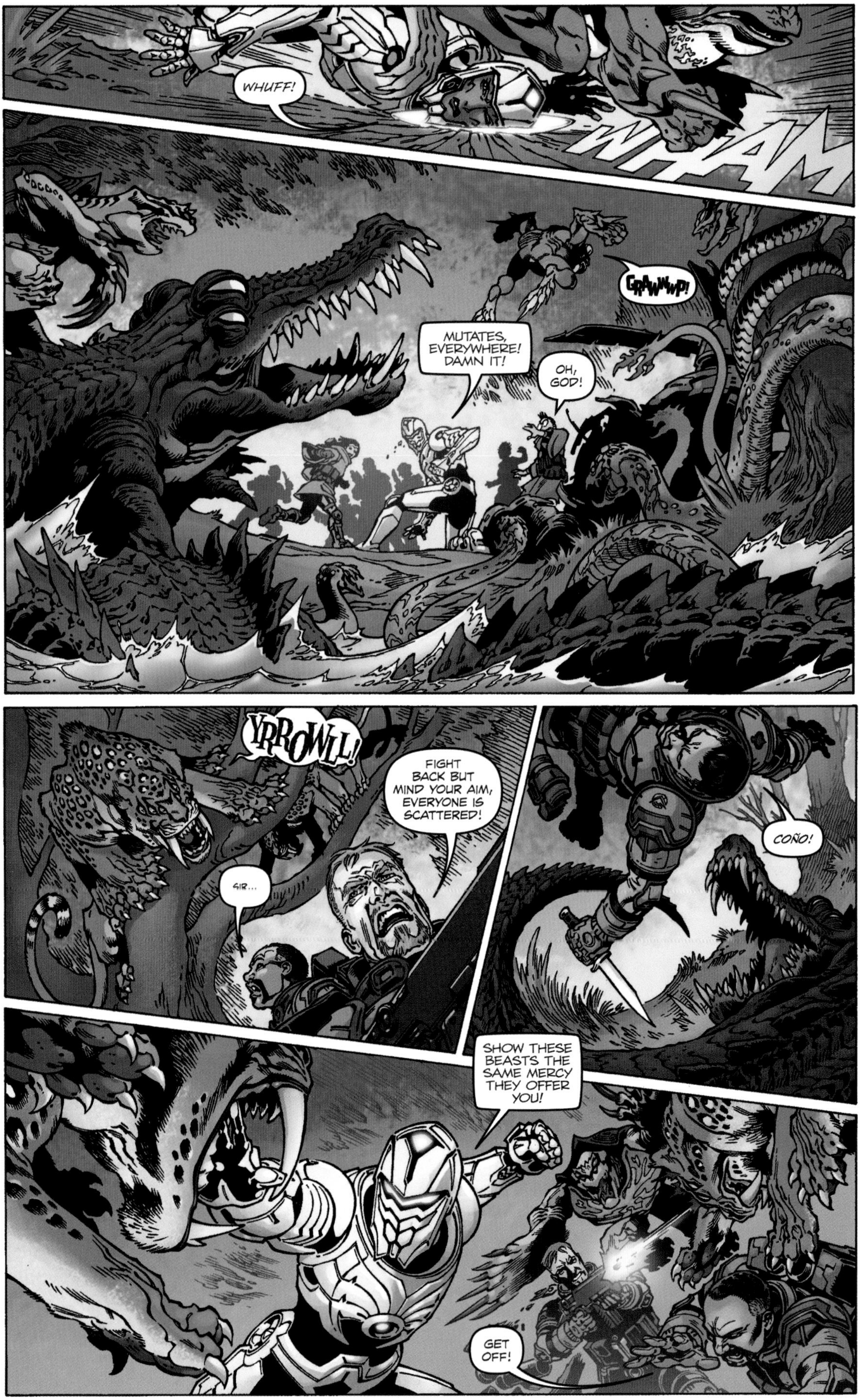
WHUFF!
WHAM
GRAWWWP!
MUTATES, EVERYWHERE! DAMN IT!
OH, GOD!
YRROWLL!
FIGHT BACK BUT MIND YOUR AIM, EVERYONE IS SCATTERED!
SIR...
COÑO!
SHOW THESE BEASTS THE SAME MERCY THEY OFFER YOU!
GET OFF!

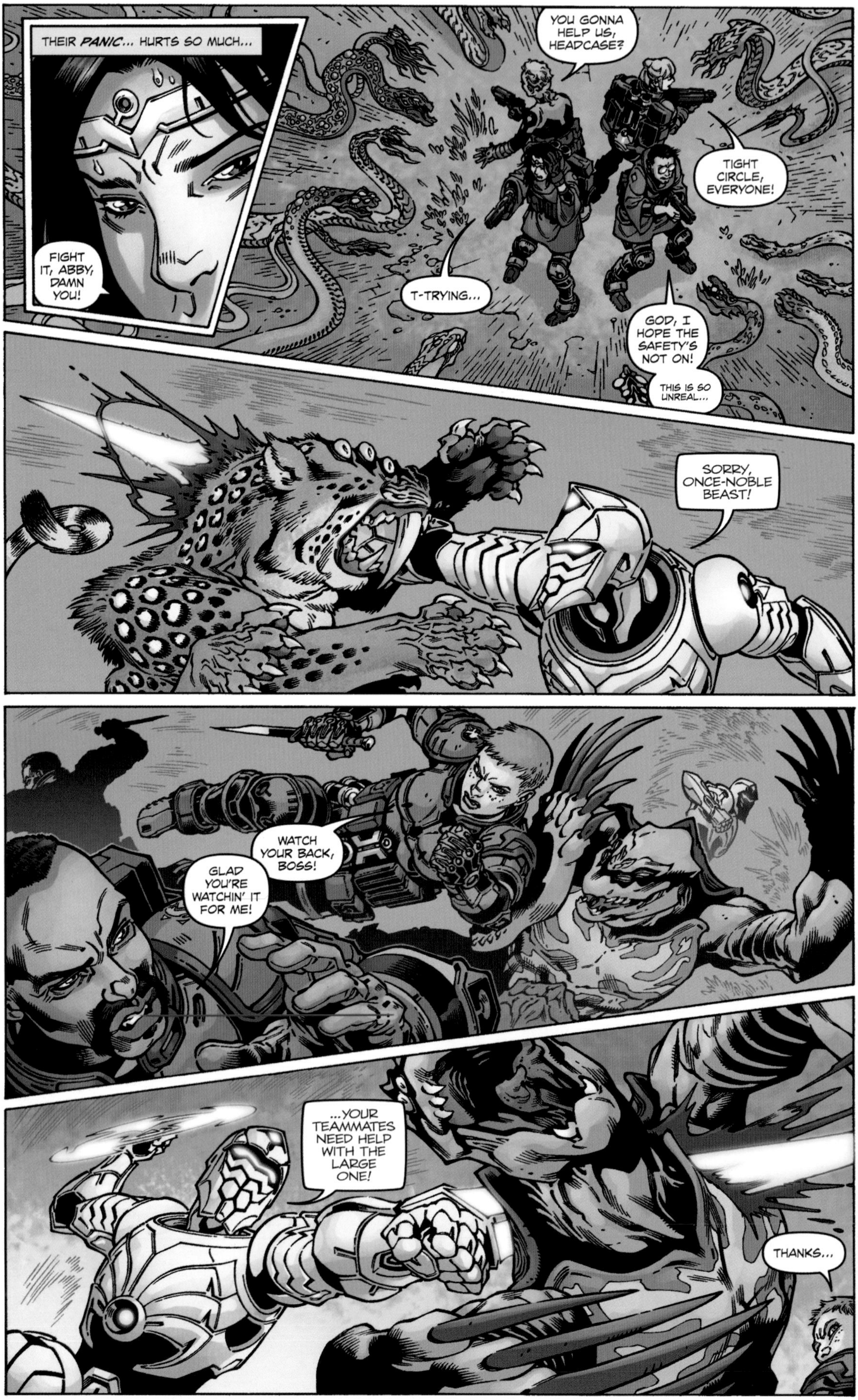
THEIR PANIC... HURTS SO MUCH...
FIGHT IT, ABBY, DAMN YOU!
YOU GONNA HELP US, HEADCASE?
T-TRYING...
TIGHT CIRCLE, EVERYONE!
GOD, I HOPE THE SAFETY'S NOT ON!
THIS IS SO UNREAL...
SORRY, ONCE-NOBLE BEAST!
WATCH YOUR BACK, BOSS!
GLAD YOU'RE WATCHIN' IT FOR ME!
...YOUR TEAMMATES NEED HELP WITH THE LARGE ONE!
THANKS...

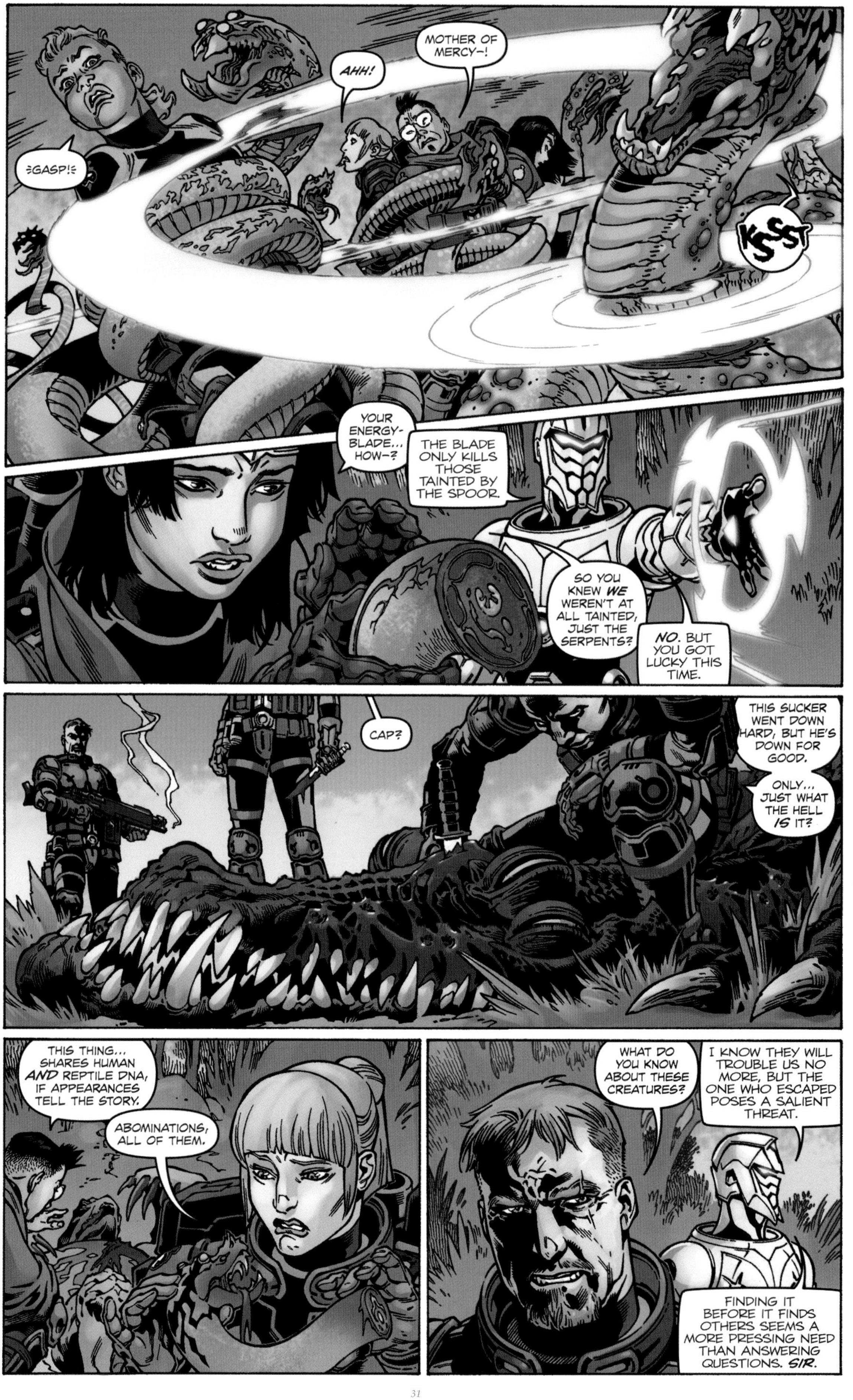

GASP!
AHH!
MOTHER OF MERCY-!
KSSST
YOUR ENERGY-BLADE... HOW-?
THE BLADE ONLY KILLS THOSE TAINTED BY THE SPOOR.
SO YOU KNEW WE WEREN'T AT ALL TAINTED, JUST THE SERPENTS?
NO. BUT YOU GOT LUCKY THIS TIME.
CAP?
THIS SUCKER WENT DOWN HARD, BUT HE'S DOWN FOR GOOD.
ONLY... JUST WHAT THE HELL IS IT?
THIS THING... SHARES HUMAN AND REPTILE DNA, IF APPEARANCES TELL THE STORY.
ABOMINATIONS, ALL OF THEM.
WHAT DO YOU KNOW ABOUT THESE CREATURES?
I KNOW THEY WILL TROUBLE US NO MORE, BUT THE ONE WHO ESCAPED POSES A SALIENT THREAT.
FINDING IT BEFORE IT FINDS OTHERS SEEMS A MORE PRESSING NEED THAN ANSWERING QUESTIONS. SIR.

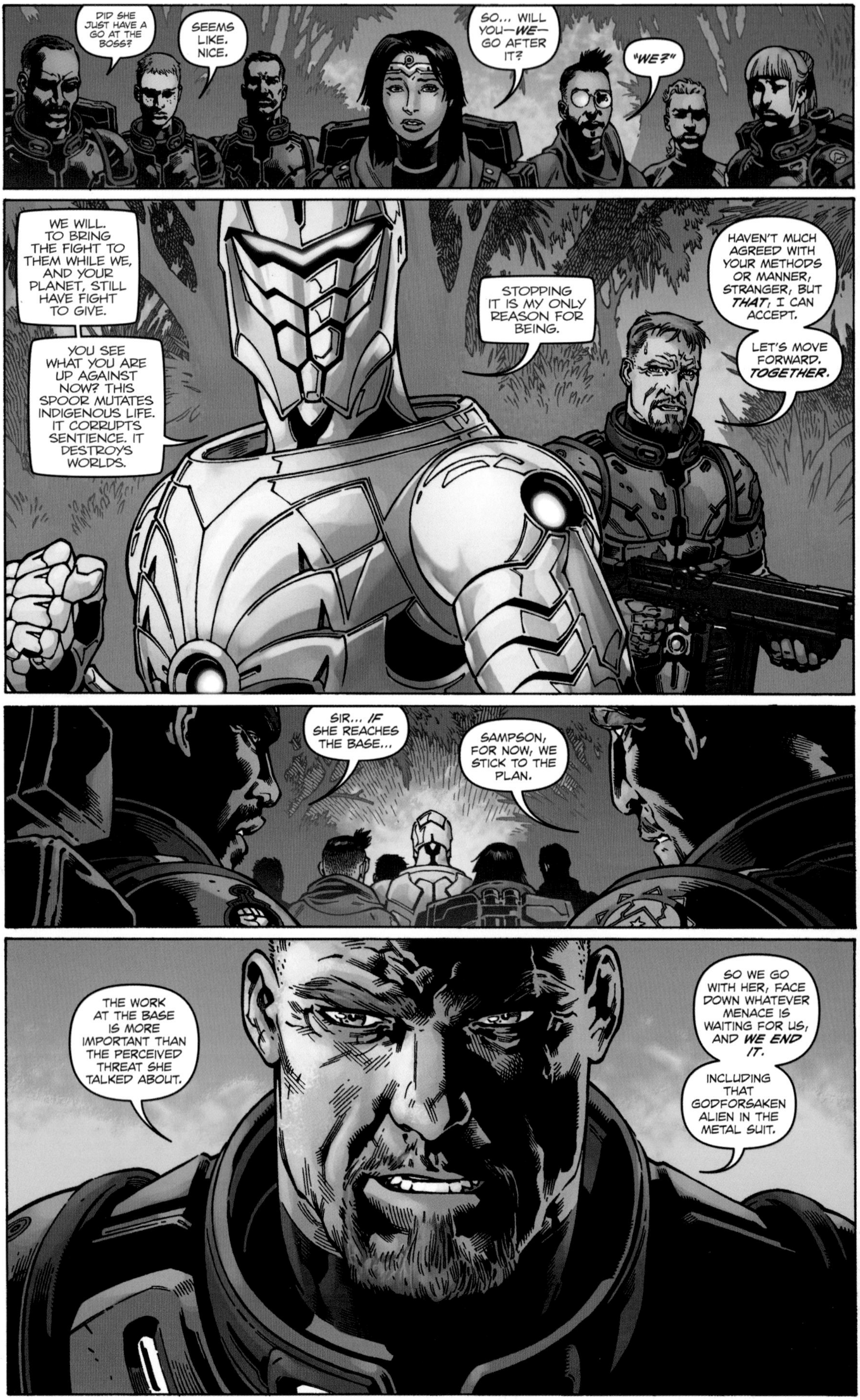
DID SHE JUST HAVE A GO AT THE BOSS?
SEEMS LIKE. NICE.
SO... WILL YOU—WE—GO AFTER IT?
"WE?"
WE WILL. TO BRING THE FIGHT TO THEM WHILE WE, AND YOUR PLANET, STILL HAVE FIGHT TO GIVE.
YOU SEE WHAT YOU ARE UP AGAINST NOW? THIS SPOOR MUTATES INDIGENOUS LIFE. IT CORRUPTS SENTIENCE. IT DESTROYS WORLDS.
STOPPING IT IS MY ONLY REASON FOR BEING.
HAVEN'T MUCH AGREED WITH YOUR METHODS OR MANNER, STRANGER, BUT THAT, I CAN ACCEPT.
LET'S MOVE FORWARD. TOGETHER.
SIR... IF SHE REACHES THE BASE...
SAMPSON, FOR NOW, WE STICK TO THE PLAN.
THE WORK AT THE BASE IS MORE IMPORTANT THAN THE PERCEIVED THREAT SHE TALKED ABOUT.
SO WE GO WITH HER, FACE DOWN WHATEVER MENACE IS WAITING FOR US, AND WE END IT.
INCLUDING THAT GODFORSAKEN ALIEN IN THE METAL SUIT.

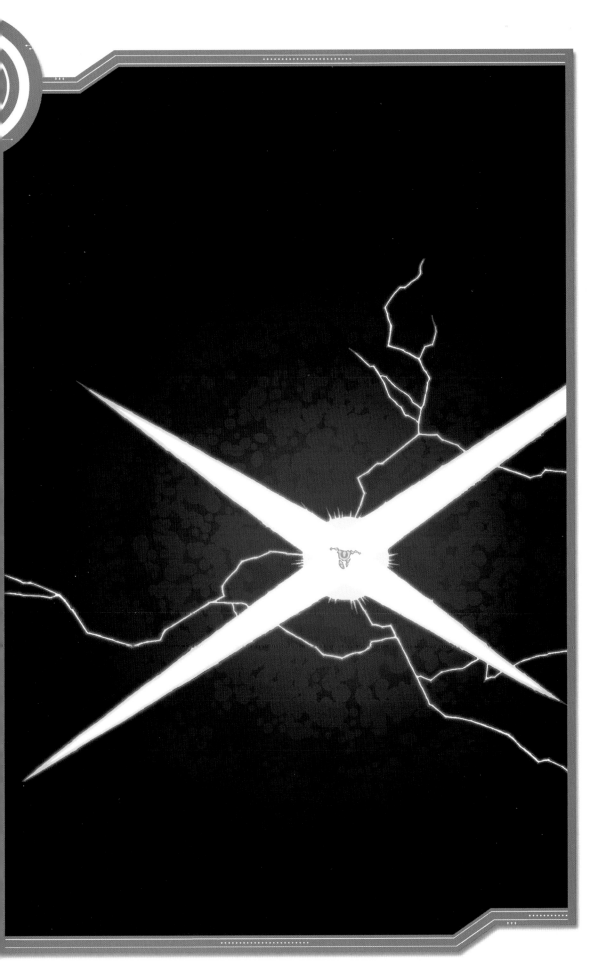

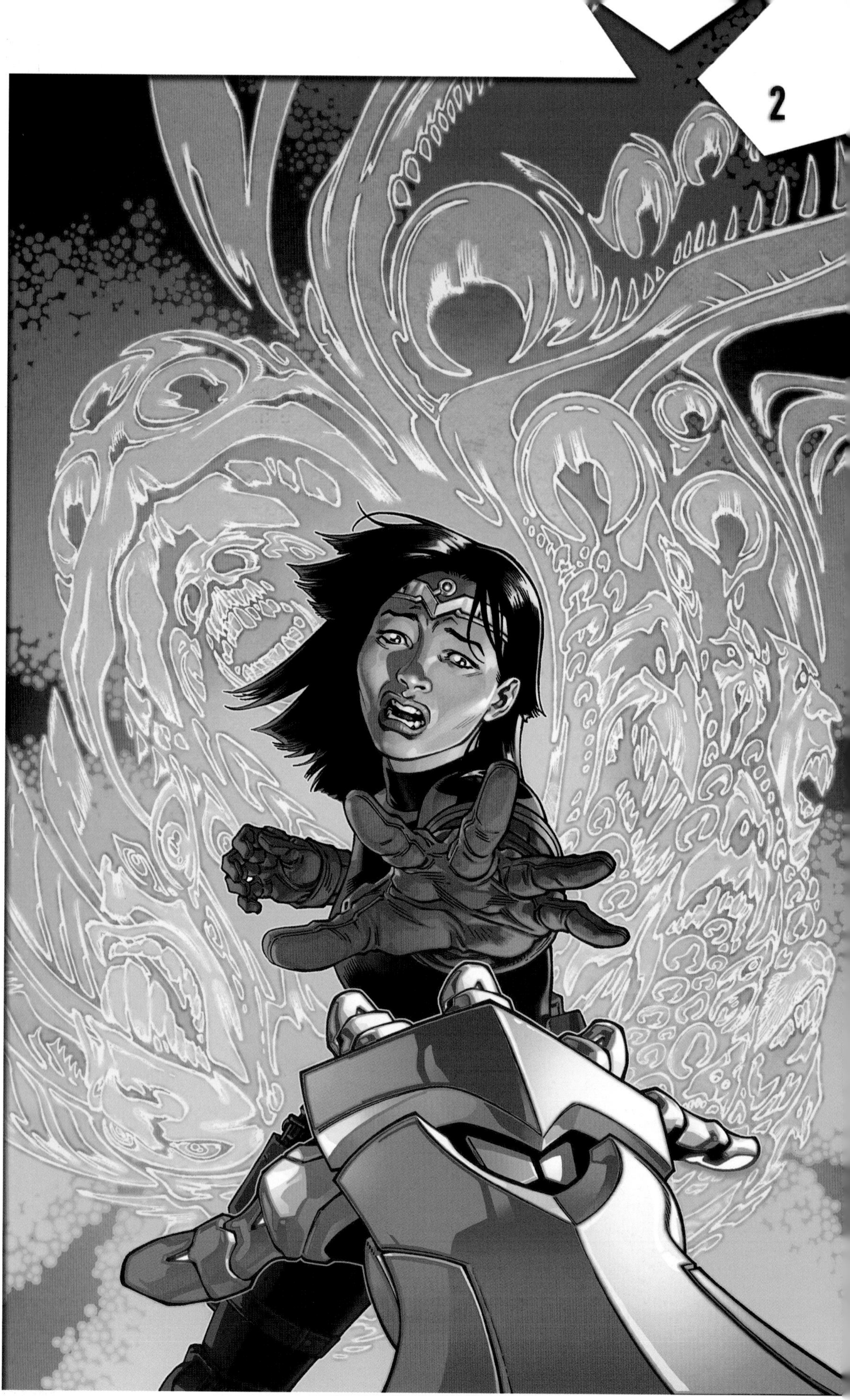
2

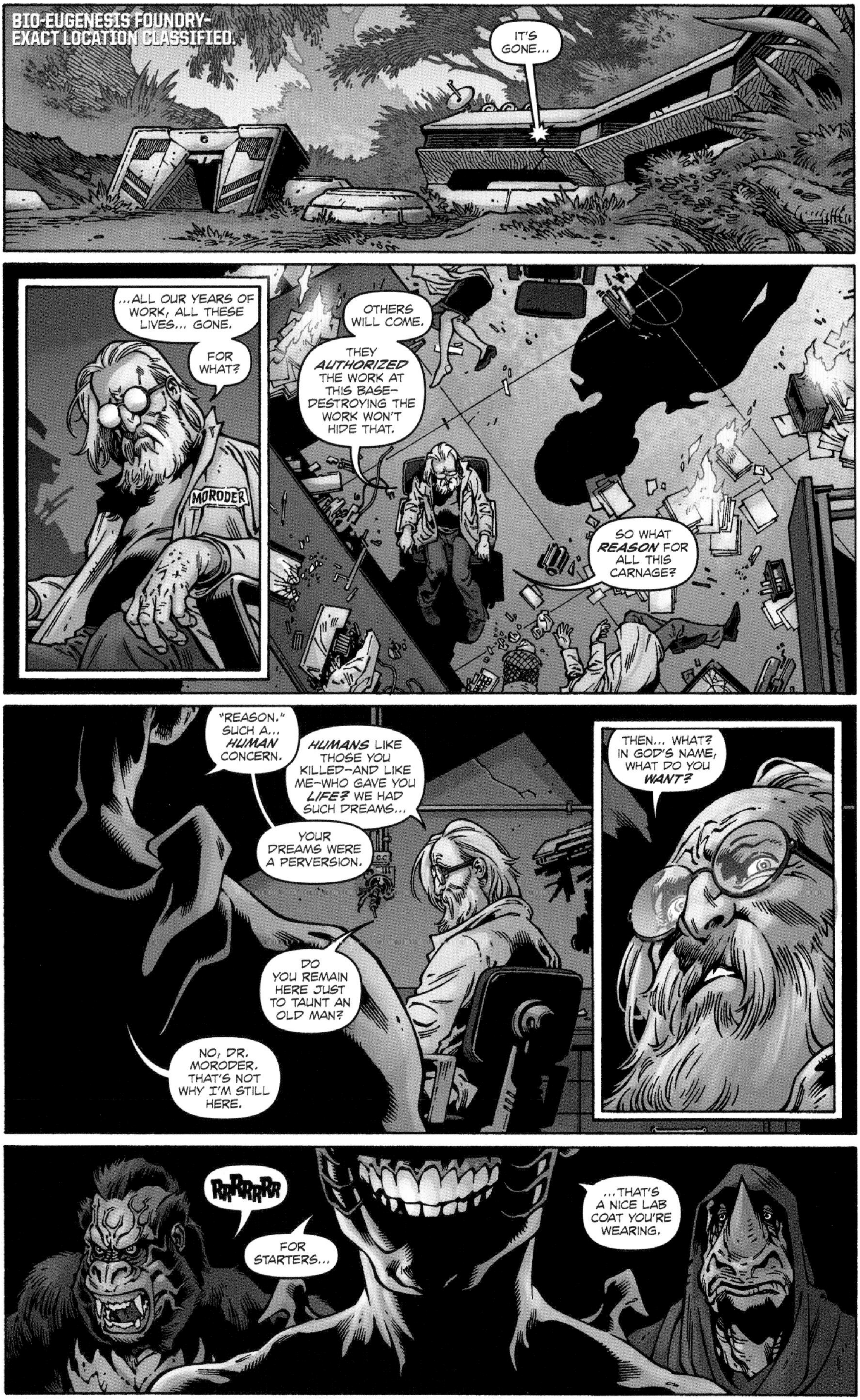
BIO-EUGENESIS FOUNDRY–
EXACT LOCATION CLASSIFIED.
IT'S GONE...
...ALL OUR YEARS OF WORK, ALL THESE LIVES... GONE.
FOR WHAT?
OTHERS WILL COME.
THEY *AUTHORIZED* THE WORK AT THIS BASE– DESTROYING THE WORK WON'T HIDE THAT.
MORODER
SO WHAT *REASON* FOR ALL THIS CARNAGE?
"REASON." SUCH A... *HUMAN* CONCERN.
HUMANS LIKE THOSE YOU KILLED–AND LIKE ME–WHO GAVE YOU *LIFE?* WE HAD SUCH DREAMS...
YOUR DREAMS WERE A PERVERSION.
THEN... WHAT? IN GOD'S NAME, WHAT DO YOU *WANT?*
DO YOU REMAIN HERE JUST TO TAUNT AN OLD MAN?
NO, DR. MORODER. THAT'S NOT WHY I'M STILL HERE.
RRRRRRR
FOR STARTERS...
...THAT'S A NICE LAB COAT YOU'RE WEARING.

IT'S LIKE I'VE ALWAYS SAID, WHENEVER YOU TRY TO PLAY GOD...

...ALONG COMES A *BIGGER GOD* TO SHOW YOU HOW IT'S DONE.

HMMFF.

YOU HAVE NEVER SAID THAT BEFORE.

YOU DIDN'T EVEN HAVE THE GIFT OF SPEECH UNTIL LAST WEEK.

YET HERE I AM NOW, FULLY AWAKENED.

MMRR-- RIGHT ABOUT... ONE THING.

THEY... COME NOW. THEY COME... FOR US.

HE IS RIGHT. THE HUMANS WILL SEEK RETRIBUTION.

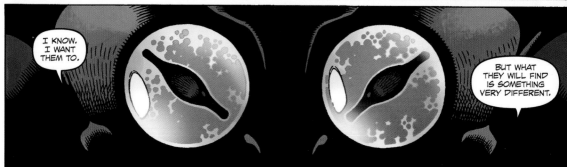

I KNOW. I WANT THEM TO.

BUT WHAT THEY WILL FIND IS SOMETHING VERY DIFFERENT.

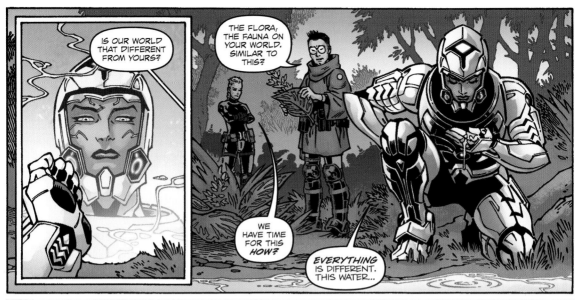

IS OUR WORLD THAT DIFFERENT FROM YOURS?

THE FLORA, THE FAUNA ON YOUR WORLD. SIMILAR TO THIS?

WE HAVE TIME FOR THIS *HOW?*

EVERYTHING IS DIFFERENT. THIS WATER...

FEELS COLD AND REFRESHING, YES? MOUNTAIN STREAMS ALWAYS—

NO.

TO ME, IT IS METALLIC, ODORLESS.

I TASTE *NOTHING.*

ER, OKAY, THEN.

ONYX, THE TRANSPORT VEHICLES ARE NEARLY READY, THEY—

I *FEEL* NOTHING. NOT ANY MORE.

I AM READY *RIGHT NOW.*

DELAYING ANY LONGER IS FOLLY.

CATCH UP TO ME WHEN YOU'RE ABLE.

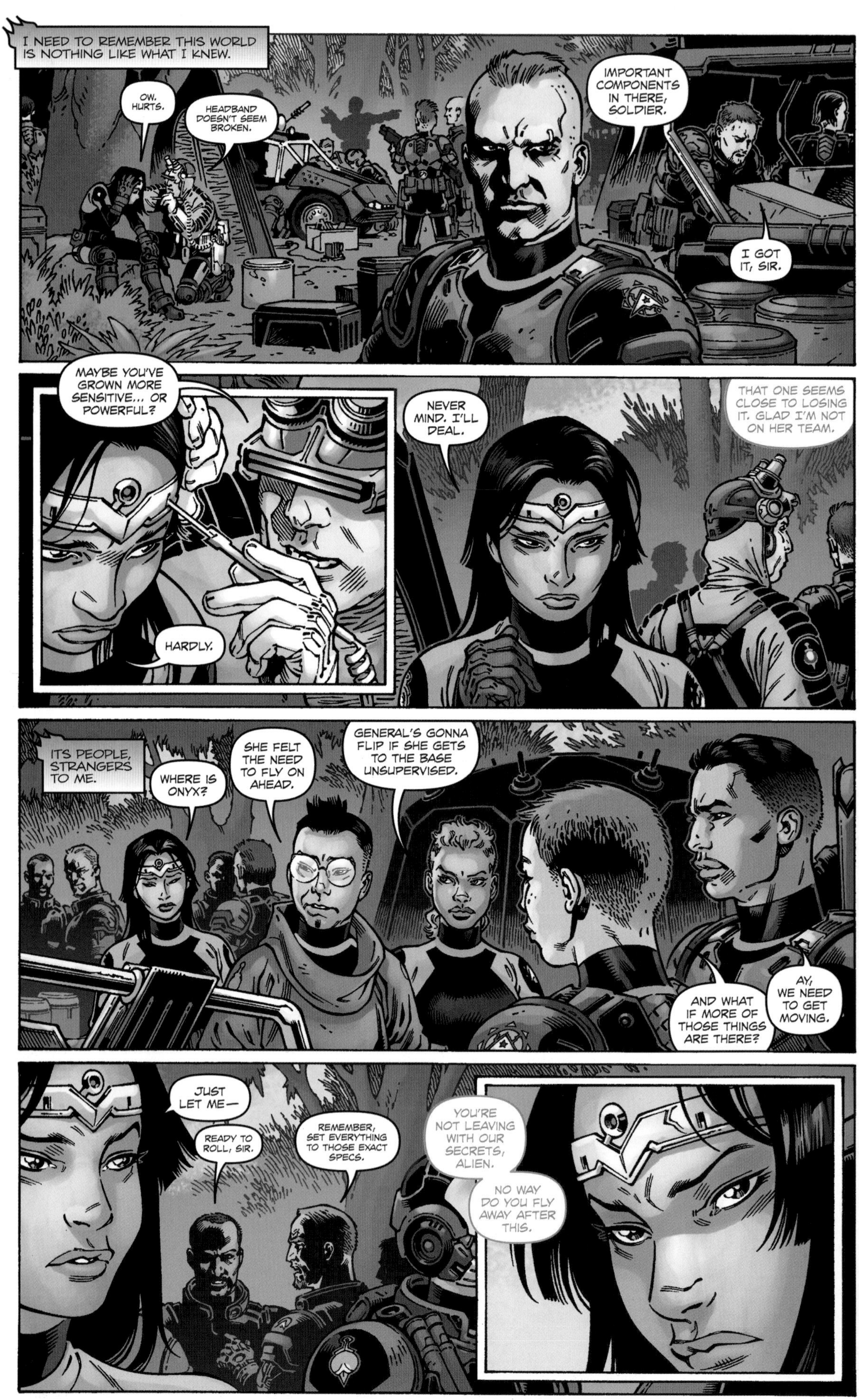
I NEED TO REMEMBER THIS WORLD IS NOTHING LIKE WHAT I KNEW.
OW. HURTS.
HEADBAND DOESN'T SEEM BROKEN.
IMPORTANT COMPONENTS IN THERE, SOLDIER.
I GOT IT, SIR.
MAYBE YOU'VE GROWN MORE SENSITIVE... OR POWERFUL?
HARDLY.
NEVER MIND. I'LL DEAL.
THAT ONE SEEMS CLOSE TO LOSING IT. GLAD I'M NOT ON HER TEAM.
ITS PEOPLE, STRANGERS TO ME.
WHERE IS ONYX?
SHE FELT THE NEED TO FLY ON AHEAD.
GENERAL'S GONNA FLIP IF SHE GETS TO THE BASE UNSUPERVISED.
AND WHAT IF MORE OF THOSE THINGS ARE THERE?
AY, WE NEED TO GET MOVING.
JUST LET ME—
READY TO ROLL, SIR.
REMEMBER, SET EVERYTHING TO THOSE EXACT SPECS.
YOU'RE NOT LEAVING WITH OUR SECRETS, ALIEN.
NO WAY DO YOU FLY AWAY AFTER THIS.

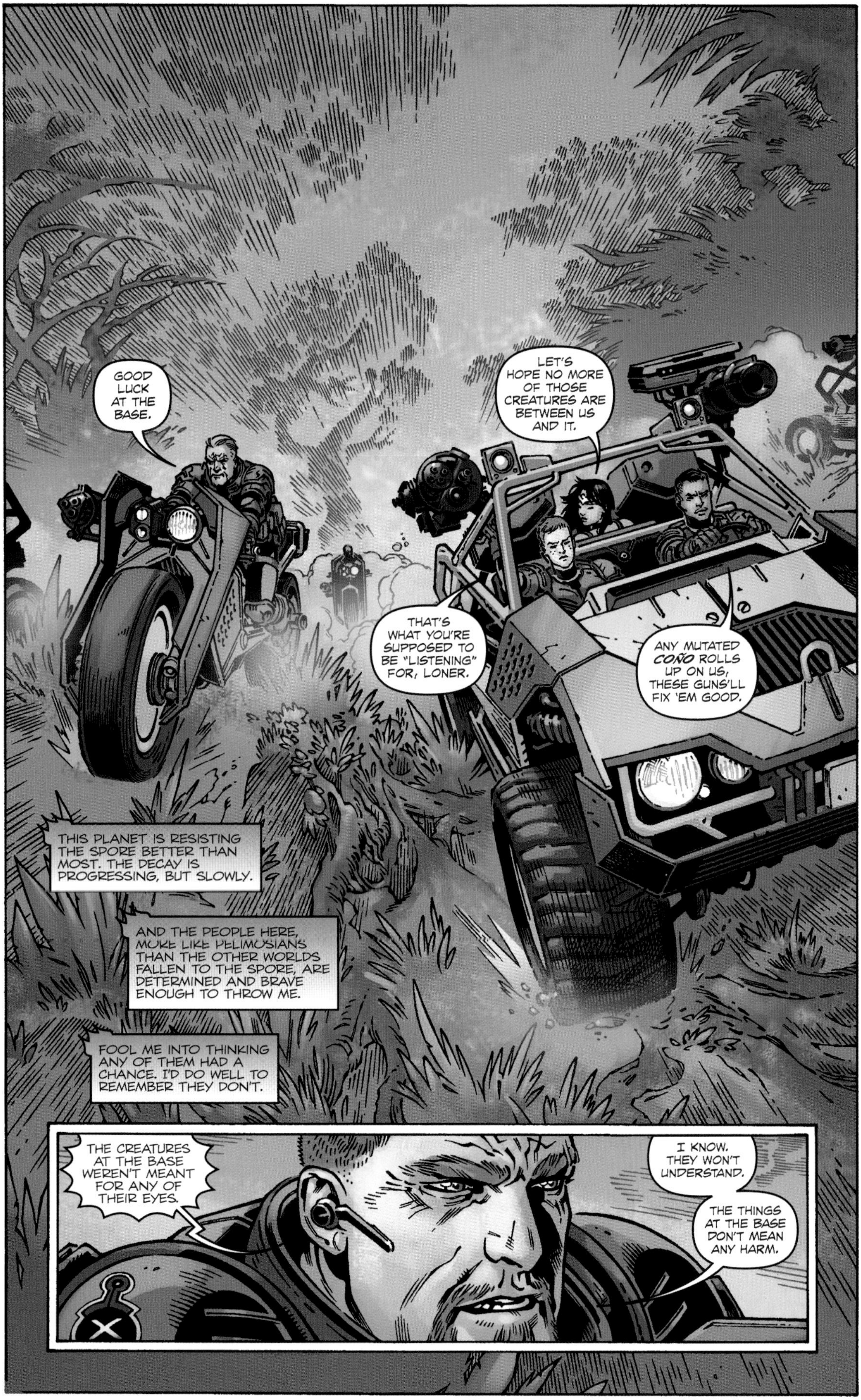
GOOD LUCK AT THE BASE.
LET'S HOPE NO MORE OF THOSE CREATURES ARE BETWEEN US AND IT.
THAT'S WHAT YOU'RE SUPPOSED TO BE "LISTENING" FOR, LONER.
ANY MUTATED ***COÑO*** ROLLS UP ON US, THESE GUNS'LL FIX 'EM GOOD.
THIS PLANET IS RESISTING THE SPORE BETTER THAN MOST. THE DECAY IS PROGRESSING, BUT SLOWLY.
AND THE PEOPLE HERE, MORE LIKE PELIMOSIANS THAN THE OTHER WORLDS FALLEN TO THE SPORE, ARE DETERMINED AND BRAVE ENOUGH TO THROW ME.
FOOL ME INTO THINKING ANY OF THEM HAD A CHANCE. I'D DO WELL TO REMEMBER THEY DON'T.
THE CREATURES AT THE BASE WEREN'T MEANT FOR ANY OF THEIR EYES.
I KNOW. THEY WON'T UNDERSTAND.
THE THINGS AT THE BASE DON'T MEAN ANY HARM.

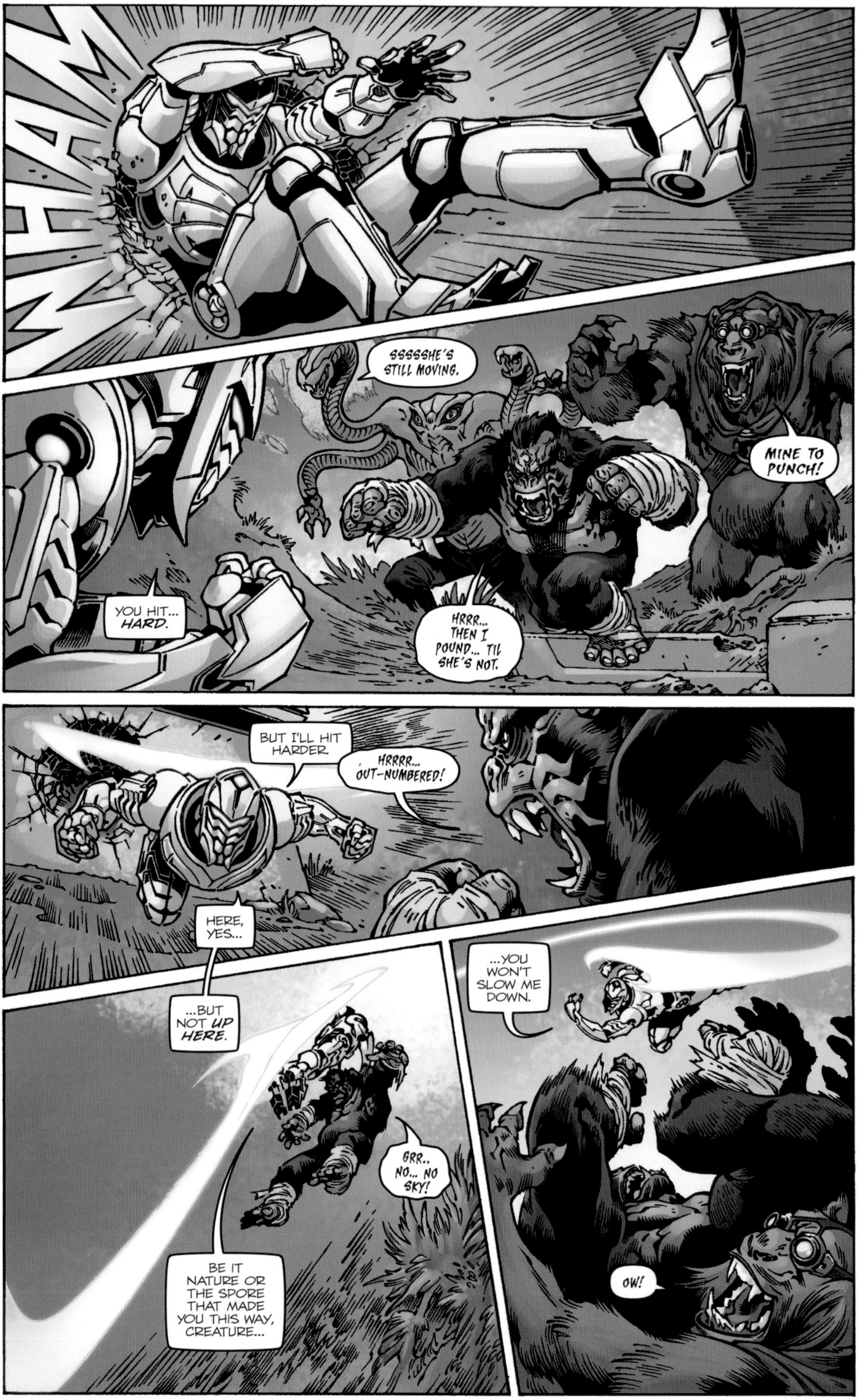
WHAM
SSSSSHE'S STILL MOVING.
MINE TO PUNCH!
YOU HIT... HARD.
HRRR... THEN I POUND... TIL SHE'S NOT.
BUT I'LL HIT HARDER.
HRRRR... OUT-NUMBERED!
HERE, YES...
...BUT NOT UP HERE.
GRR.. NO... NO SKY!
BE IT NATURE OR THE SPORE THAT MADE YOU THIS WAY, CREATURE...
...YOU WON'T SLOW ME DOWN.
OW!

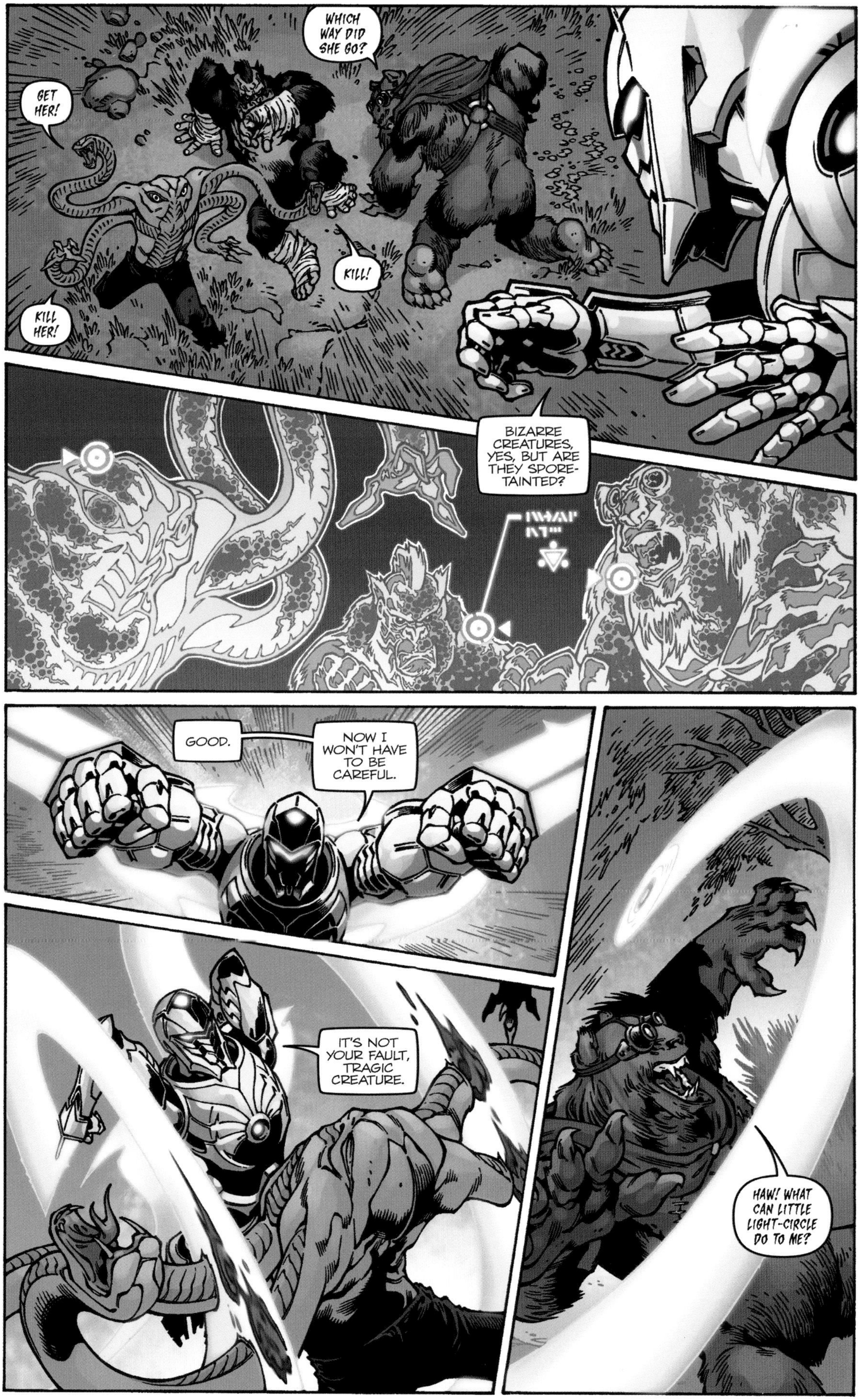
WHICH WAY DID SHE GO?
GET HER!
KILL!
KILL HER!
BIZARRE CREATURES, YES, BUT ARE THEY SPORE-TAINTED?
GOOD.
NOW I WON'T HAVE TO BE CAREFUL.
IT'S NOT YOUR FAULT, TRAGIC CREATURE.
HAW! WHAT CAN LITTLE LIGHT-CIRCLE DO TO ME?

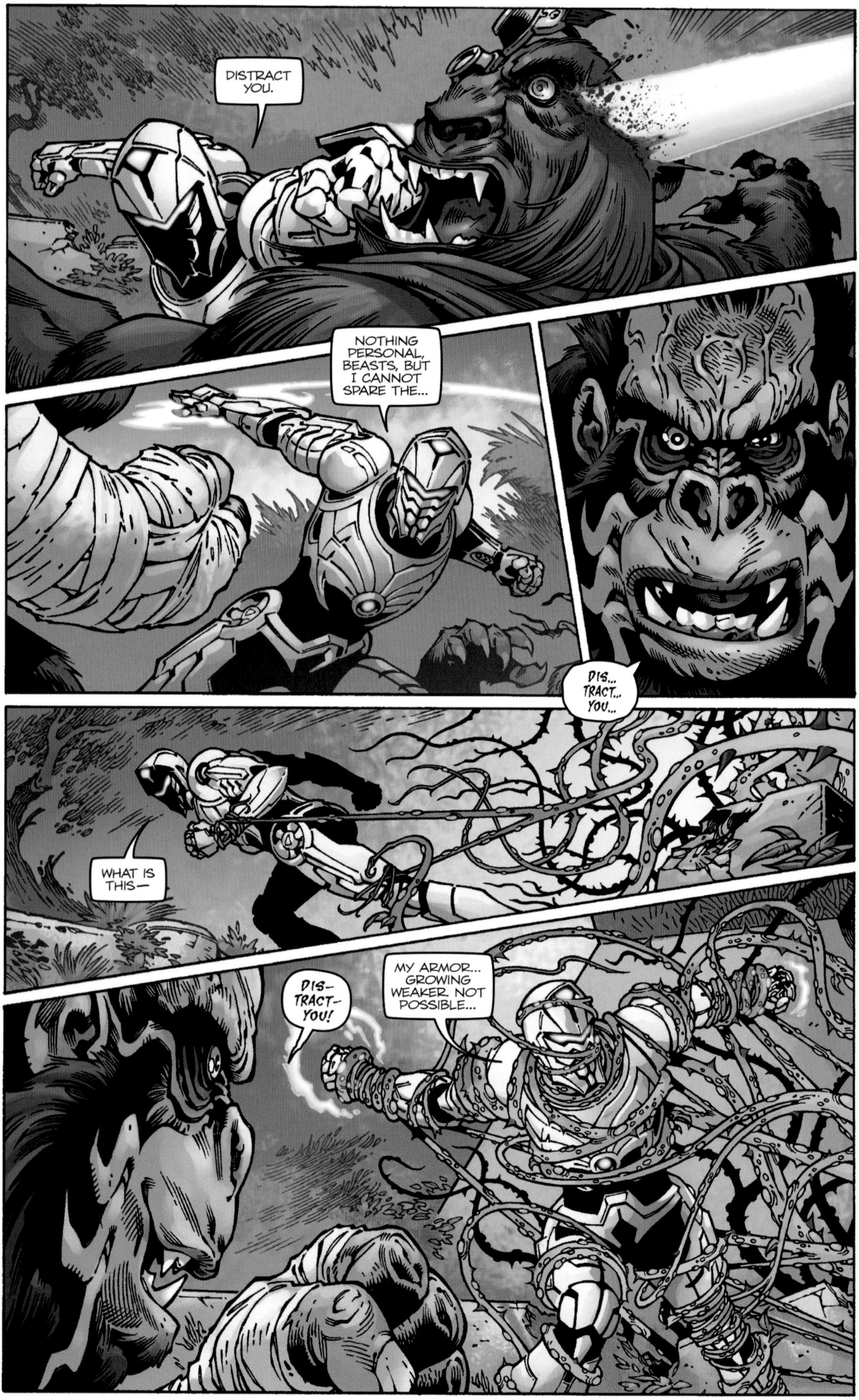
DISTRACT YOU.
NOTHING PERSONAL, BEASTS, BUT I CANNOT SPARE THE...
DIS... TRACT... YOU...
WHAT IS THIS—
DIS-TRACT-YOU!
MY ARMOR... GROWING WEAKER NOT POSSIBLE...

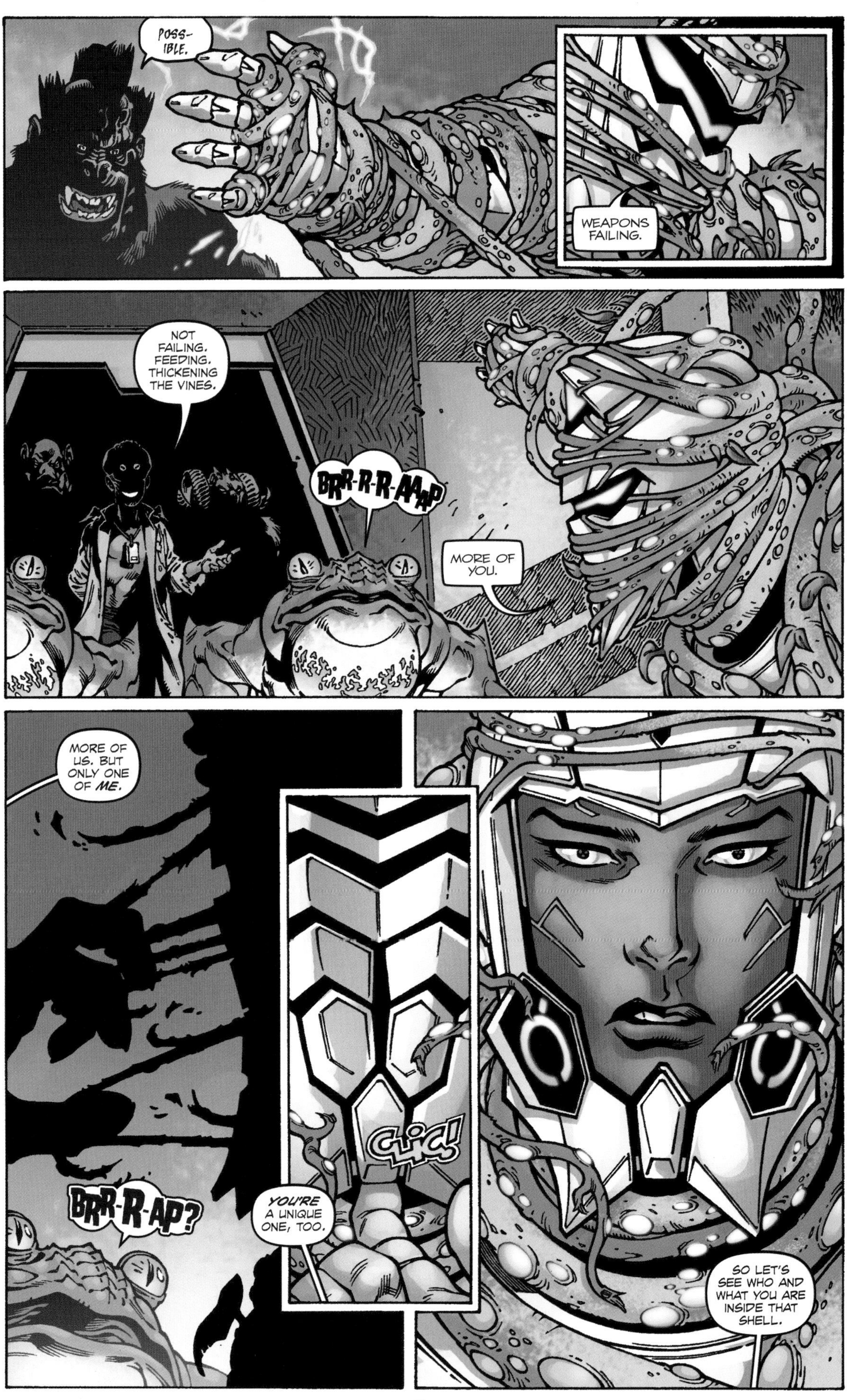
POSS-IBLE.
WEAPONS FAILING.
NOT FAILING. FEEDING. THICKENING THE VINES.
BRR-R-R-AAAP
MORE OF YOU.
MORE OF US. BUT ONLY ONE OF *ME*.
CLIC!
BRR-R-AP?
YOU'RE A UNIQUE ONE, TOO.
SO LET'S SEE WHO AND WHAT YOU ARE INSIDE THAT SHELL.

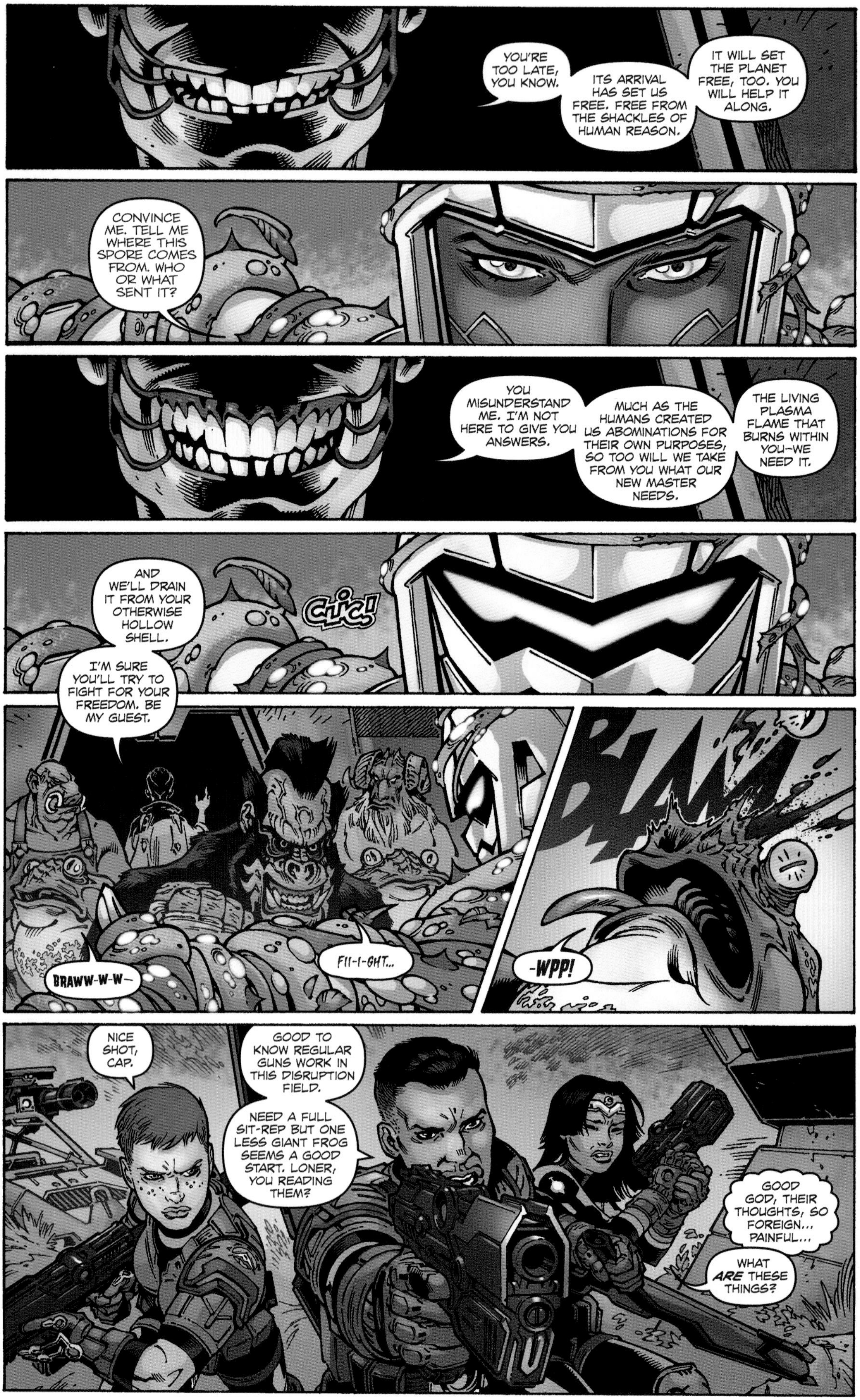

YOU'RE TOO LATE, YOU KNOW.
ITS ARRIVAL HAS SET US FREE. FREE FROM THE SHACKLES OF HUMAN REASON.
IT WILL SET THE PLANET FREE, TOO. YOU WILL HELP IT ALONG.
CONVINCE ME. TELL ME WHERE THIS SPORE COMES FROM. WHO OR WHAT SENT IT?
YOU MISUNDERSTAND ME. I'M NOT HERE TO GIVE YOU ANSWERS.
MUCH AS THE HUMANS CREATED US ABOMINATIONS FOR THEIR OWN PURPOSES, SO TOO WILL WE TAKE FROM YOU WHAT OUR NEW MASTER NEEDS.
THE LIVING PLASMA FLAME THAT BURNS WITHIN YOU—WE NEED IT.
AND WE'LL DRAIN IT FROM YOUR OTHERWISE HOLLOW SHELL.
CLIC!
I'M SURE YOU'LL TRY TO FIGHT FOR YOUR FREEDOM. BE MY GUEST.
BRAWW-W-W—
FII-I-GHT...
BLAM
-WPP!
NICE SHOT, CAP.
GOOD TO KNOW REGULAR GUNS WORK IN THIS DISRUPTION FIELD.
NEED A FULL SIT-REP BUT ONE LESS GIANT FROG SEEMS A GOOD START. LONER, YOU READING THEM?
GOOD GOD, THEIR THOUGHTS, SO FOREIGN... PAINFUL...
WHAT ARE THESE THINGS?

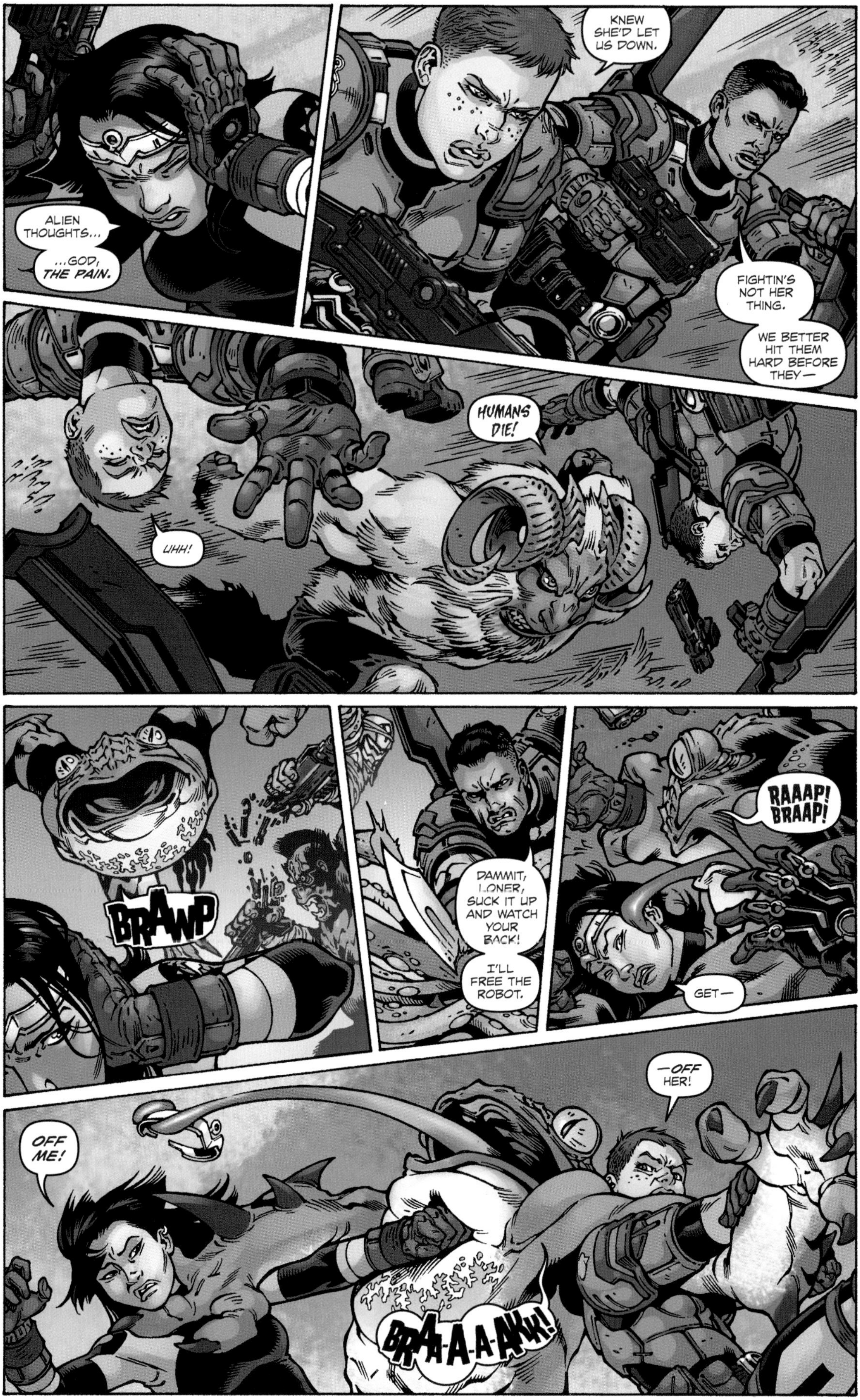
ALIEN THOUGHTS...
...GOD, THE PAIN.
KNEW SHE'D LET US DOWN.
FIGHTIN'S NOT HER THING.
WE BETTER HIT THEM HARD BEFORE THEY—
HUMANS DIE!
UHH!
BRAWP
DAMMIT, LONER, SUCK IT UP AND WATCH YOUR BACK!
I'LL FREE THE ROBOT.
RAAAP! BRAAP!
GET—
—OFF HER!
OFF ME!
BRA-A-A-AKK!

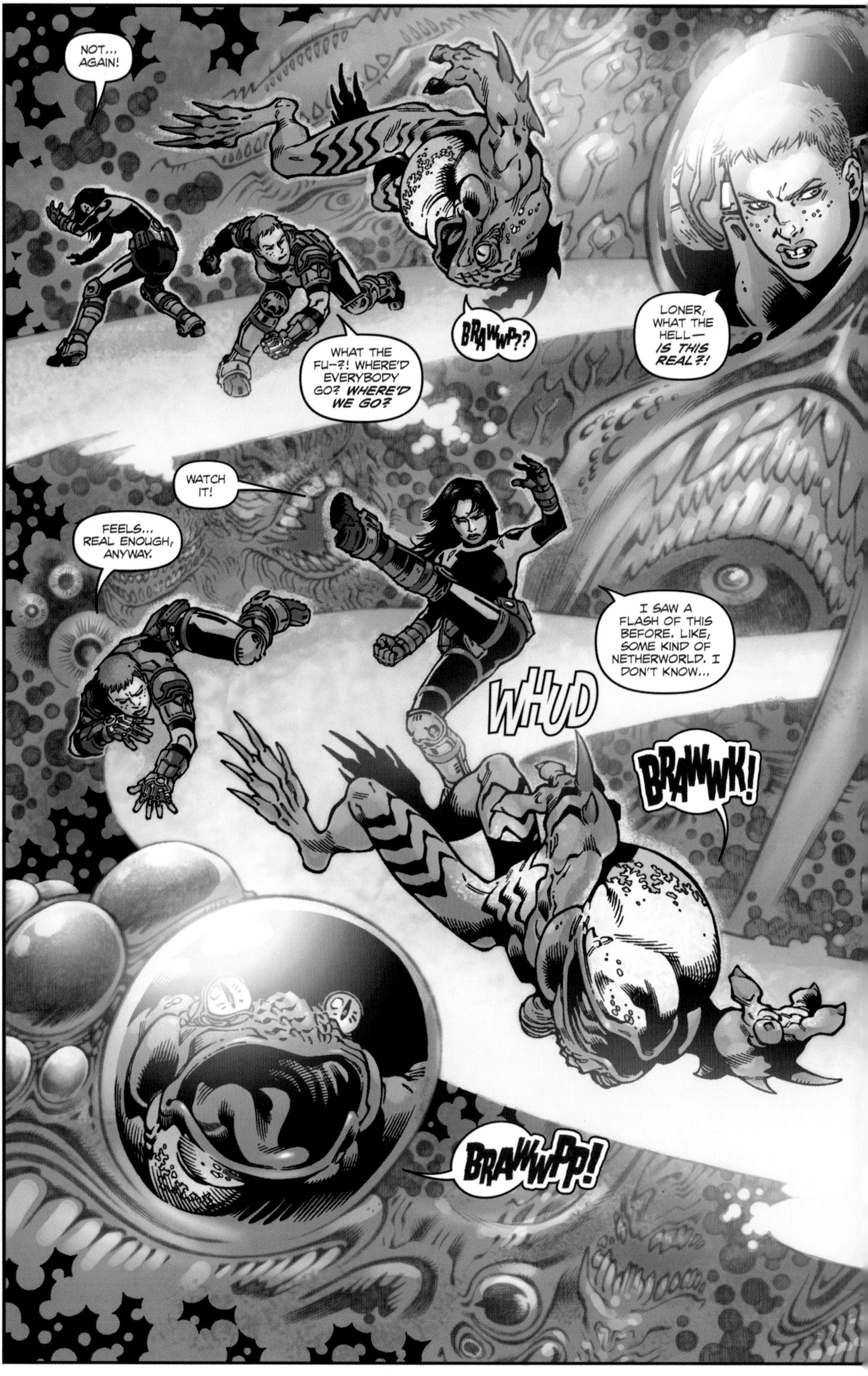
NOT... AGAIN!
WHAT THE FU-?! WHERE'D EVERYBODY GO? WHERE'D WE GO?
BRAWWP??
LONER, WHAT THE HELL— IS THIS REAL?!
WATCH IT!
FEELS... REAL ENOUGH, ANYWAY.
I SAW A FLASH OF THIS BEFORE. LIKE, SOME KIND OF NETHERWORLD. I DON'T KNOW...
WHUD
BRAWWK!
BRAWWPP!

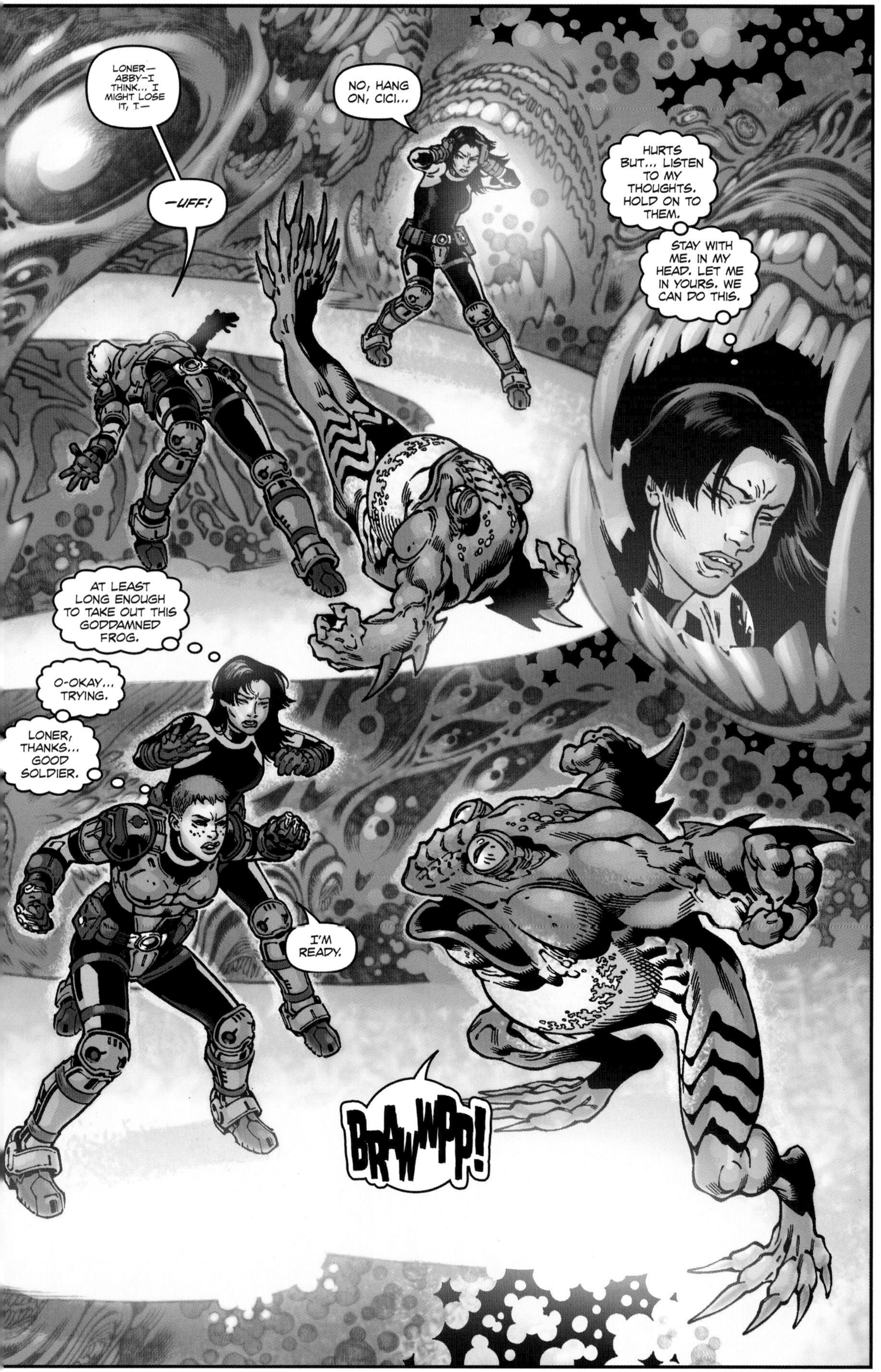

LONER— ABBY—I THINK... I MIGHT LOSE IT, T—
—UFF!
NO, HANG ON, CICI...
HURTS BUT... LISTEN TO MY THOUGHTS. HOLD ON TO THEM.
STAY WITH ME. IN MY HEAD. LET ME IN YOURS. WE CAN DO THIS.
AT LEAST LONG ENOUGH TO TAKE OUT THIS GODDAMNED FROG.
O-OKAY... TRYING.
LONER, THANKS... GOOD SOLDIER.
I'M READY.
BRAWWPP!

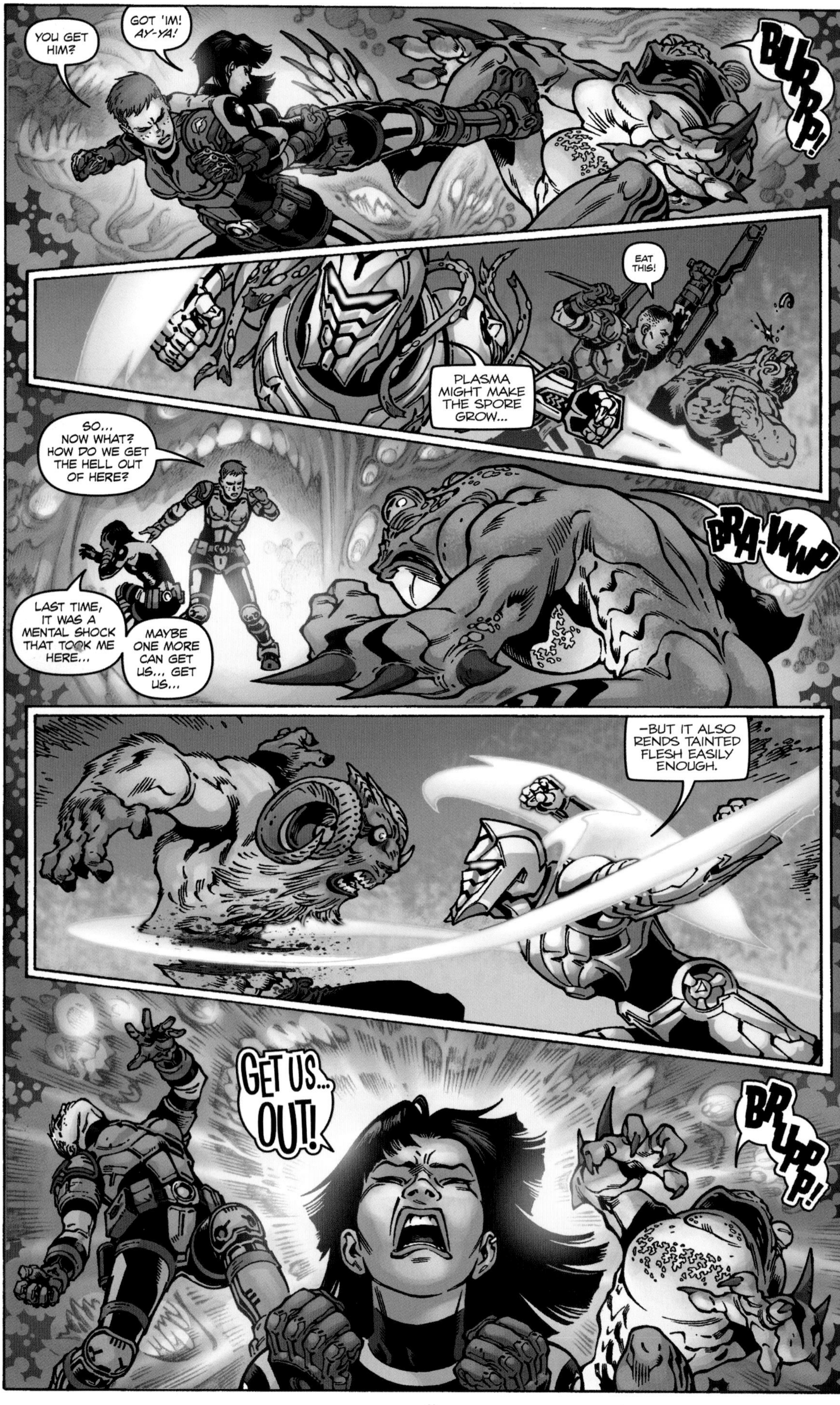
YOU GET HIM?
GOT 'IM! AY-YA!
BURRP!
EAT THIS!
PLASMA MIGHT MAKE THE SPORE GROW...
SO... NOW WHAT? HOW DO WE GET THE HELL OUT OF HERE?
BRA-WWP
LAST TIME, IT WAS A MENTAL SHOCK THAT TOOK ME HERE...
MAYBE ONE MORE CAN GET US... GET US...
–BUT IT ALSO RENDS TAINTED FLESH EASILY ENOUGH.
GET US... OUT!
BRUPP!

WE'RE... BACK?

CICI...

YES. YOUR PSYCHIC EXPLOSION FLOORED EVERYONE ELSE.

EVERYONE BUT THEIR LEADER HE'S GONE.

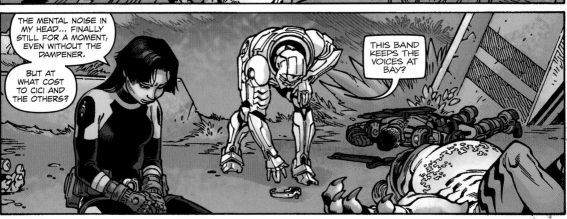

THE MENTAL NOISE IN MY HEAD... FINALLY STILL FOR A MOMENT, EVEN WITHOUT THE DAMPENER.

BUT AT WHAT COST TO CICI AND THE OTHERS?

THIS BAND KEEPS THE VOICES AT BAY?

SUPPOSED TO, ANYWAY. BUT WHY DON'T *YOUR* THOUGHTS FLOOD MY HEAD LIKE EVERYONE ELSE'S?

I UNDERSTAND NOTHING OF YOUR PLANET OR YOUR MENTAL MAKE-UP.

PERHAPS MY METAL ARMOR INHIBITS IT.

PERHAPS I'M JUST TOO ALIEN FOR YOU TO UNDERSTAND WHAT IS INSIDE ME.

ALIENS. MUTATES. I'M SO OUT OF MY ELEMENT HERE.

NO MORE THAN ME. BUT COME ON, WE CAN'T AFFORD THE TIME—THERE MIGHT BE MORE OF THESE MONSTROSITIES WAITING TO ATTACK.

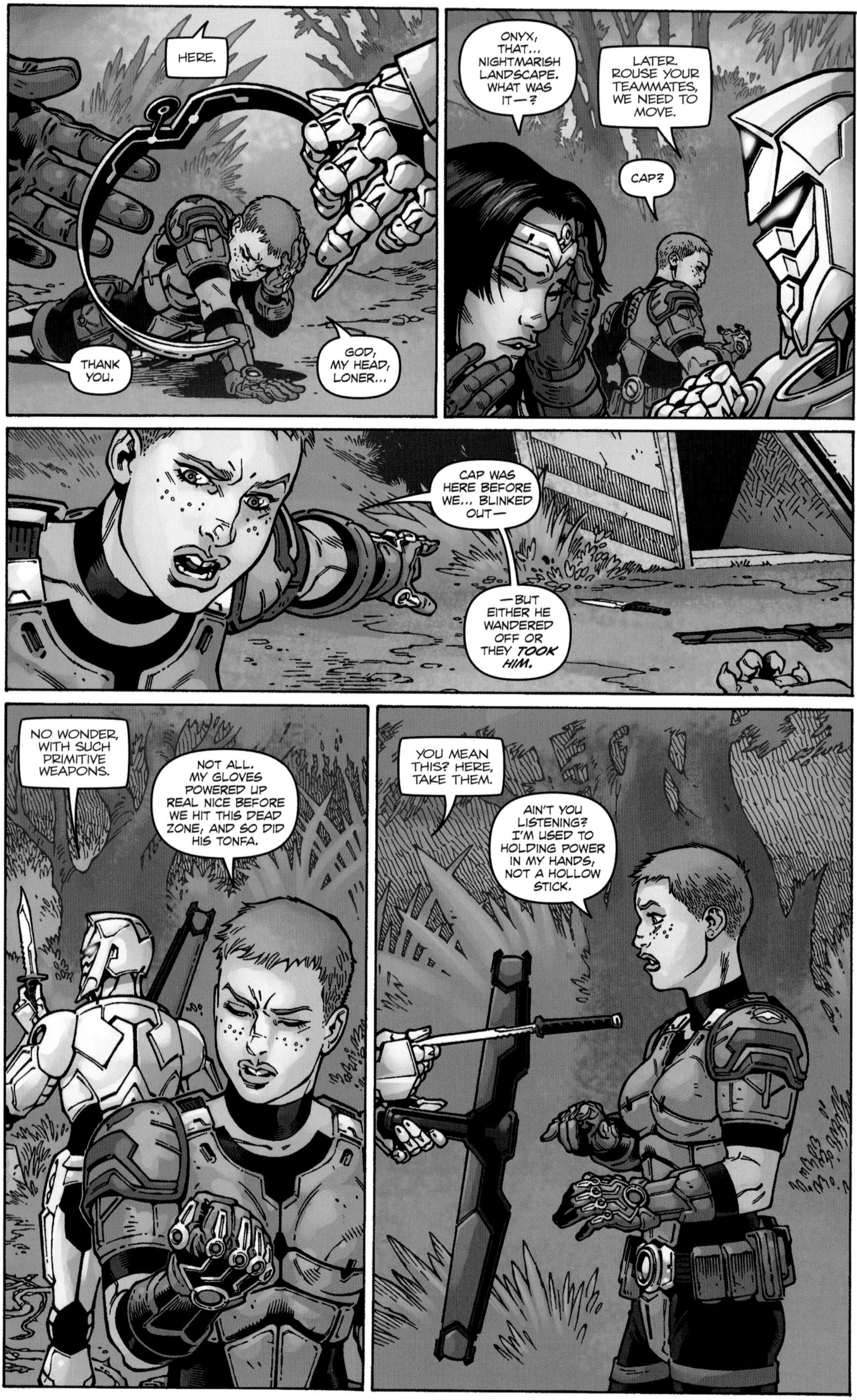
HERE.
THANK YOU.
GOD, MY HEAD, LONER...
ONYX, THAT... NIGHTMARISH LANDSCAPE. WHAT WAS IT—?
LATER. ROUSE YOUR TEAMMATES, WE NEED TO MOVE.
CAP?
CAP WAS HERE BEFORE WE... BLINKED OUT—
—BUT EITHER HE WANDERED OFF OR THEY TOOK HIM.
NO WONDER, WITH SUCH PRIMITIVE WEAPONS.
NOT ALL. MY GLOVES POWERED UP REAL NICE BEFORE WE HIT THIS DEAD ZONE, AND SO DID HIS TONFA.
YOU MEAN THIS? HERE, TAKE THEM.
AIN'T YOU LISTENING? I'M USED TO HOLDING POWER IN MY HANDS, NOT A HOLLOW STICK.

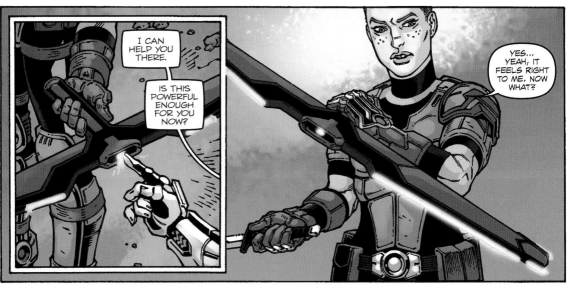

I CAN HELP YOU THERE.

IS THIS POWERFUL ENOUGH FOR YOU NOW?

YES... YEAH, IT FEELS RIGHT TO ME. NOW WHAT?

NOW THE FIGHTERS AMONG YOU NEED TO PREPARE TO FIGHT FOR YOUR PLANET'S VERY EXISTENCE.

BUT BEFORE WE GO INSIDE...

...THERE'S THE MATTER OF THE BATTLE'S FEW SURVIVORS TO BE DEALT WITH.

LEAVE THAT UNSAVORY BUSINESS TO ME.

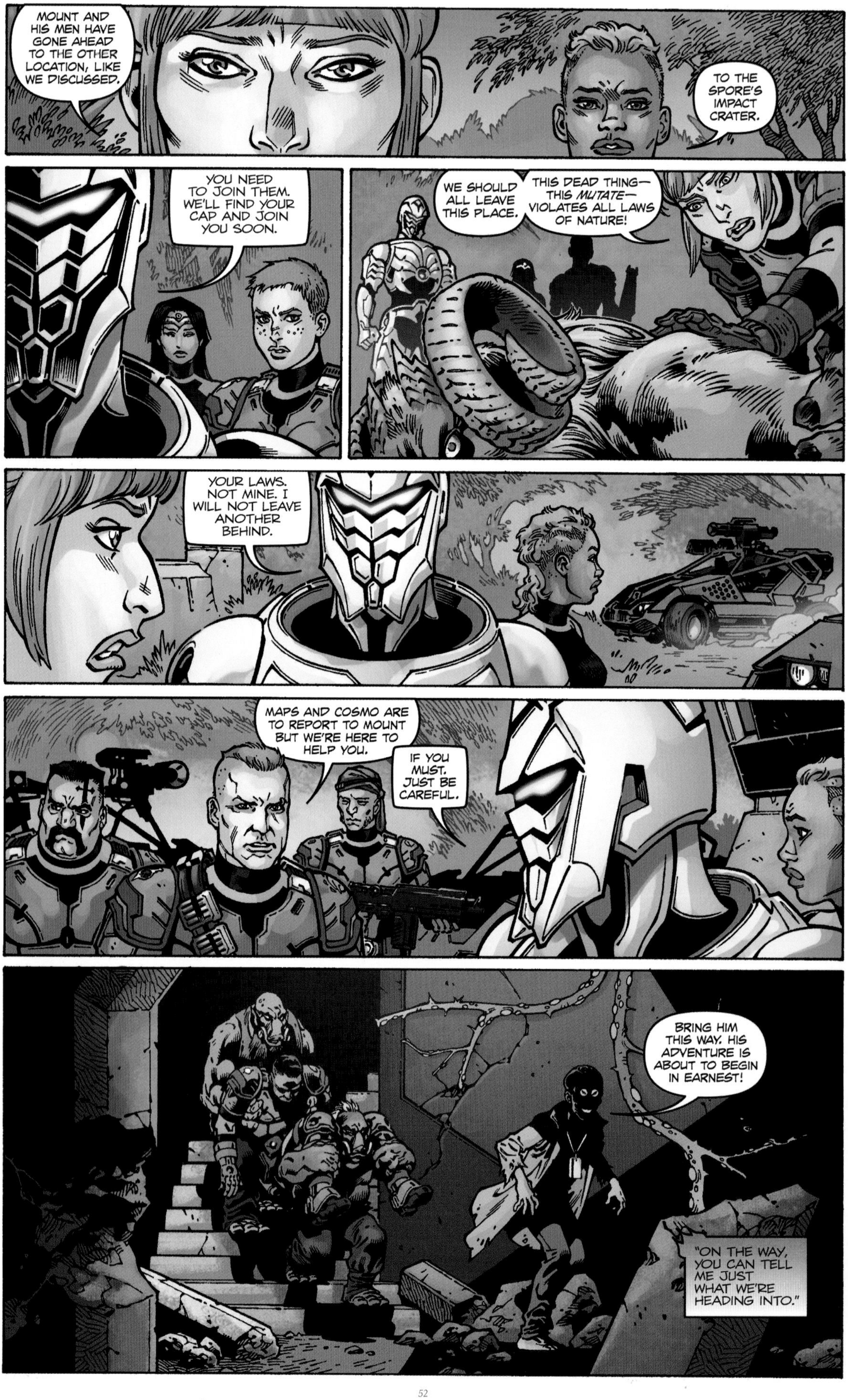
MOUNT AND HIS MEN HAVE GONE AHEAD TO THE OTHER LOCATION, LIKE WE DISCUSSED.
TO THE SPORE'S IMPACT CRATER.
YOU NEED TO JOIN THEM. WE'LL FIND YOUR CAP AND JOIN YOU SOON.
WE SHOULD ALL LEAVE THIS PLACE.
THIS DEAD THING— THIS *MUTATE*— VIOLATES ALL LAWS OF NATURE!
YOUR LAWS. NOT MINE. I WILL NOT LEAVE ANOTHER BEHIND.
MAPS AND COSMO ARE TO REPORT TO MOUNT BUT WE'RE HERE TO HELP YOU.
IF YOU MUST. JUST BE CAREFUL.
BRING HIM THIS WAY. HIS ADVENTURE IS ABOUT TO BEGIN IN EARNEST!
"ON THE WAY, YOU CAN TELL ME JUST WHAT WE'RE HEADING INTO."

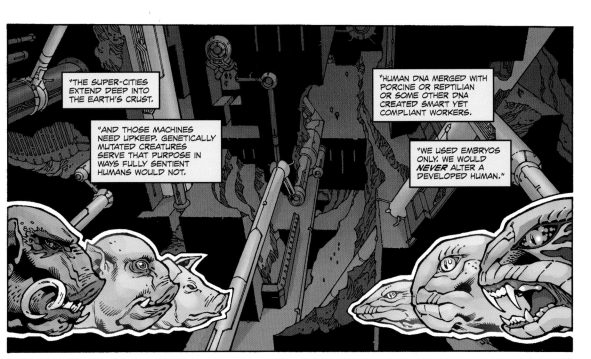

"THE SUPER-CITIES EXTEND DEEP INTO THE EARTH'S CRUST.

"AND THOSE MACHINES NEED UPKEEP. GENETICALLY MUTATED CREATURES SERVE THAT PURPOSE IN WAYS FULLY SENTIENT HUMANS WOULD NOT.

"HUMAN DNA MERGED WITH PORCINE OR REPTILIAN OR SOME OTHER DNA CREATED SMART YET COMPLIANT WORKERS.

"WE USED EMBRYOS ONLY. WE WOULD *NEVER* ALTER A DEVELOPED HUMAN."

"NEVER."

UHHHH

WHAT THE HELL...?

NO, MAN, GOD, DON'T...!

LET HIM. PANIC WILL HASTEN THE END RESULT.

SNORT!

HUMAN... STRUGGLE...

"SUBMISSION.

"COMPREHENSION."

NNNN!

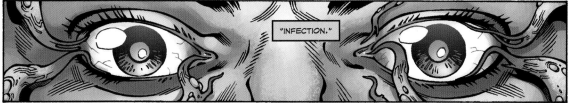

"INFECTION."

"AND SUBJUGATION."

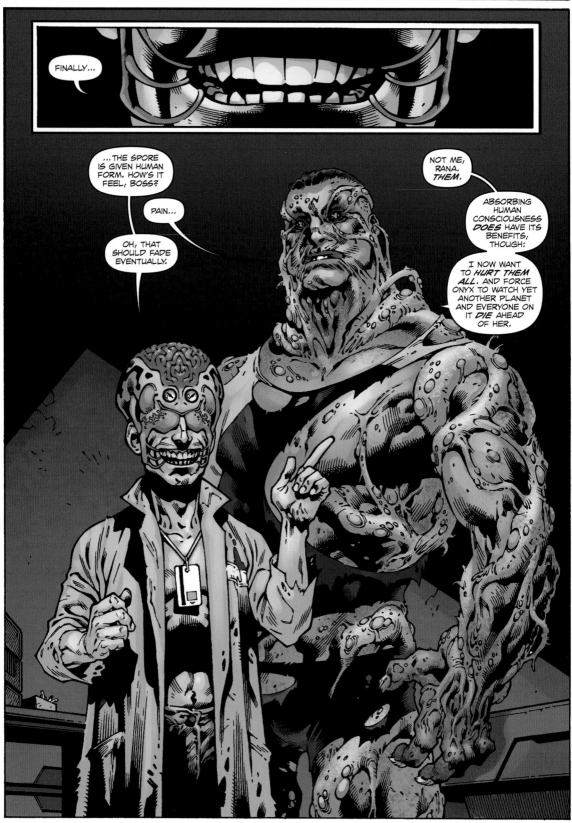

FINALLY...

...THE SPORE IS GIVEN HUMAN FORM. HOW'S IT FEEL, BOSS?

PAIN...

OH, THAT SHOULD FADE EVENTUALLY.

NOT ME, RANA, *THEM*.

ABSORBING HUMAN CONSCIOUSNESS *DOES* HAVE ITS BENEFITS, THOUGH:

I NOW WANT TO *HURT THEM ALL*. AND FORCE ONYX TO WATCH YET ANOTHER PLANET AND EVERYONE ON IT *DIE* AHEAD OF HER.

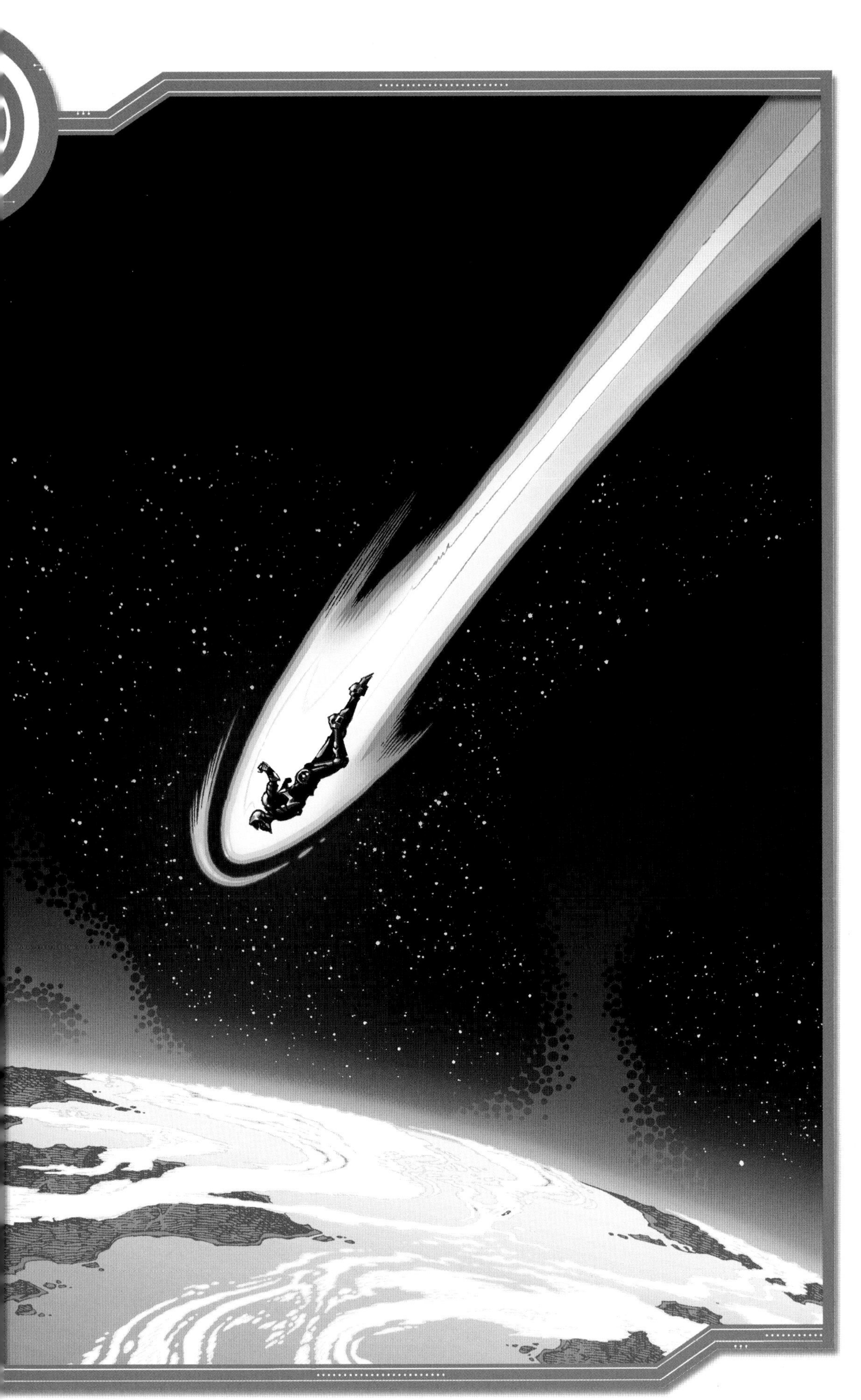

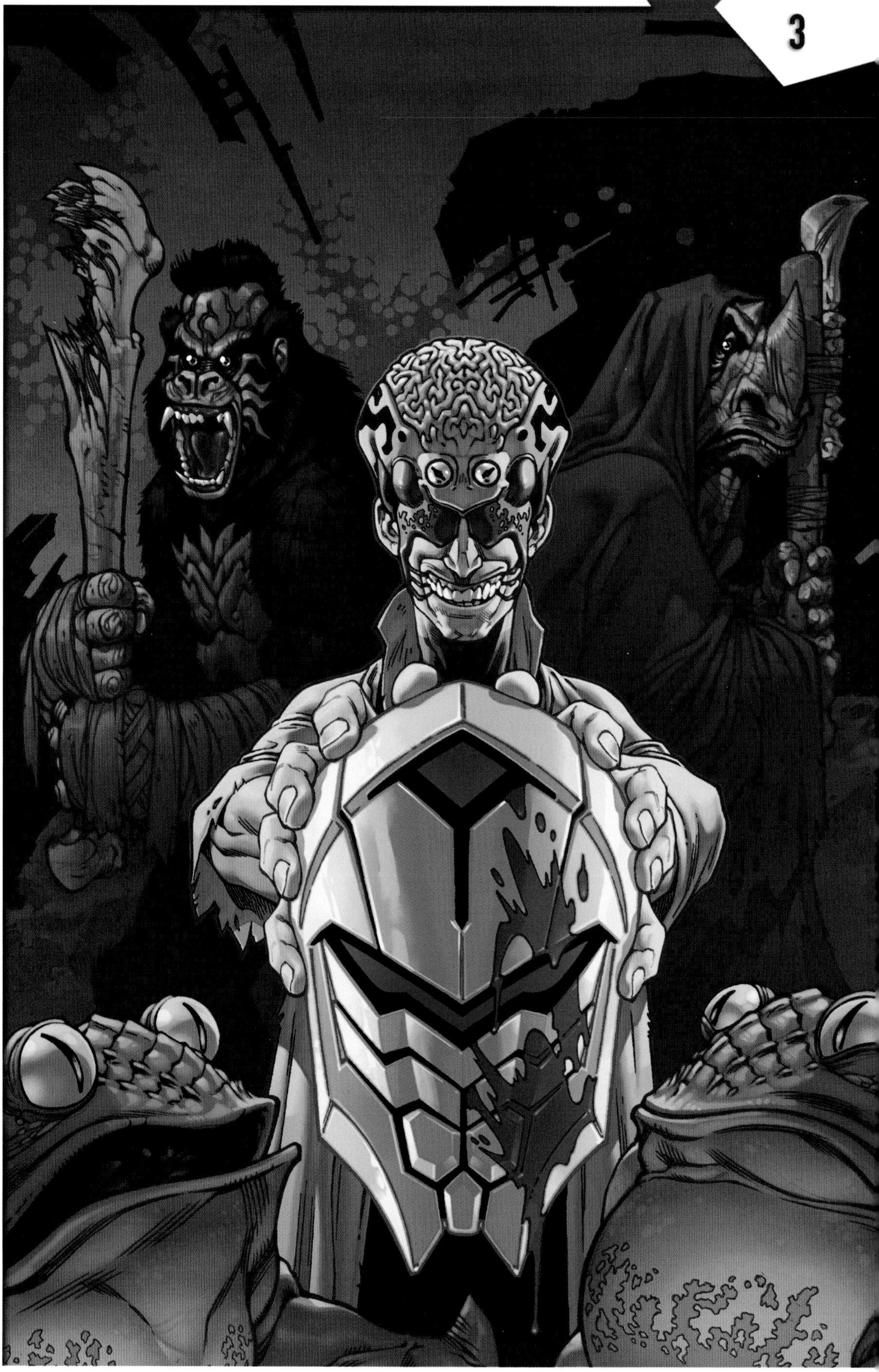

3

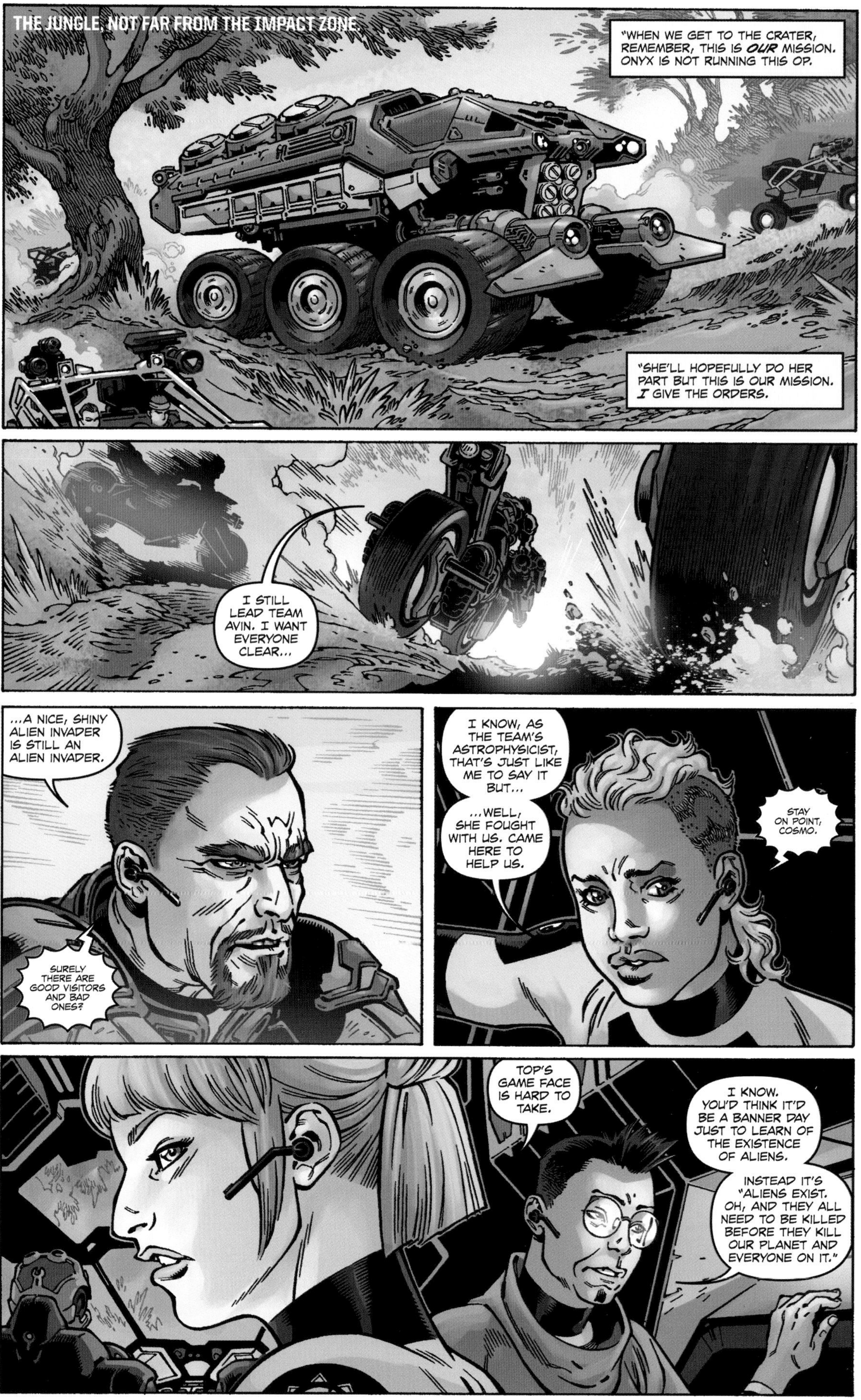
THE JUNGLE, NOT FAR FROM THE IMPACT ZONE.
"WHEN WE GET TO THE CRATER, REMEMBER, THIS IS OUR MISSION. ONYX IS NOT RUNNING THIS OP.
"SHE'LL HOPEFULLY DO HER PART BUT THIS IS OUR MISSION. I GIVE THE ORDERS.
I STILL LEAD TEAM AVIN. I WANT EVERYONE CLEAR...
...A NICE, SHINY ALIEN INVADER IS STILL AN ALIEN INVADER.
SURELY THERE ARE GOOD VISITORS AND BAD ONES?
I KNOW, AS THE TEAM'S ASTROPHYSICIST, THAT'S JUST LIKE ME TO SAY IT BUT...
...WELL, SHE FOUGHT WITH US. CAME HERE TO HELP US.
STAY ON POINT, COSMO.
TOP'S GAME FACE IS HARD TO TAKE.
I KNOW. YOU'D THINK IT'D BE A BANNER DAY JUST TO LEARN OF THE EXISTENCE OF ALIENS.
INSTEAD IT'S "ALIENS EXIST. OH, AND THEY ALL NEED TO BE KILLED BEFORE THEY KILL OUR PLANET AND EVERYONE ON IT."

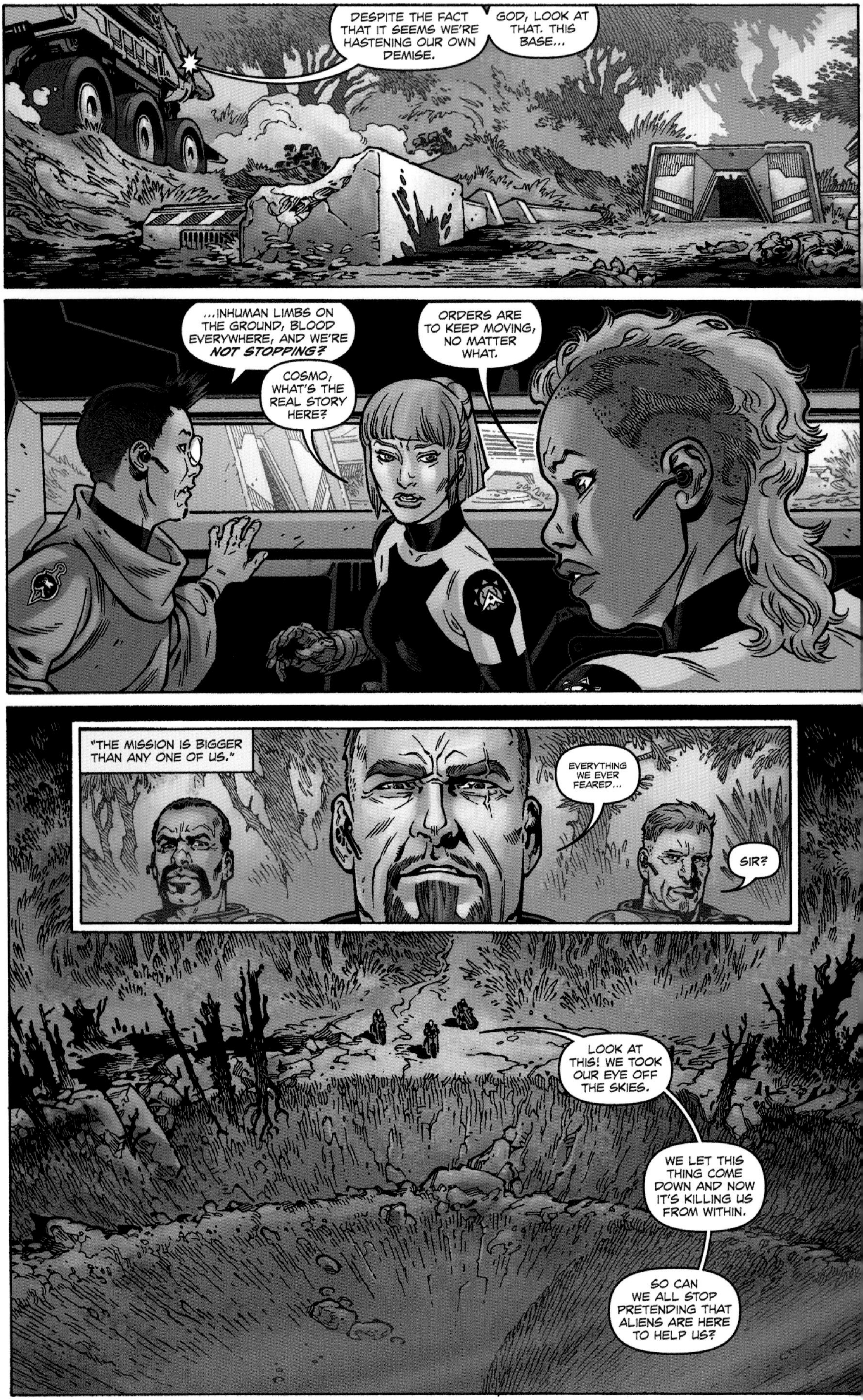
DESPITE THE FACT THAT IT SEEMS WE'RE HASTENING OUR OWN DEMISE.
GOD, LOOK AT THAT. THIS BASE...
...INHUMAN LIMBS ON THE GROUND, BLOOD EVERYWHERE, AND WE'RE *NOT STOPPING?*
COSMO, WHAT'S THE REAL STORY HERE?
ORDERS ARE TO KEEP MOVING, NO MATTER WHAT.
"THE MISSION IS BIGGER THAN ANY ONE OF US."
EVERYTHING WE EVER FEARED...
SIR?
LOOK AT THIS! WE TOOK OUR EYE OFF THE SKIES.
WE LET THIS THING COME DOWN AND NOW IT'S KILLING US FROM WITHIN.
SO CAN WE ALL STOP PRETENDING THAT ALIENS ARE HERE TO HELP US?

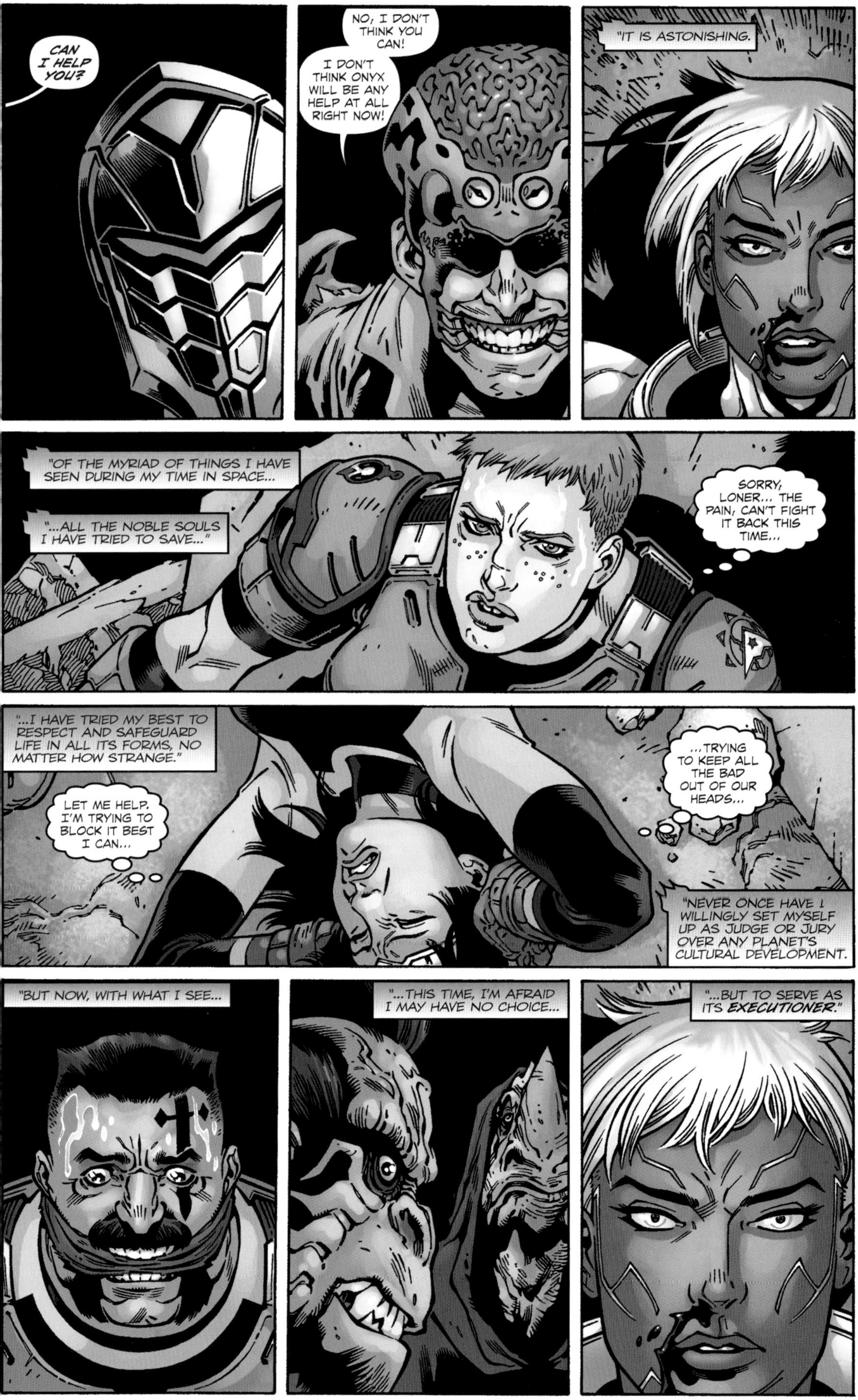
CAN I HELP YOU?
NO, I DON'T THINK YOU CAN!
I DON'T THINK ONYX WILL BE ANY HELP AT ALL RIGHT NOW!
"IT IS ASTONISHING.
"OF THE MYRIAD OF THINGS I HAVE SEEN DURING MY TIME IN SPACE...
"...ALL THE NOBLE SOULS I HAVE TRIED TO SAVE..."
SORRY, LONER... THE PAIN, CAN'T FIGHT IT BACK THIS TIME...
"...I HAVE TRIED MY BEST TO RESPECT AND SAFEGUARD LIFE IN ALL ITS FORMS, NO MATTER HOW STRANGE."
LET ME HELP. I'M TRYING TO BLOCK IT BEST I CAN...
...TRYING TO KEEP ALL THE BAD OUT OF OUR HEADS...
"NEVER ONCE HAVE I WILLINGLY SET MYSELF UP AS JUDGE OR JURY OVER ANY PLANET'S CULTURAL DEVELOPMENT.
"BUT NOW, WITH WHAT I SEE...
"...THIS TIME, I'M AFRAID I MAY HAVE NO CHOICE...
"...BUT TO SERVE AS ITS EXECUTIONER."

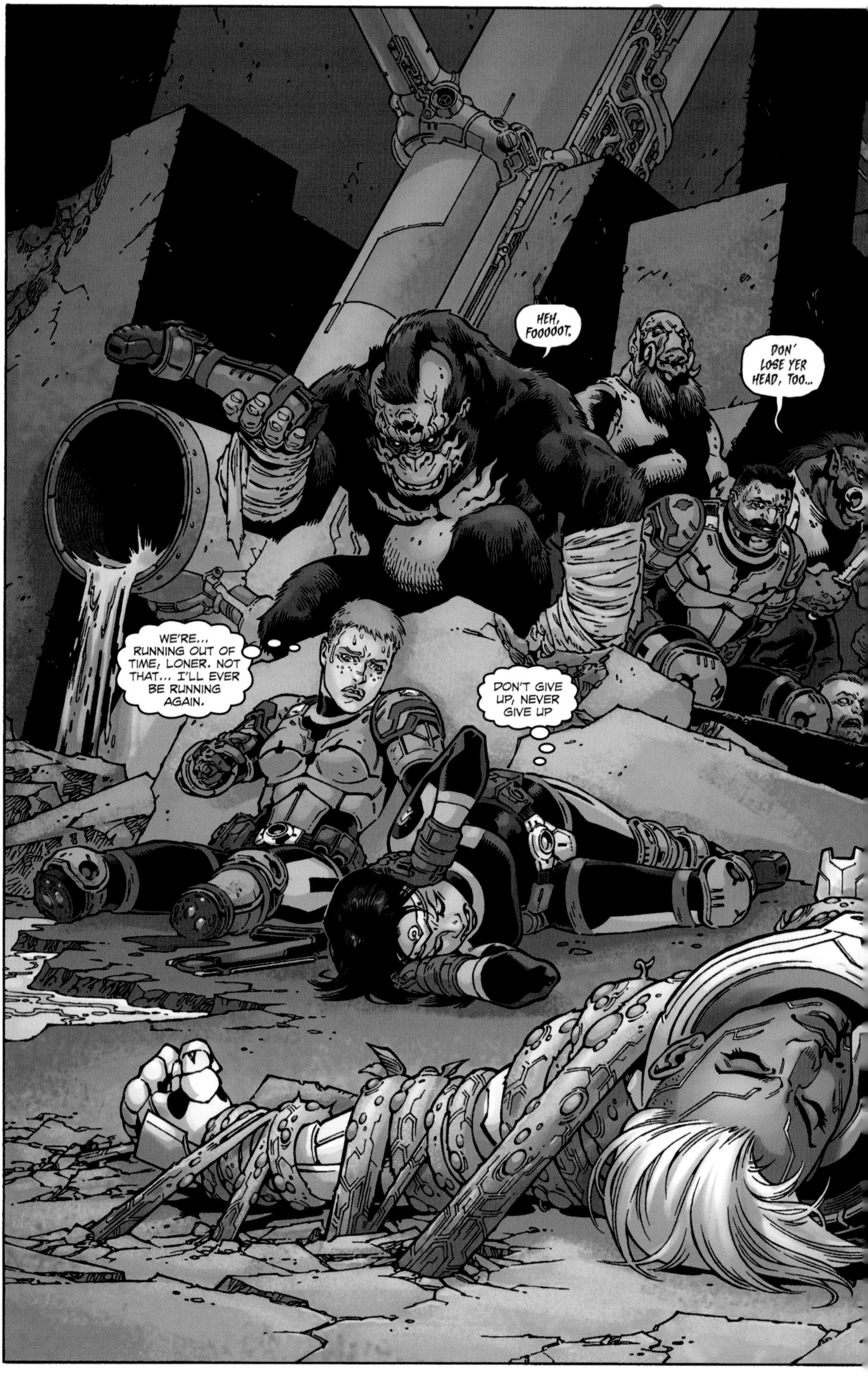
HEH, FOOOOOT.
DON' LOSE YER HEAD, TOO...
WE'RE... RUNNING OUT OF TIME, LONER. NOT THAT... I'LL EVER BE RUNNING AGAIN.
DON'T GIVE UP, NEVER GIVE UP

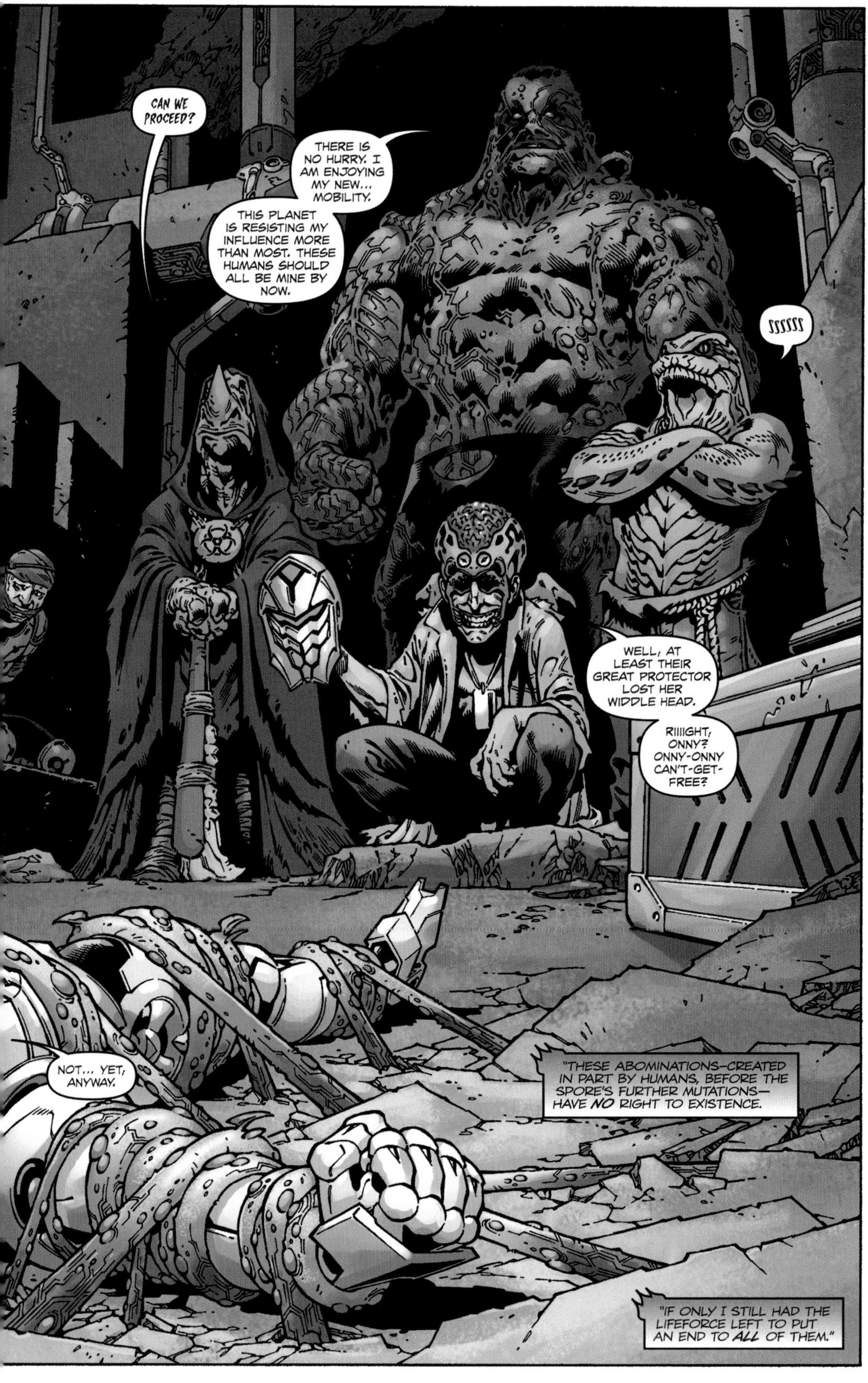
CAN WE PROCEED?
THERE IS NO HURRY. I AM ENJOYING MY NEW... MOBILITY.
THIS PLANET IS RESISTING MY INFLUENCE MORE THAN MOST. THESE HUMANS SHOULD ALL BE MINE BY NOW.
SSSSSS
WELL, AT LEAST THEIR GREAT PROTECTOR LOST HER WIDDLE HEAD.
RIIIIGHT, ONNY? ONNY-ONNY CAN'T-GET-FREE?
NOT... YET, ANYWAY.
"THESE ABOMINATIONS—CREATED IN PART BY HUMANS, BEFORE THE SPORE'S FURTHER MUTATIONS—HAVE NO RIGHT TO EXISTENCE.
"IF ONLY I STILL HAD THE LIFEFORCE LEFT TO PUT AN END TO ALL OF THEM."

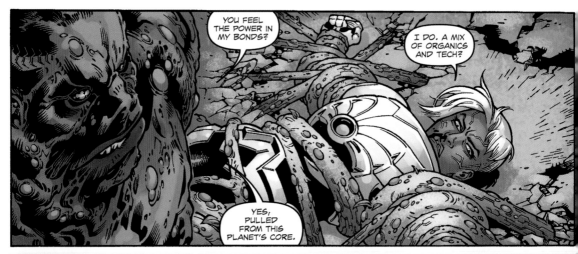

YOU FEEL THE POWER IN MY BONDS?

I DO. A MIX OF ORGANICS AND TECH?

YES, PULLED FROM THIS PLANET'S CORE.

"AND FUELED FURTHER BY THE ENERGY IN THE EARTHLING'S WEAPONS... AND *BOOTS*."

S-SADIST...

BUT I WANT *MORE*. AND I KNOW FROM WHERE IT WILL COME.

THE LIVING PLASMA INSIDE YOU WILL FEED ME THE SAME AS YOUR DEAD PLANET DID.

SPORE... TRYING TO GET IN MY HEAD... HURTS...

...CAN'T BLOCK YOUR PAIN OR STAVE OFF THE SPORE'S INFECTION MUCH LONGER...

YOU'RE DOING GREAT, LONER.

THEN LET'S PLAN OUR NEXT MOVE... WHILE WE CAN.

ON EARTH, ONLY CRAZIES WASTE TIME TELLING THEIR PLANS, JUST *EAT* HER, JUST—

SHHH

EEAAAKKKH!!

SSSSSS!

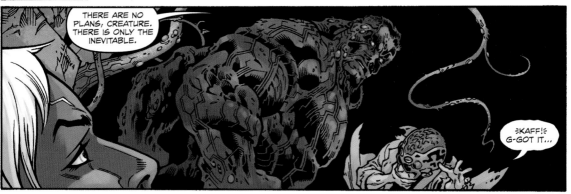

THERE ARE NO PLANS, CREATURE. THERE IS ONLY THE INEVITABLE.

≩KAFF!≩ G-GOT IT...

COME, THEN—TAKE MY PLASMA IF YOU CAN.

THE SURVIVING PELIMOSIANS WILL AVENGE ME AND *END YOU.*

AHH, YES, OTHERS *DID* SURVIVE IN ARMOR LIKE YOURS.

UNTIL THEY PURSUED ME. AND I TOOK THEIR LIFEFORCE FROM THEM.

ESPECIALLY TASTY WAS YOUR MATE WHO CONTROLLED THE FLAME THUSLY, AS I DO NOW.

KIELL... *NO.*

YES.

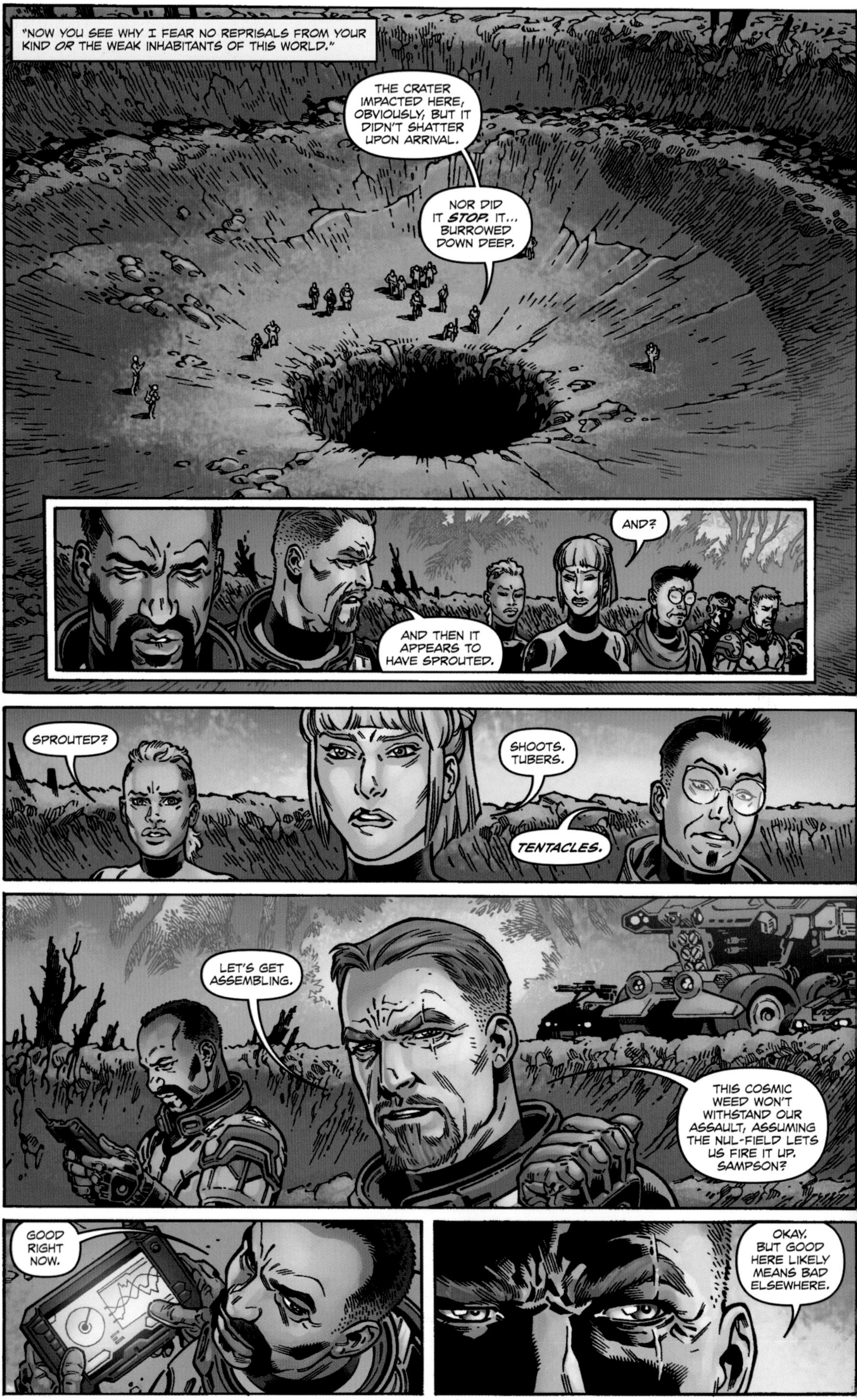
"NOW YOU SEE WHY I FEAR NO REPRISALS FROM YOUR KIND *OR* THE WEAK INHABITANTS OF THIS WORLD."
THE CRATER IMPACTED HERE, OBVIOUSLY, BUT IT DIDN'T SHATTER UPON ARRIVAL.
NOR DID IT *STOP.* IT... BURROWED DOWN DEEP.
AND?
AND THEN IT APPEARS TO HAVE SPROUTED.
SPROUTED?
SHOOTS. TUBERS.
TENTACLES.
LET'S GET ASSEMBLING.
THIS COSMIC WEED WON'T WITHSTAND OUR ASSAULT, ASSUMING THE NUL-FIELD LETS US FIRE IT UP. SAMPSON?
GOOD RIGHT NOW.
OKAY. BUT GOOD HERE LIKELY MEANS BAD ELSEWHERE.

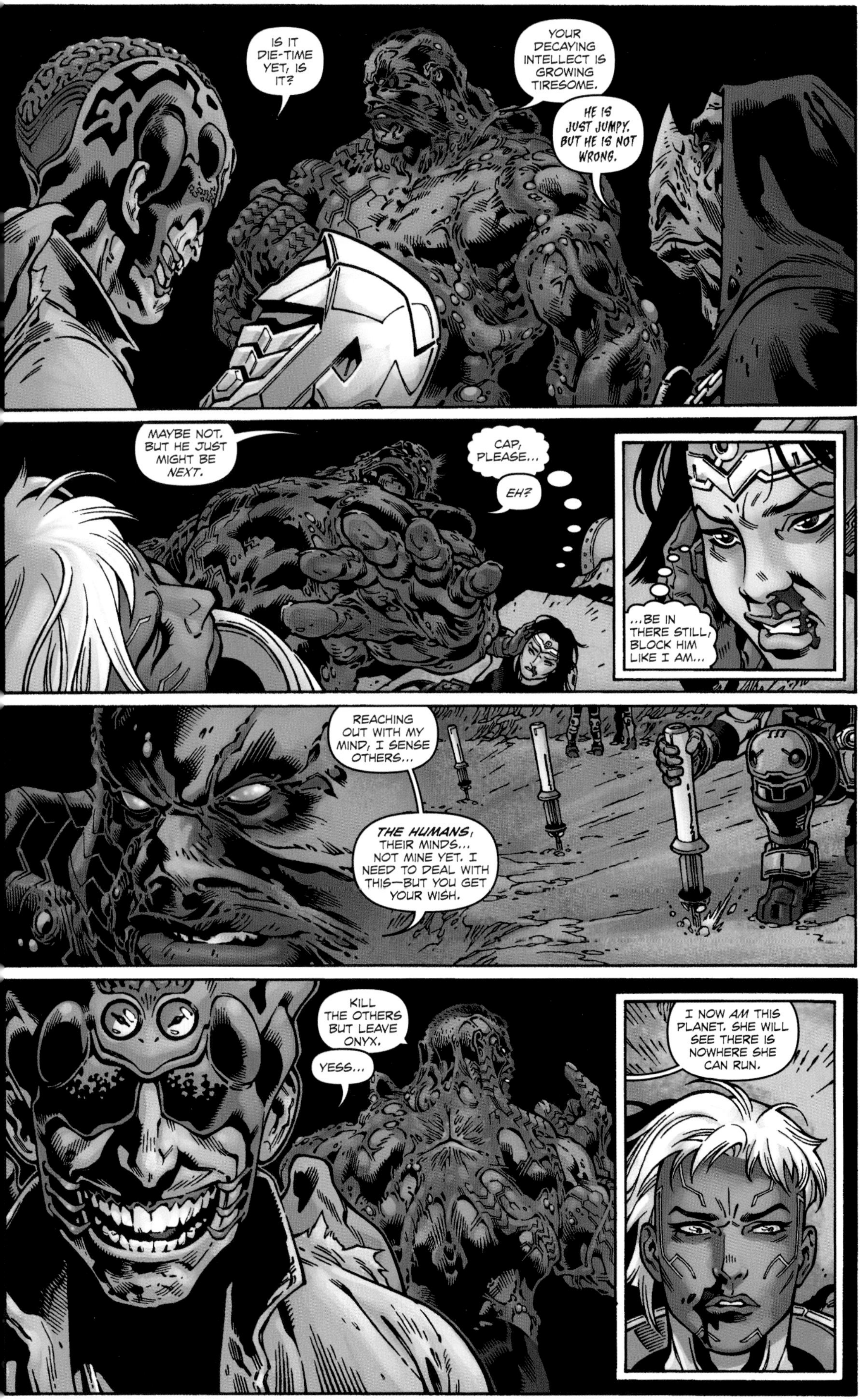
IS IT DIE-TIME YET, IS IT?
YOUR DECAYING INTELLECT IS GROWING TIRESOME.
HE IS JUST JUMPY. BUT HE IS NOT WRONG.
MAYBE NOT. BUT HE JUST MIGHT BE NEXT.
CAP, PLEASE...
EH?
...BE IN THERE STILL, BLOCK HIM LIKE I AM...
REACHING OUT WITH MY MIND, I SENSE OTHERS...
THE HUMANS, THEIR MINDS... NOT MINE YET. I NEED TO DEAL WITH THIS—BUT YOU GET YOUR WISH.
KILL THE OTHERS BUT LEAVE ONYX.
YESS...
I NOW AM THIS PLANET. SHE WILL SEE THERE IS NOWHERE SHE CAN RUN.

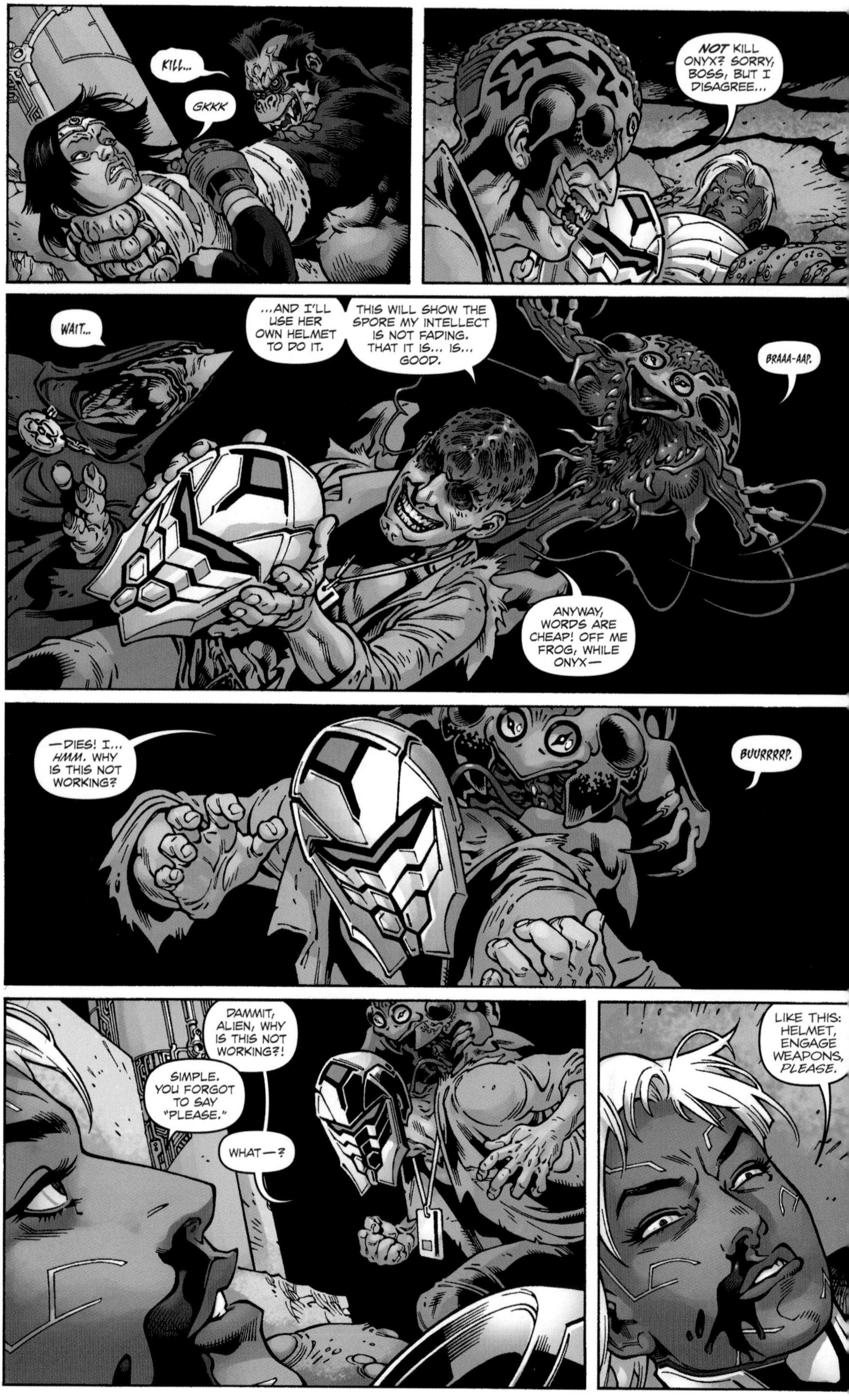
KILL...
GKKK
NOT KILL ONYX? SORRY, BOSS, BUT I DISAGREE...
WAIT...
...AND I'LL USE HER OWN HELMET TO DO IT.
THIS WILL SHOW THE SPORE MY INTELLECT IS NOT FADING. THAT IT IS... IS... GOOD.
BRAAA-AAP.
ANYWAY, WORDS ARE CHEAP! OFF ME FROG, WHILE ONYX—
—DIES! I... HMM. WHY IS THIS NOT WORKING?
BUURRRRP.
DAMMIT, ALIEN, WHY IS THIS NOT WORKING?!
SIMPLE. YOU FORGOT TO SAY "PLEASE."
WHAT—?
LIKE THIS: HELMET, ENGAGE WEAPONS, PLEASE.

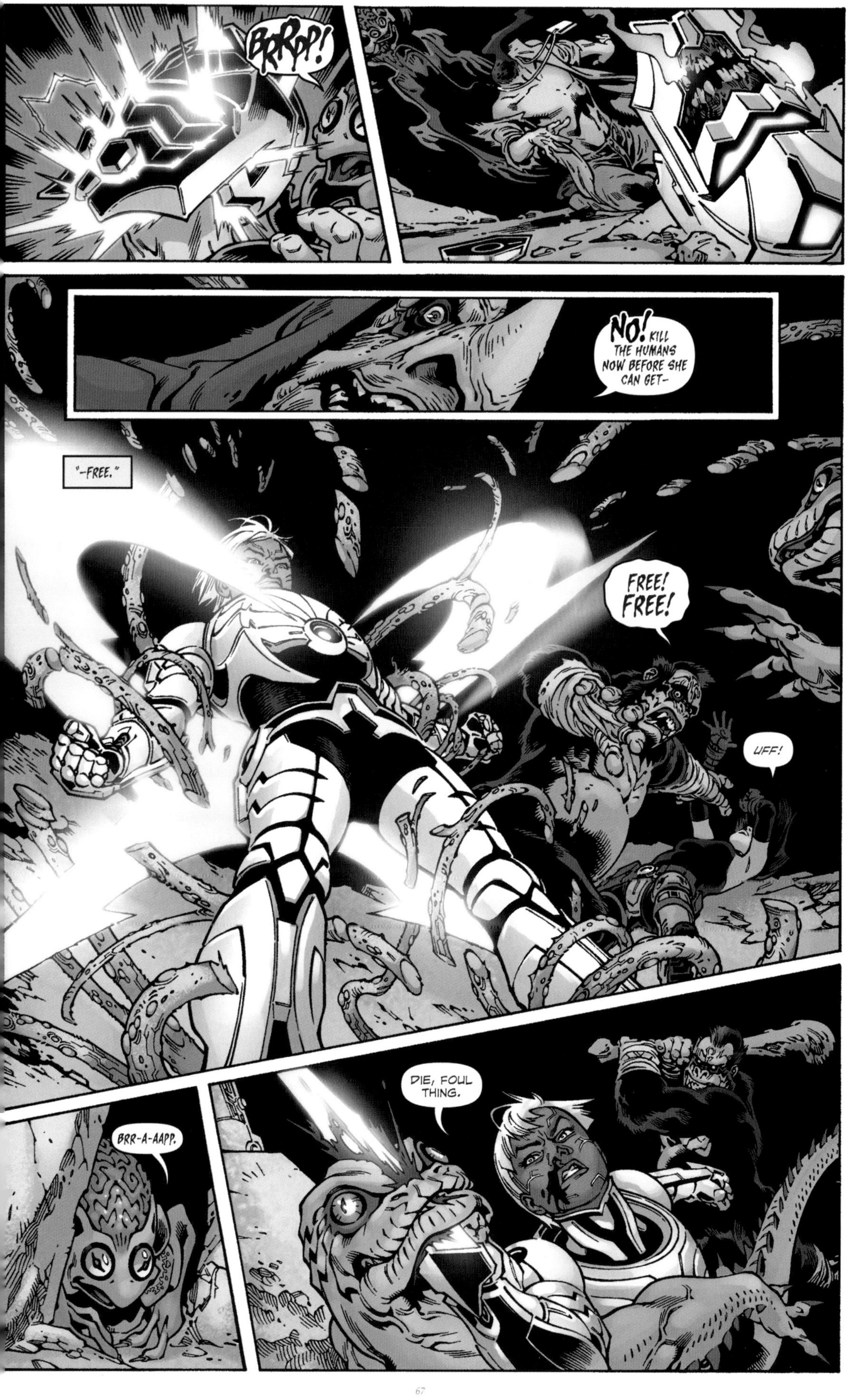
BRRDP!
NO! KILL THE HUMANS NOW BEFORE SHE CAN GET-
"-FREE."
FREE! FREE!
UFF!
BRR-A-AAPP.
DIE, FOUL THING.

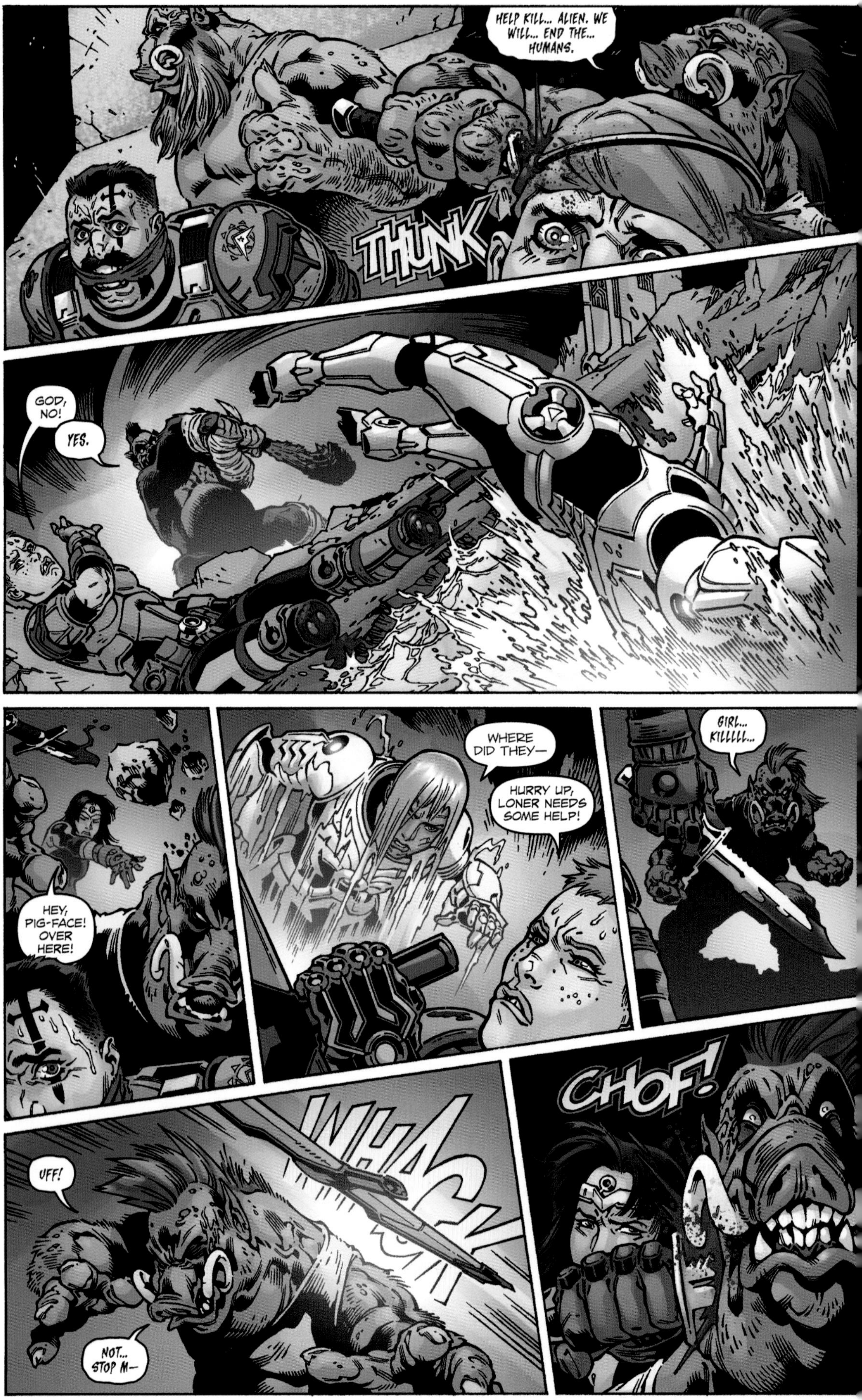
HELP KILL... ALIEN. WE WILL... END THE... HUMANS.
THUNK
GOD, NO!
YES.
HEY, PIG-FACE! OVER HERE!
WHERE DID THEY—
HURRY UP, LONER NEEDS SOME HELP!
GIRL... KILLLLL...
UFF!
WHACK
NOT... STOP M—
CHOF!

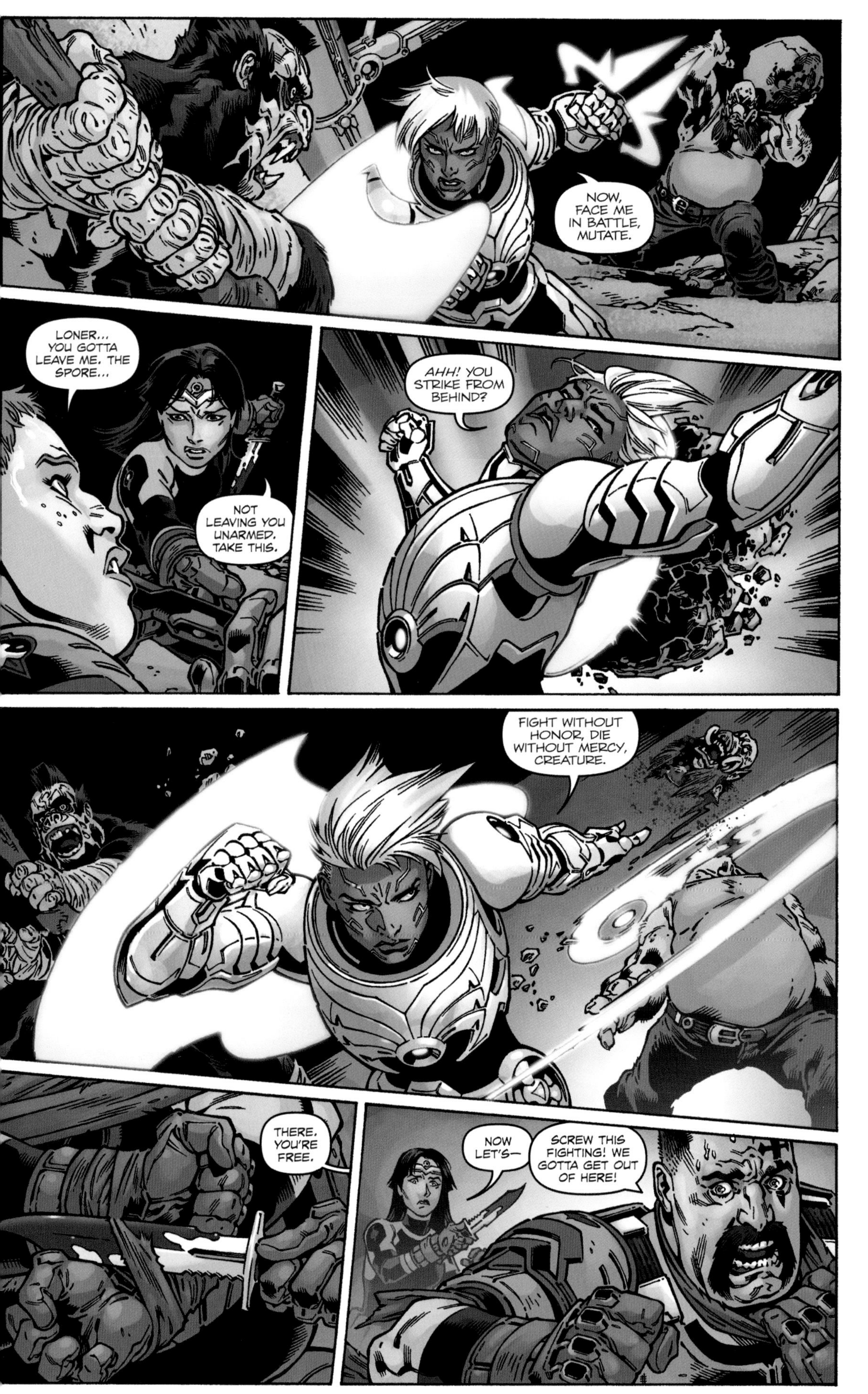
NOW, FACE ME IN BATTLE, MUTATE.
LONER... YOU GOTTA LEAVE ME. THE SPORE...
NOT LEAVING YOU UNARMED. TAKE THIS.
AHH! YOU STRIKE FROM BEHIND?
FIGHT WITHOUT HONOR, DIE WITHOUT MERCY, CREATURE.
THERE. YOU'RE FREE.
NOW LET'S—
SCREW THIS FIGHTING! WE GOTTA GET OUT OF HERE!

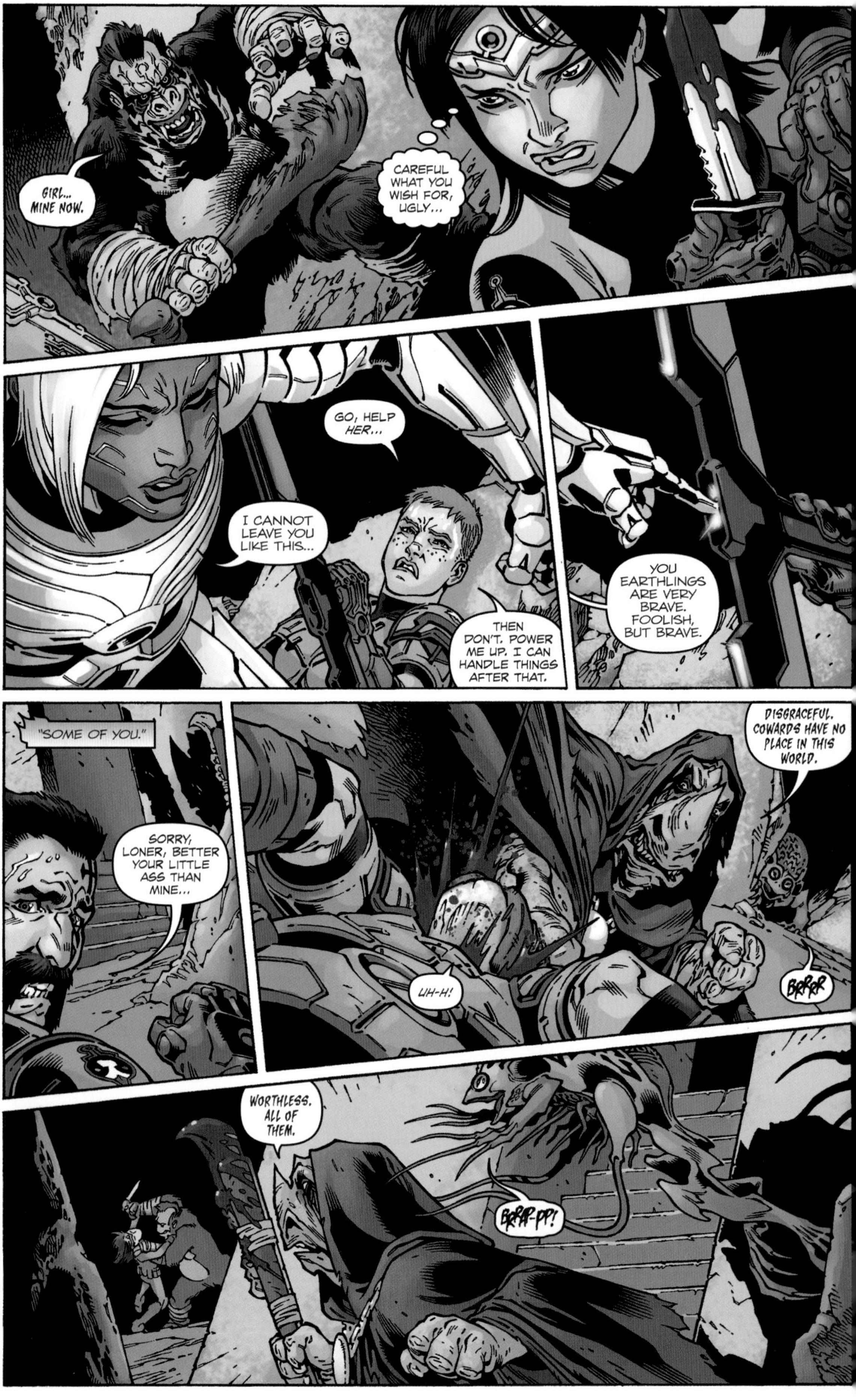
GIRL... MINE NOW.
CAREFUL WHAT YOU WISH FOR, UGLY...
GO, HELP HER...
I CANNOT LEAVE YOU LIKE THIS...
THEN DON'T. POWER ME UP. I CAN HANDLE THINGS AFTER THAT.
YOU EARTHLINGS ARE VERY BRAVE. FOOLISH, BUT BRAVE.
"SOME OF YOU."
SORRY, LONER, BETTER YOUR LITTLE ASS THAN MINE...
DISGRACEFUL. COWARDS HAVE NO PLACE IN THIS WORLD.
UH-H!
BRRRR
WORTHLESS. ALL OF THEM.
BRRAP-PP!

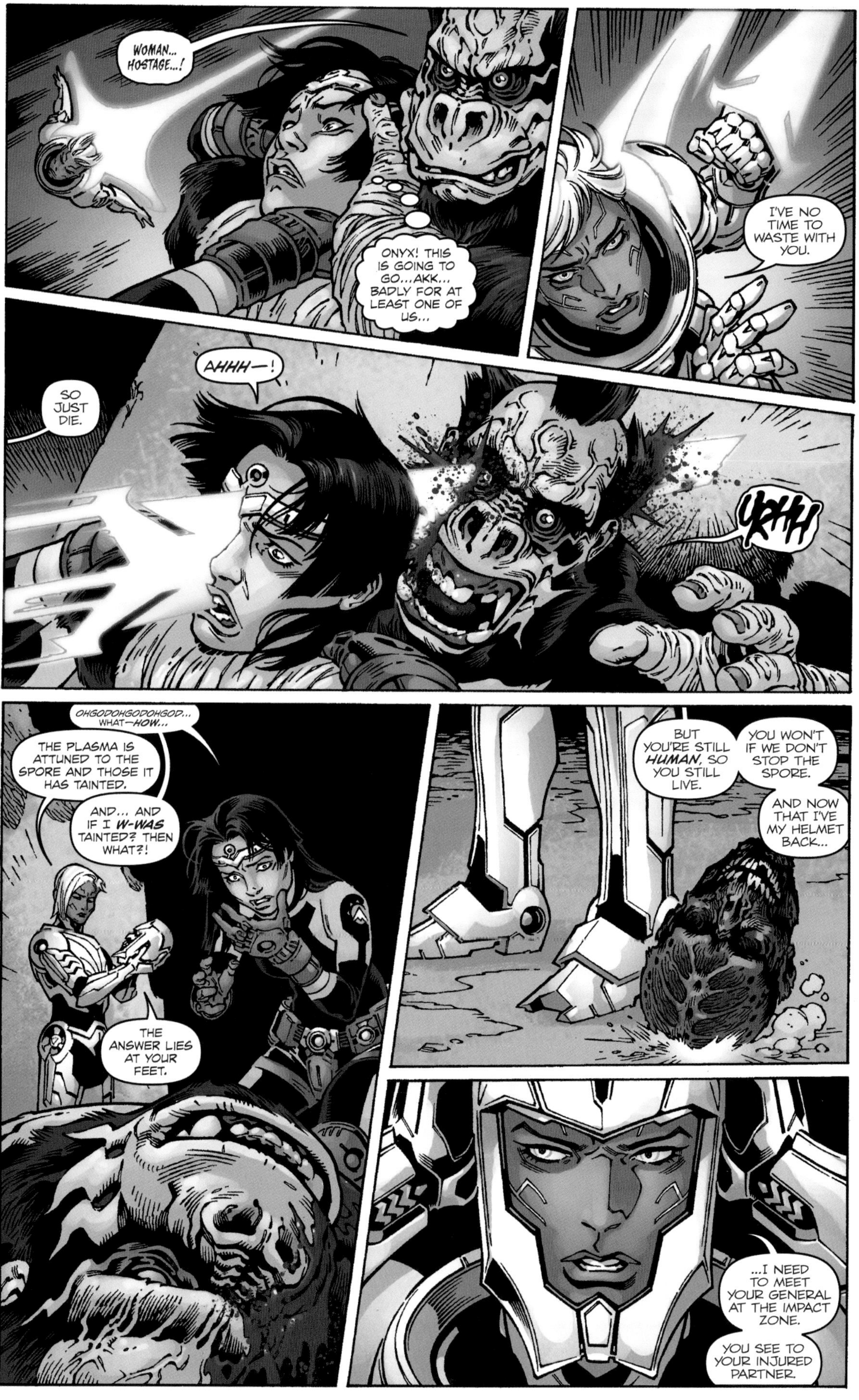
WOMAN... HOSTAGE...!
ONYX! THIS IS GOING TO GO...AKK... BADLY FOR AT LEAST ONE OF US...
I'VE NO TIME TO WASTE WITH YOU.
AHHH—!
SO JUST DIE.
URHH
OHGODOHGODOHGOD... WHAT—HOW...
THE PLASMA IS ATTUNED TO THE SPORE AND THOSE IT HAS TAINTED.
AND... AND IF I W-WAS TAINTED? THEN WHAT?!
THE ANSWER LIES AT YOUR FEET.
BUT YOU'RE STILL HUMAN, SO YOU STILL LIVE.
YOU WON'T IF WE DON'T STOP THE SPORE.
AND NOW THAT I'VE MY HELMET BACK...
...I NEED TO MEET YOUR GENERAL AT THE IMPACT ZONE.
YOU SEE TO YOUR INJURED PARTNER.

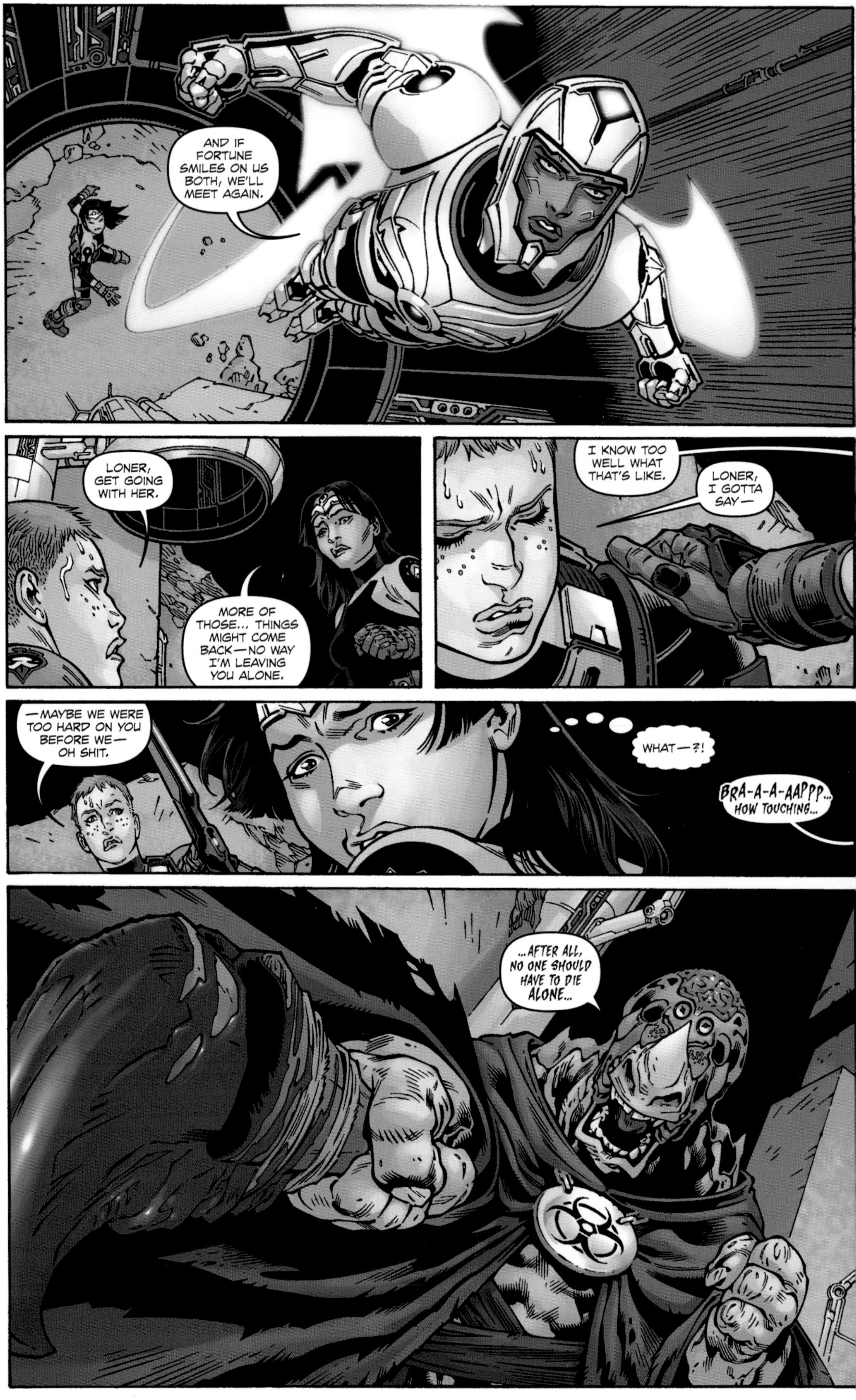
AND IF FORTUNE SMILES ON US BOTH, WE'LL MEET AGAIN.
LONER, GET GOING WITH HER.
MORE OF THOSE... THINGS MIGHT COME BACK—NO WAY I'M LEAVING YOU ALONE.
I KNOW TOO WELL WHAT THAT'S LIKE.
LONER, I GOTTA SAY—
—MAYBE WE WERE TOO HARD ON YOU BEFORE WE— OH SHIT.
WHAT—?!
BRA-A-A-AAPPP... HOW TOUCHING...
...AFTER ALL, NO ONE SHOULD HAVE TO DIE ALONE...

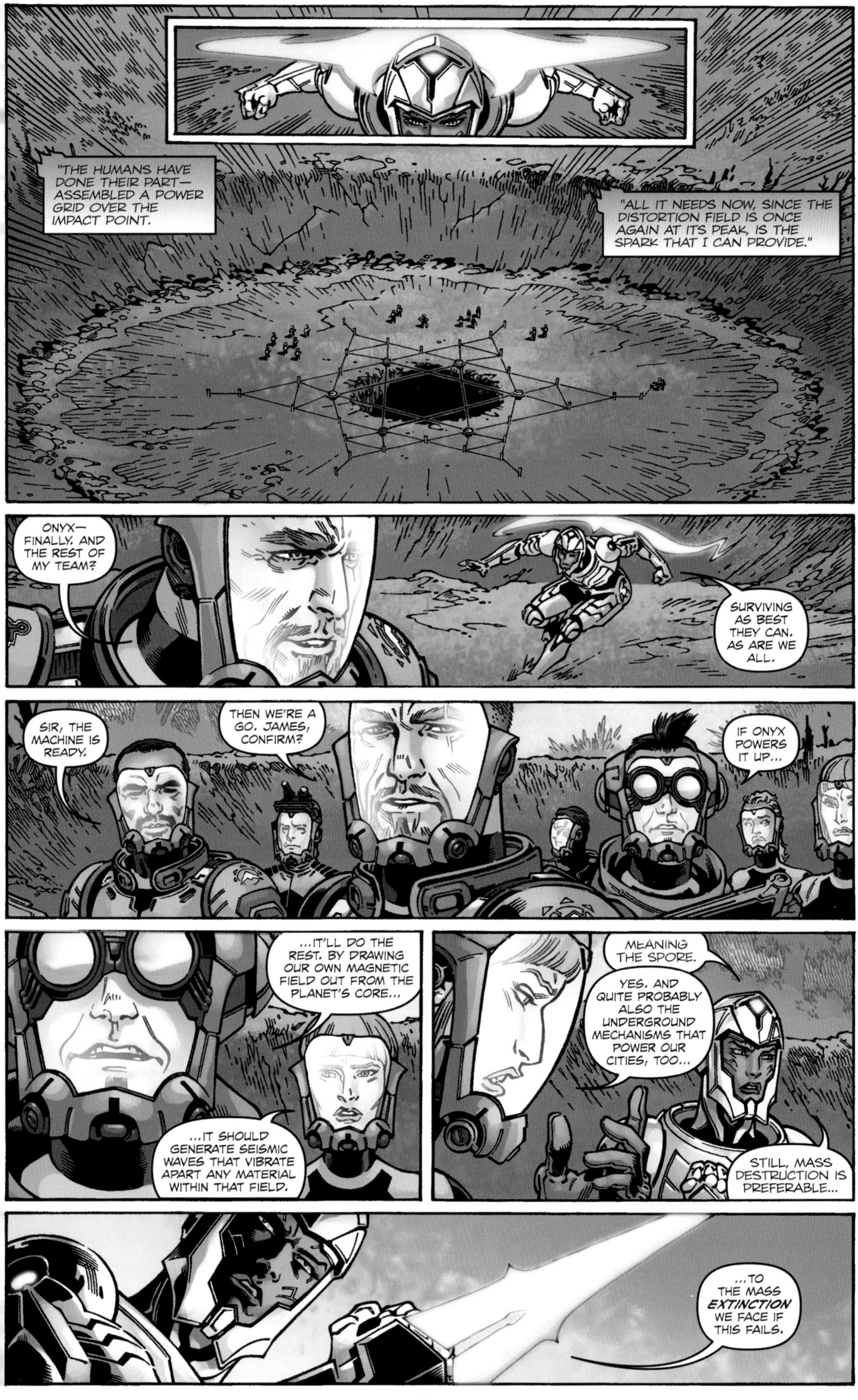
"THE HUMANS HAVE DONE THEIR PART—ASSEMBLED A POWER GRID OVER THE IMPACT POINT.
"ALL IT NEEDS NOW, SINCE THE DISTORTION FIELD IS ONCE AGAIN AT ITS PEAK, IS THE SPARK THAT I CAN PROVIDE."
ONYX—FINALLY. AND THE REST OF MY TEAM?
SURVIVING AS BEST THEY CAN. AS ARE WE ALL.
SIR, THE MACHINE IS READY.
THEN WE'RE A GO. JAMES, CONFIRM?
IF ONYX POWERS IT UP...
...IT'LL DO THE REST. BY DRAWING OUR OWN MAGNETIC FIELD OUT FROM THE PLANET'S CORE...
...IT SHOULD GENERATE SEISMIC WAVES THAT VIBRATE APART ANY MATERIAL WITHIN THAT FIELD.
MEANING THE SPORE.
YES. AND QUITE PROBABLY ALSO THE UNDERGROUND MECHANISMS THAT POWER OUR CITIES, TOO...
STILL, MASS DESTRUCTION IS PREFERABLE...
...TO THE MASS EXTINCTION WE FACE IF THIS FAILS.

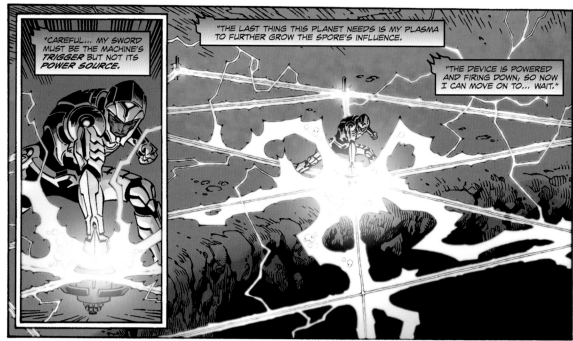

"CAREFUL... MY SWORD MUST BE THE MACHINE'S *TRIGGER* BUT NOT ITS *POWER SOURCE.*

"THE LAST THING THIS PLANET NEEDS IS MY PLASMA TO FURTHER GROW THE SPORE'S INFLUENCE.

"THE DEVICE IS POWERED AND FIRING DOWN, SO NOW I CAN MOVE ON TO... *WAIT.*"

I CANNOT DISENGAGE.

JAMES, THE MACHINE FEELS LIKE IT'S... *SYPHONING...*

THESE READINGS ARE... *IMPOSSIBLE!* ENERGY LEVELS, SPIKING...

SIR, I KNOW THIS IS UNPROVEN, BUT SOMETHING IS WRONG.

WE NEED TO SHUT IT DOWN. ONYX IS...

ONYX IS *DONE.* I MEANT WHAT I SAID BEFORE: EARTH IS OUR PLANET.

SAMPSON, THIS IS IT: *CODE BACKHAND!*

READY ON MY MARK, BOSS.

N-N-NNNNN-

SIR, WHAT IN THE HELL...?

STAY *BACK*, SOLDIER!

GUH!

EASY, MAPS.

BUT THEY'RE KILLING HER...

AND US, TOO, IF WE MAKE A WRONG MOVE HERE.

EARTH DOESN'T WANT OR NEED YOUR OTHERWORLDLY WARS, ALIEN...

ESPECIALLY ONE YOU'VE ALREADY LOST. THE SPORE HAS REACHED THE PLANET'S CORE.

NEVER... GIVE UP...

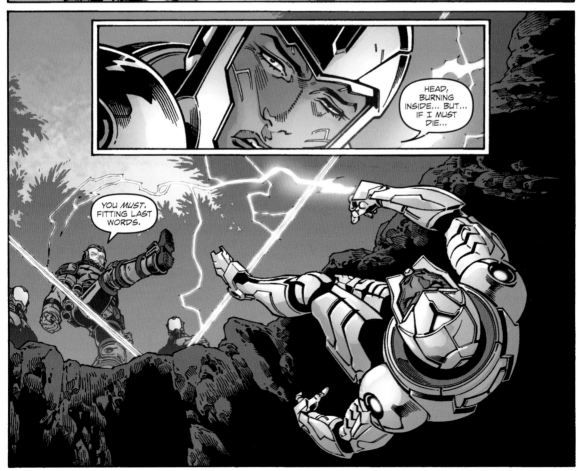

HEAD, BURNING INSIDE... BUT... IF I MUST DIE...

YOU *MUST*. FITTING LAST WORDS.

MY GOD. SHE'S... *GONE.*

MOUNT, YOU'VE LOST YOUR MIND!

SOMEONE, GRAB HIM, OR...

I DON'T THINK SO. THOSE MEN ARE WITH *ME.*

I'M NOT WITH YOU, YOU SICK SONUVA—

HKKK

NO!

THEY'RE *ALL* WITH ME.

HSSSSS

THIS ENTIRE PLANET IS NOW *MINE.*

THIS ENTIRE PLANET IS NOW MINE.

THIS ENTIRE PLANET IS NOW MINE.

THIS ENTIRE PLANET IS NOW MINE.

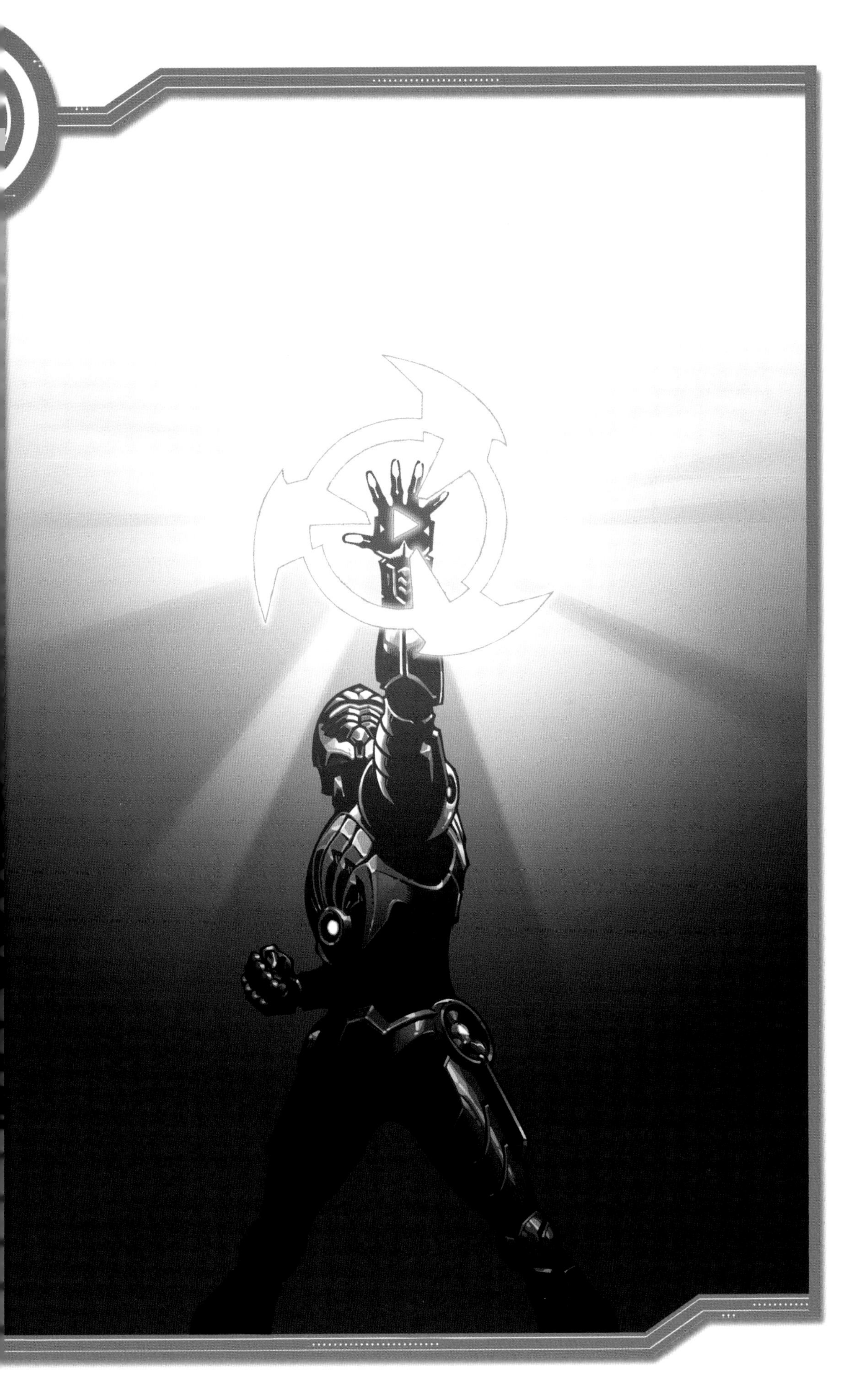

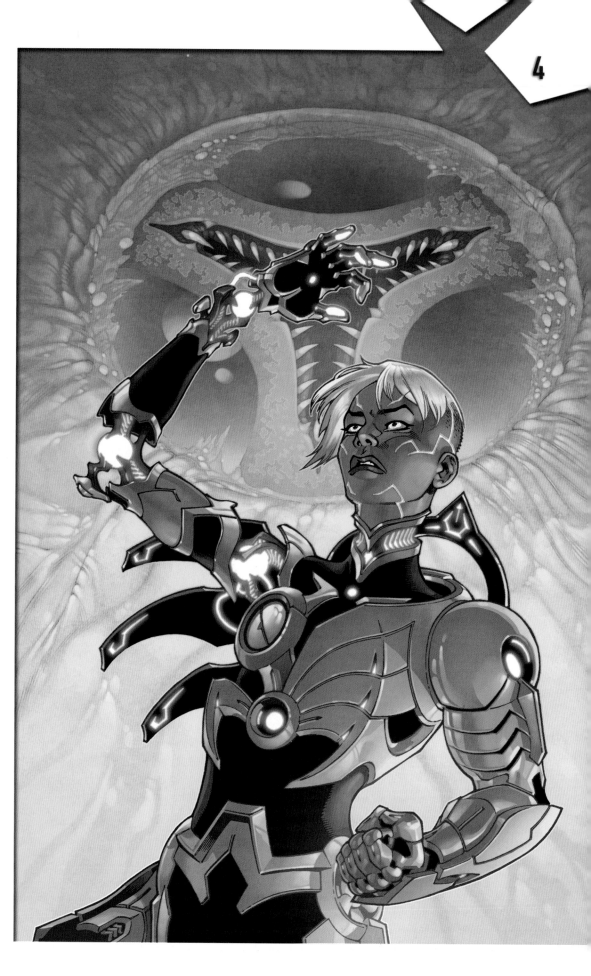

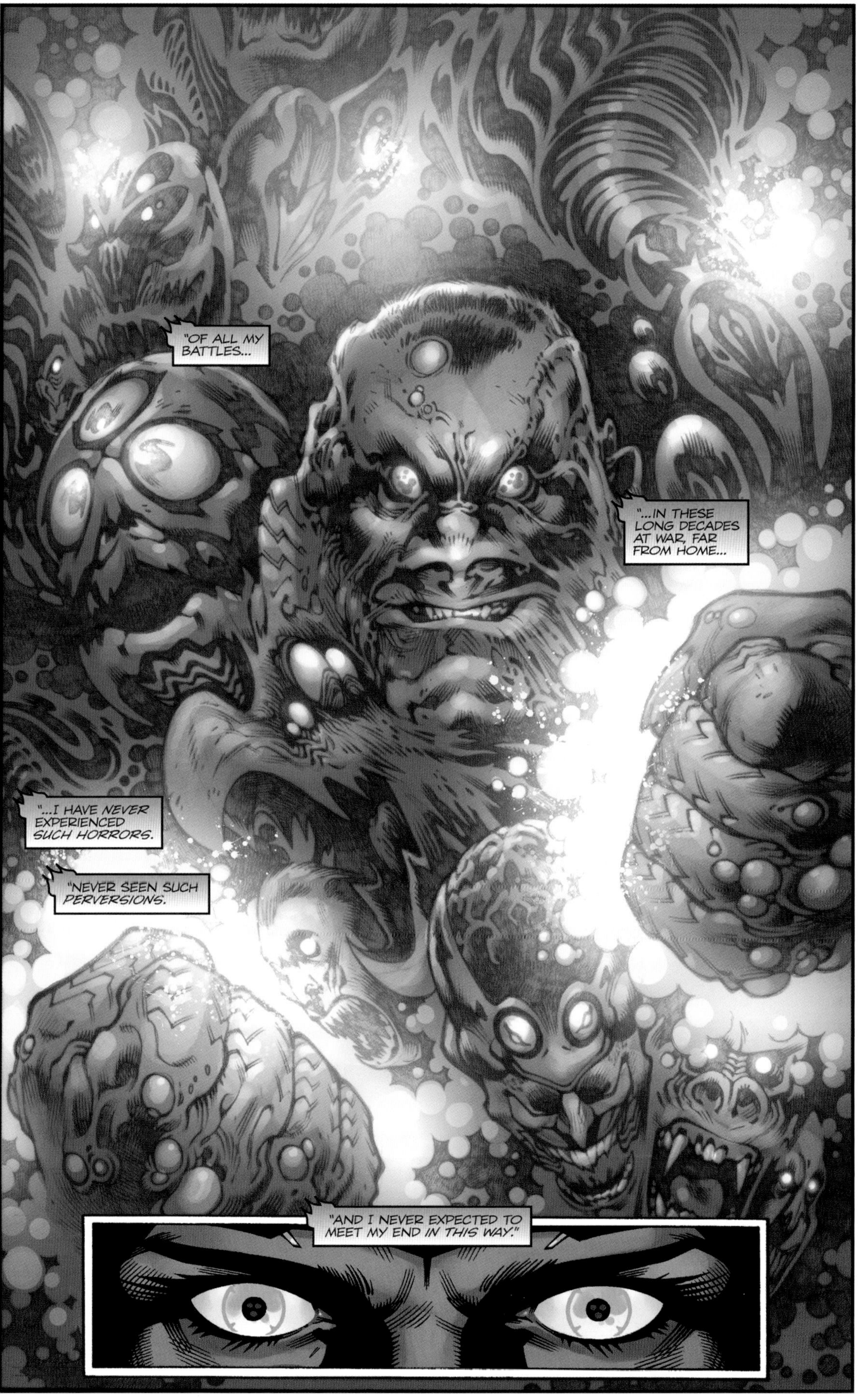
"OF ALL MY BATTLES...
"...IN THESE LONG DECADES AT WAR, FAR FROM HOME...
"...I HAVE NEVER EXPERIENCED SUCH HORRORS.
"NEVER SEEN SUCH PERVERSIONS.
"AND I NEVER EXPECTED TO MEET MY END IN THIS WAY."

"I STILL HAVE NO SUCH PLANS.

"IF ONLY I HAD ENOUGH REMAINING LIFEFORCE TO ALLOW ME TO MOVE...

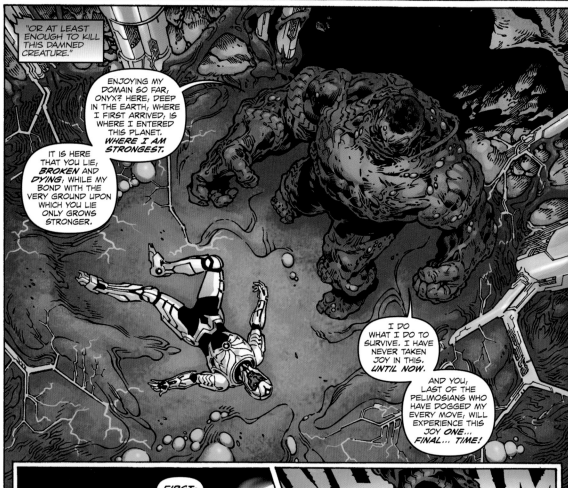

"OR AT LEAST ENOUGH TO KILL THIS DAMNED CREATURE."

ENJOYING MY DOMAIN SO FAR, ONYX? HERE, DEEP IN THE EARTH, WHERE I FIRST ARRIVED, IS WHERE I ENTERED THIS PLANET. **WHERE I AM STRONGEST.**

IT IS HERE THAT YOU LIE, **BROKEN** AND **DYING**, WHILE MY BOND WITH THE VERY GROUND UPON WHICH YOU LIE ONLY GROWS STRONGER.

I DO WHAT I DO TO SURVIVE. I HAVE NEVER TAKEN JOY IN THIS. **UNTIL NOW.**

AND YOU, LAST OF THE PELIMOSIANS WHO HAVE DOGGED MY EVERY MOVE, WILL EXPERIENCE THIS JOY *ONE... FINAL... TIME!*

FIRST-HAND.

WHAM

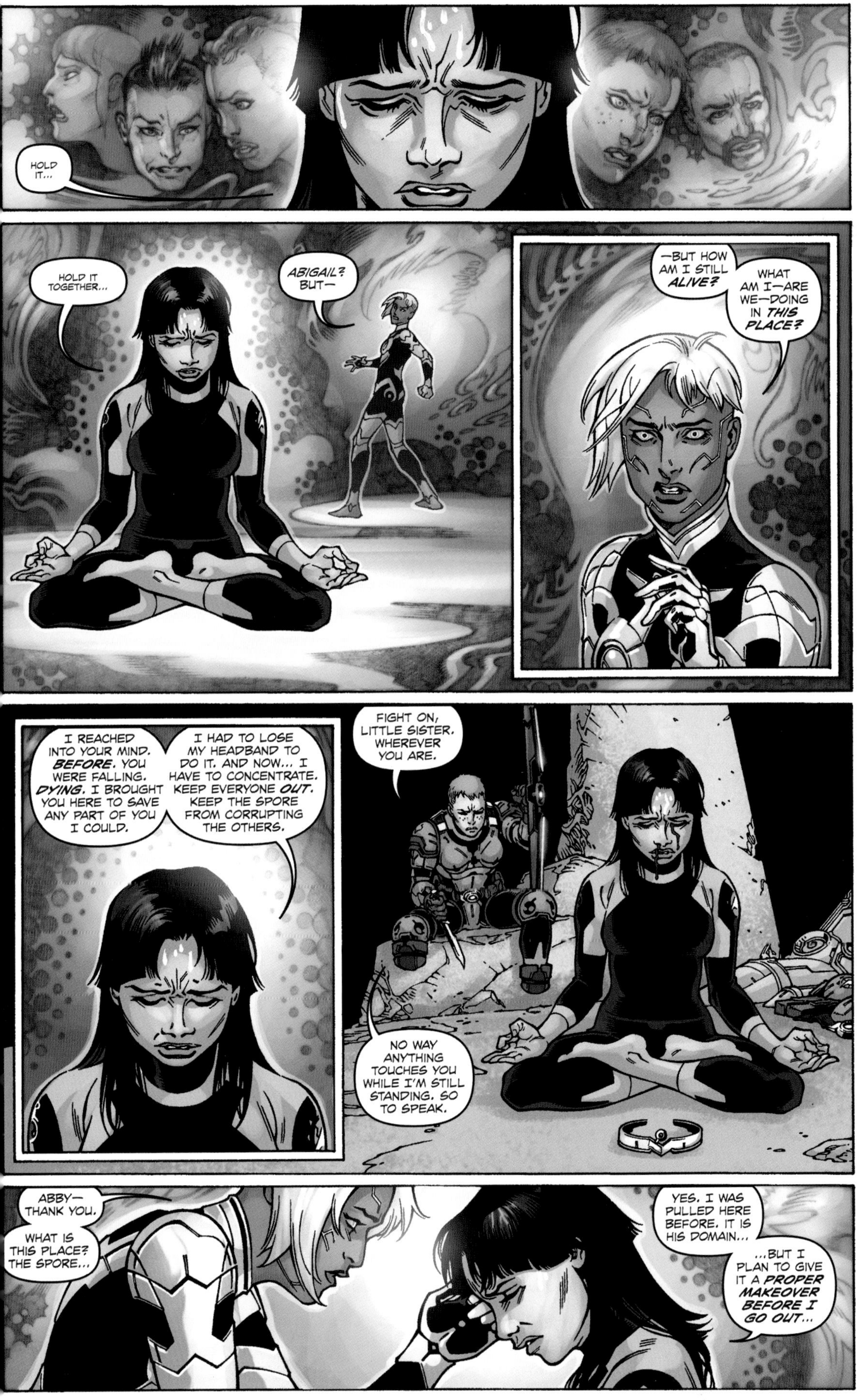
HOLD IT...
HOLD IT TOGETHER...
ABIGAIL? BUT—
—BUT HOW AM I STILL ALIVE?
WHAT AM I—ARE WE—DOING IN THIS PLACE?
I REACHED INTO YOUR MIND. BEFORE. YOU WERE FALLING. DYING. I BROUGHT YOU HERE TO SAVE ANY PART OF YOU I COULD.
I HAD TO LOSE MY HEADBAND TO DO IT. AND NOW... I HAVE TO CONCENTRATE. KEEP EVERYONE OUT. KEEP THE SPORE FROM CORRUPTING THE OTHERS.
FIGHT ON, LITTLE SISTER. WHEREVER YOU ARE.
NO WAY ANYTHING TOUCHES YOU WHILE I'M STILL STANDING. SO TO SPEAK.
ABBY— THANK YOU.
WHAT IS THIS PLACE? THE SPORE...
YES. I WAS PULLED HERE BEFORE. IT IS HIS DOMAIN...
...BUT I PLAN TO GIVE IT A PROPER MAKEOVER BEFORE I GO OUT...

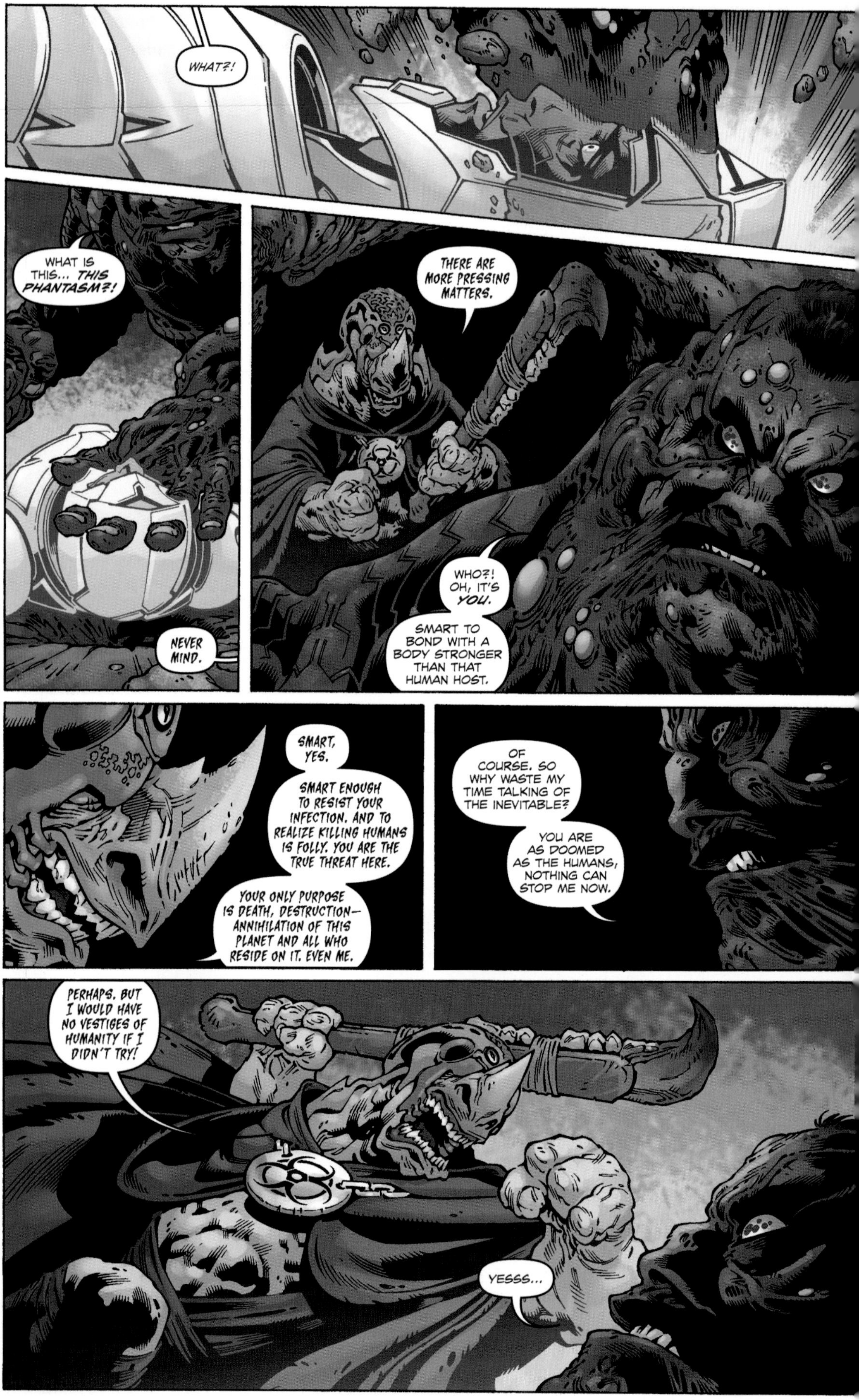
WHAT?!
WHAT IS THIS... THIS PHANTASM?!
NEVER MIND.
THERE ARE MORE PRESSING MATTERS.
WHO?! OH, IT'S YOU.
SMART TO BOND WITH A BODY STRONGER THAN THAT HUMAN HOST.
SMART, YES.
SMART ENOUGH TO RESIST YOUR INFECTION. AND TO REALIZE KILLING HUMANS IS FOLLY. YOU ARE THE TRUE THREAT HERE.
YOUR ONLY PURPOSE IS DEATH, DESTRUCTION—ANNIHILATION OF THIS PLANET AND ALL WHO RESIDE ON IT. EVEN ME.
OF COURSE. SO WHY WASTE MY TIME TALKING OF THE INEVITABLE?
YOU ARE AS DOOMED AS THE HUMANS, NOTHING CAN STOP ME NOW.
PERHAPS. BUT I WOULD HAVE NO VESTIGES OF HUMANITY IF I DIDN'T TRY!
YESSS...

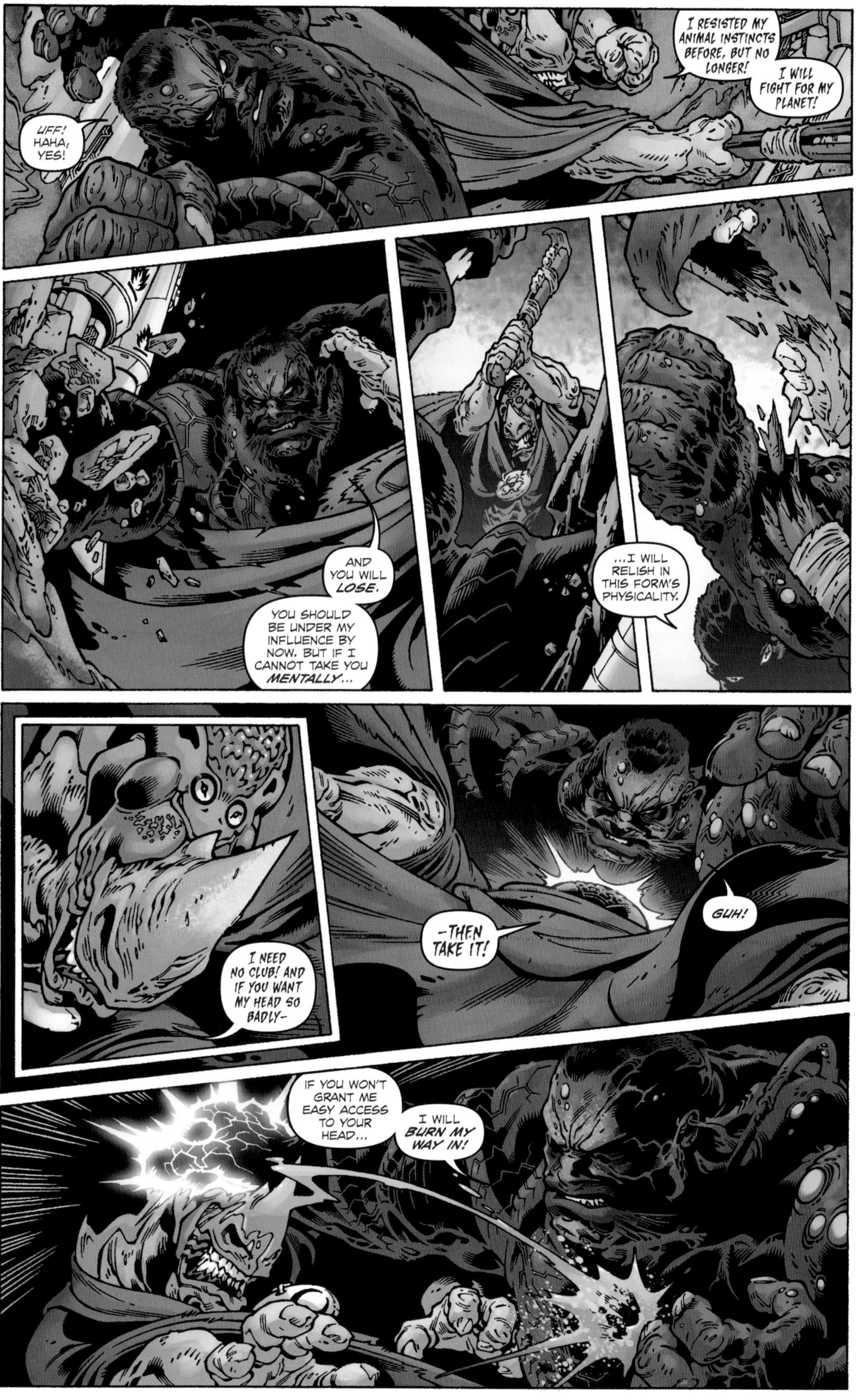
I RESISTED MY ANIMAL INSTINCTS BEFORE, BUT NO LONGER!
I WILL FIGHT FOR MY PLANET!
UFF! HAHA, YES!
AND YOU WILL *LOSE.*
YOU SHOULD BE UNDER MY INFLUENCE BY NOW. BUT IF I CANNOT TAKE YOU *MENTALLY*...
...I WILL RELISH IN THIS FORM'S PHYSICALITY.
I NEED NO CLUB! AND IF YOU WANT MY HEAD SO BADLY-
-THEN TAKE IT!
GUH!
IF YOU WON'T GRANT ME EASY ACCESS TO YOUR HEAD...
I WILL *BURN MY WAY IN!*

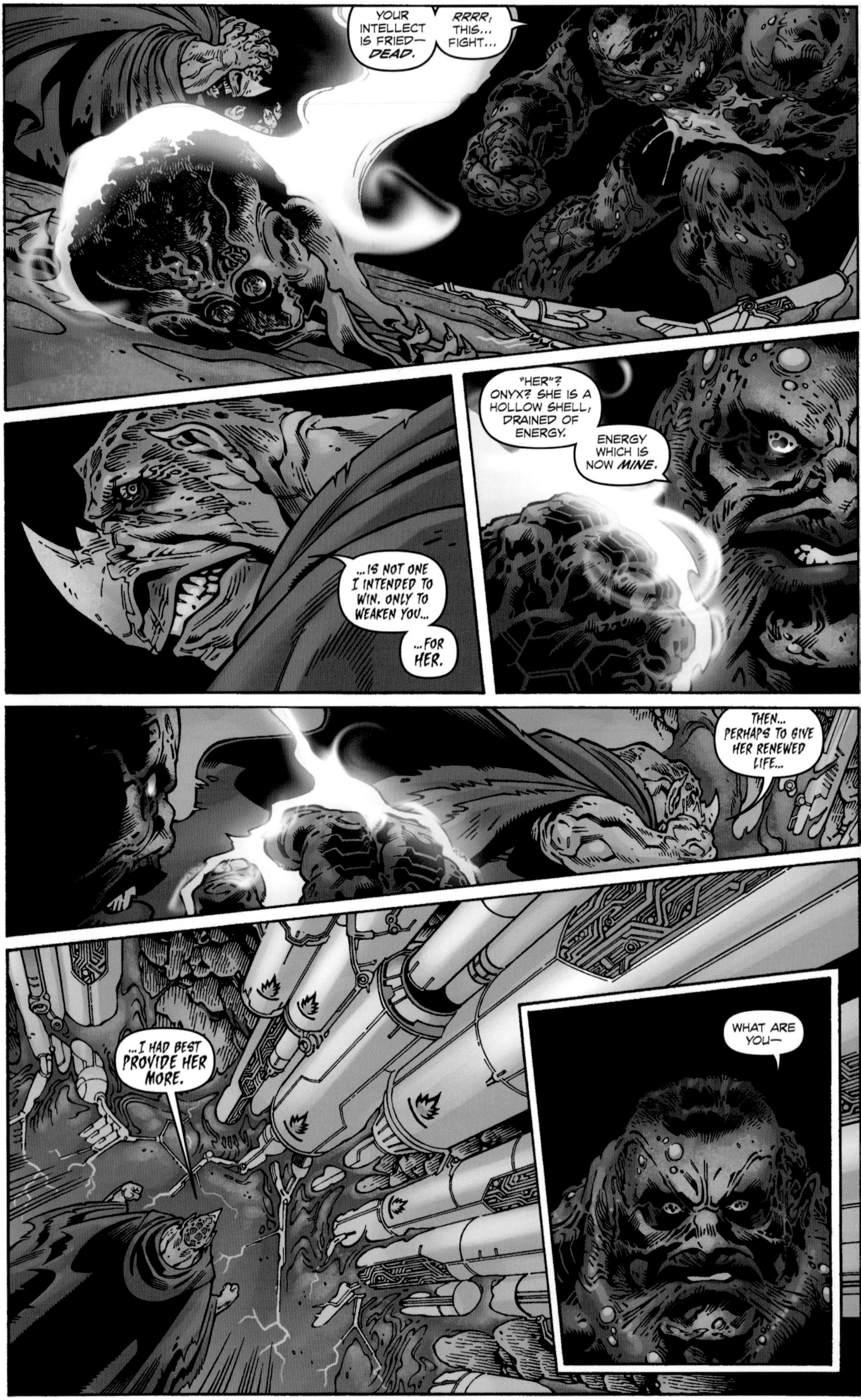
YOUR INTELLECT IS FRIED— DEAD.
RRRR, THIS... FIGHT...
...IS NOT ONE I INTENDED TO WIN. ONLY TO WEAKEN YOU...
...FOR HER.
"HER"? ONYX? SHE IS A HOLLOW SHELL, DRAINED OF ENERGY.
ENERGY WHICH IS NOW MINE.
THEN... PERHAPS TO GIVE HER RENEWED LIFE...
...I HAD BEST PROVIDE HER MORE.
WHAT ARE YOU—

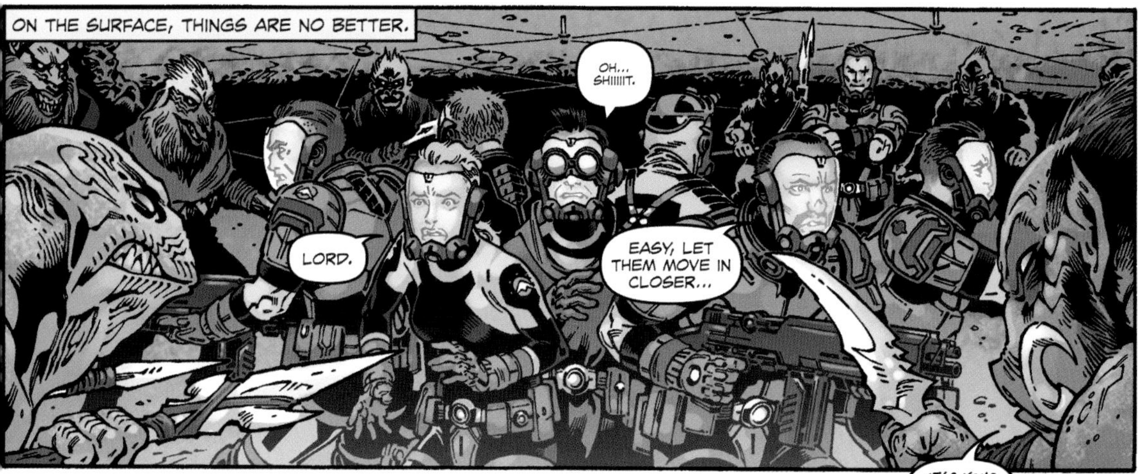
ON THE SURFACE, THINGS ARE NO BETTER.
OH... SHIIIIIT.
LORD.
EASY, LET THEM MOVE IN CLOSER...
IT'S YOUR FACE I'LL EAT FIRST. I-

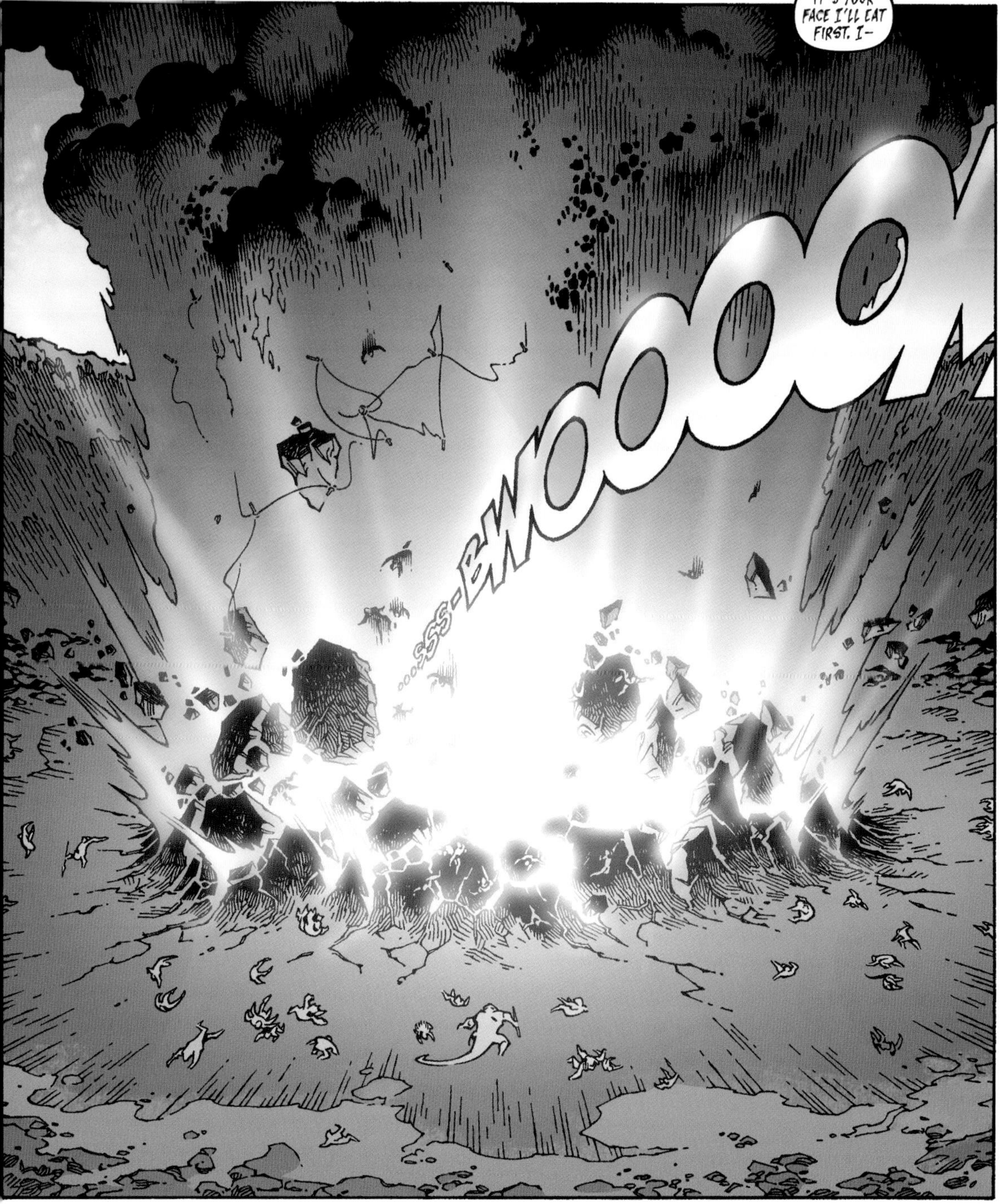
...SSS-BWOOOOOM

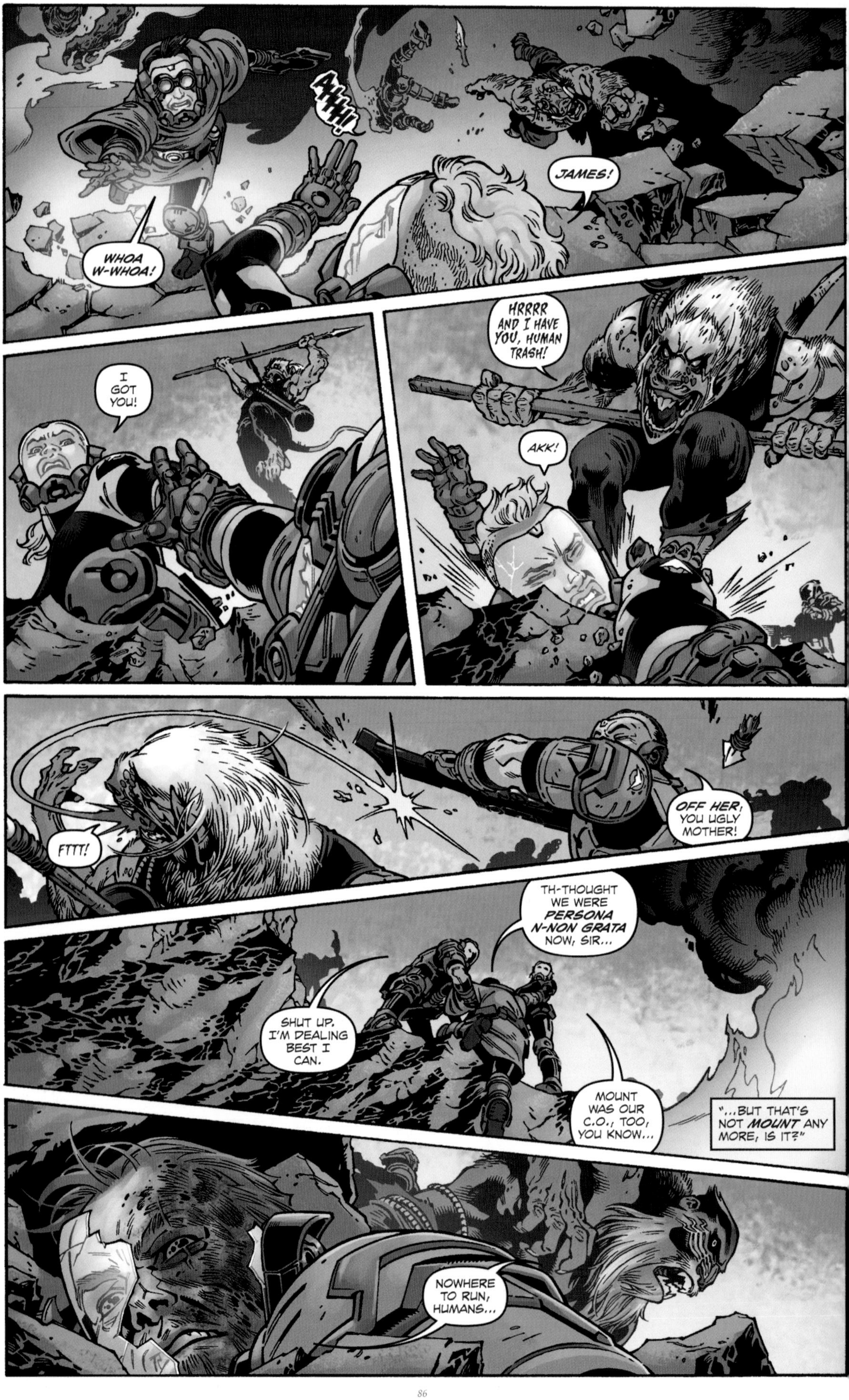
AAHH!
JAMES!
WHOA W-WHOA!
HRRRR AND I HAVE YOU, HUMAN TRASH!
I GOT YOU!
AKK!
OFF HER, YOU UGLY MOTHER!
FTTT!
TH-THOUGHT WE WERE PERSONA N-NON GRATA NOW, SIR...
SHUT UP. I'M DEALING BEST I CAN.
MOUNT WAS OUR C.O., TOO, YOU KNOW...
"...BUT THAT'S NOT MOUNT ANY MORE, IS IT?"
NOWHERE TO RUN, HUMANS...

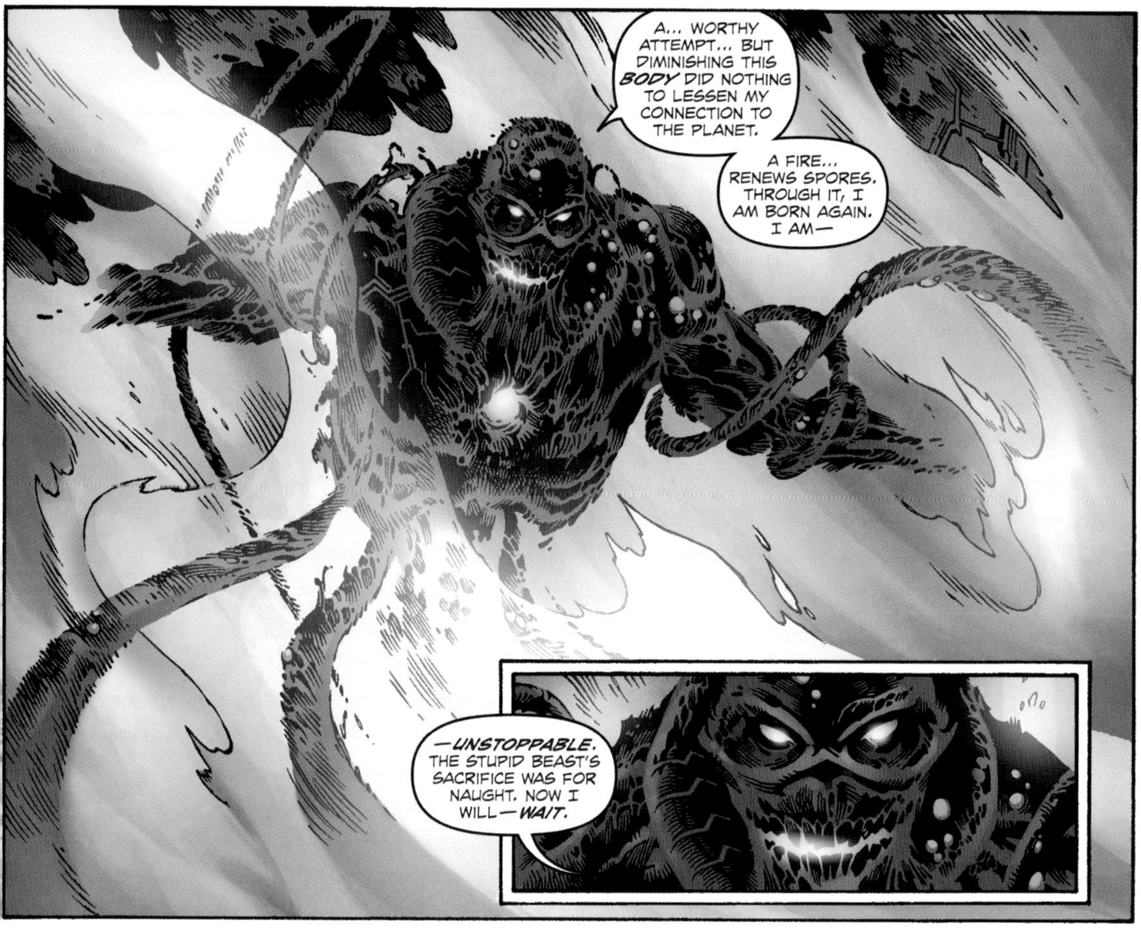
A... WORTHY ATTEMPT... BUT DIMINISHING THIS *BODY* DID NOTHING TO LESSEN MY CONNECTION TO THE PLANET.
A FIRE... RENEWS SPORES. THROUGH IT, I AM BORN AGAIN. I AM—
—*UNSTOPPABLE*. THE STUPID BEAST'S SACRIFICE WAS FOR NAUGHT. NOW I WILL—*WAIT*.

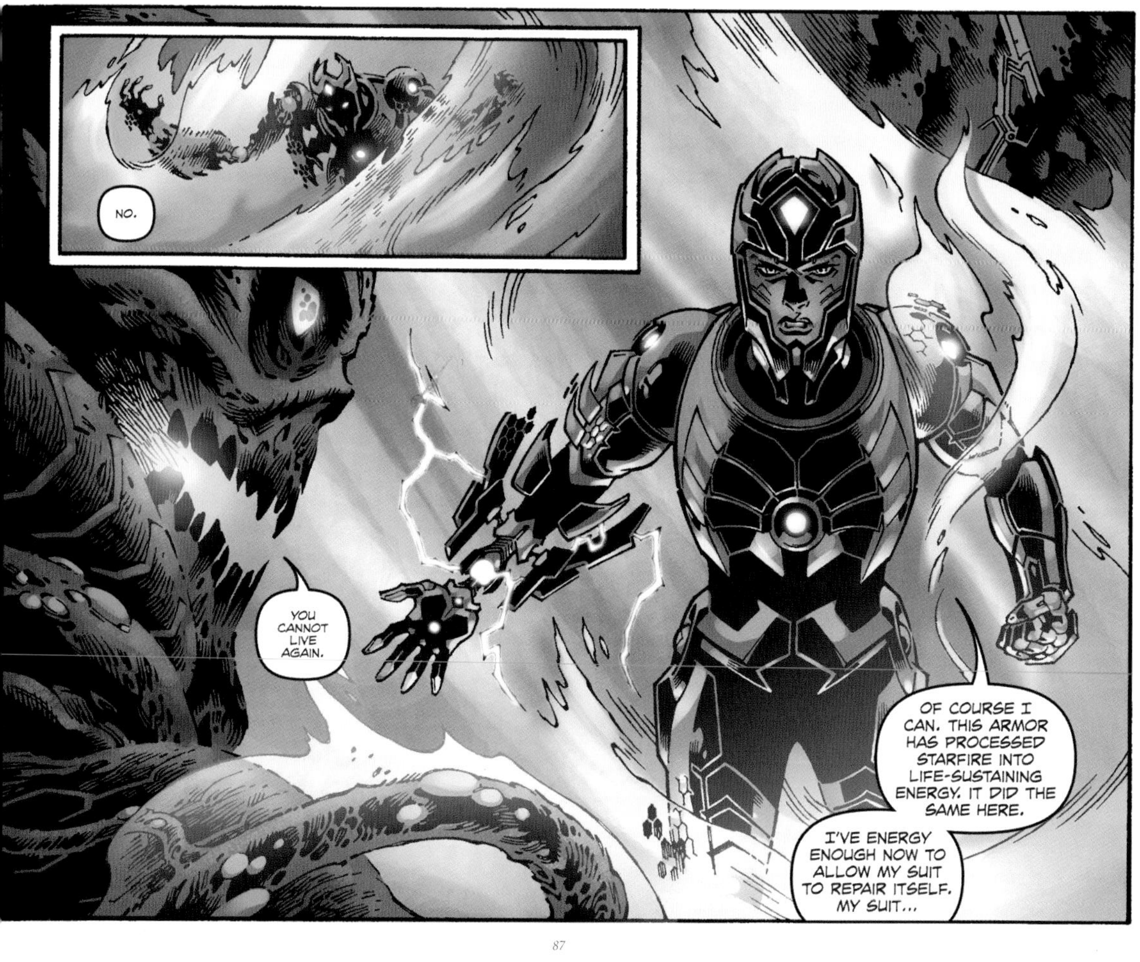
NO.
YOU CANNOT LIVE AGAIN.
OF COURSE I CAN. THIS ARMOR HAS PROCESSED STARFIRE INTO LIFE-SUSTAINING ENERGY. IT DID THE SAME HERE.
I'VE ENERGY ENOUGH NOW TO ALLOW MY SUIT TO REPAIR ITSELF. MY SUIT...

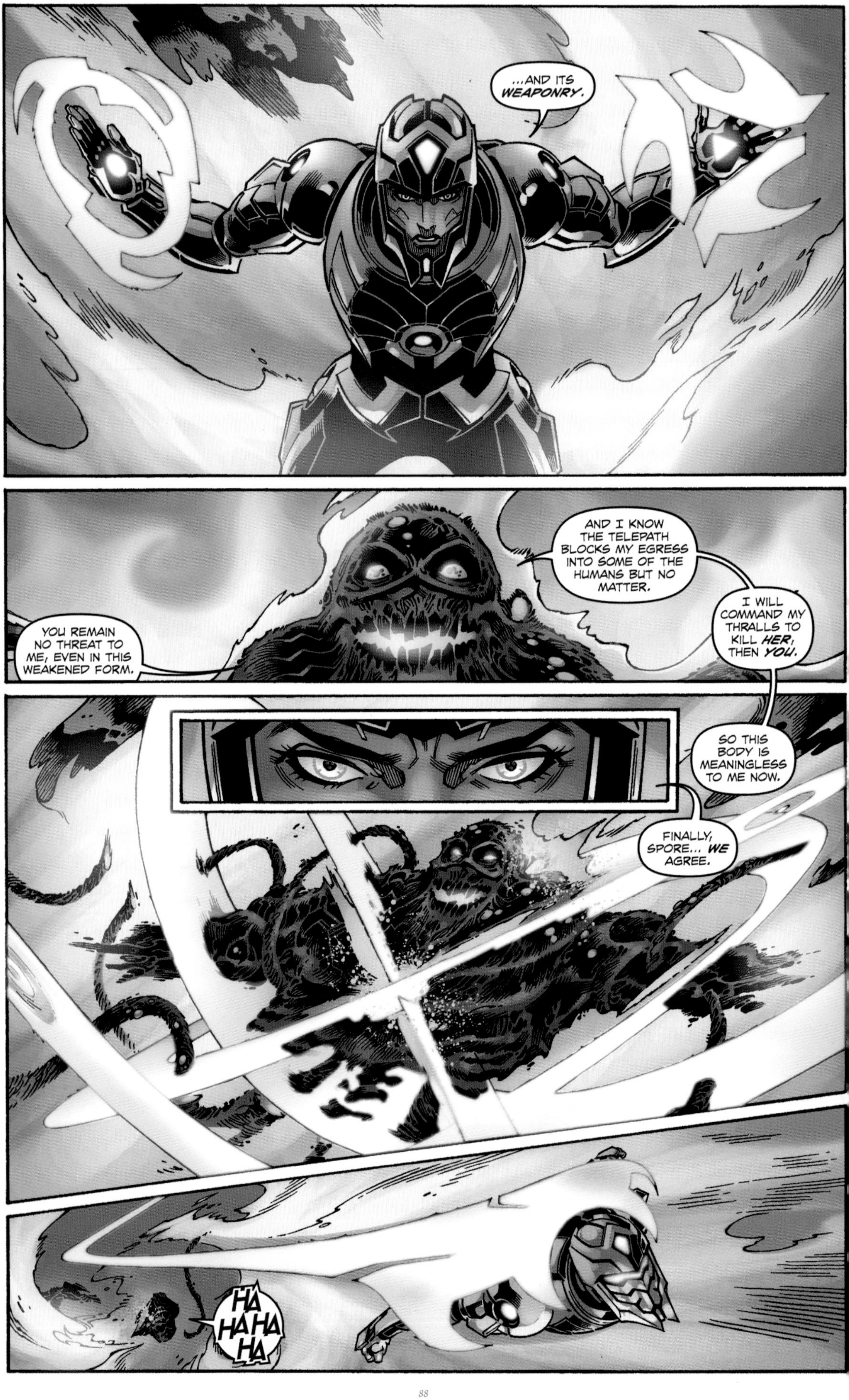
...AND ITS WEAPONRY.
AND I KNOW THE TELEPATH BLOCKS MY EGRESS INTO SOME OF THE HUMANS BUT NO MATTER.
YOU REMAIN NO THREAT TO ME, EVEN IN THIS WEAKENED FORM.
I WILL COMMAND MY THRALLS TO KILL HER, THEN YOU.
SO THIS BODY IS MEANINGLESS TO ME NOW.
FINALLY, SPORE... WE AGREE.
HA HA HA HA

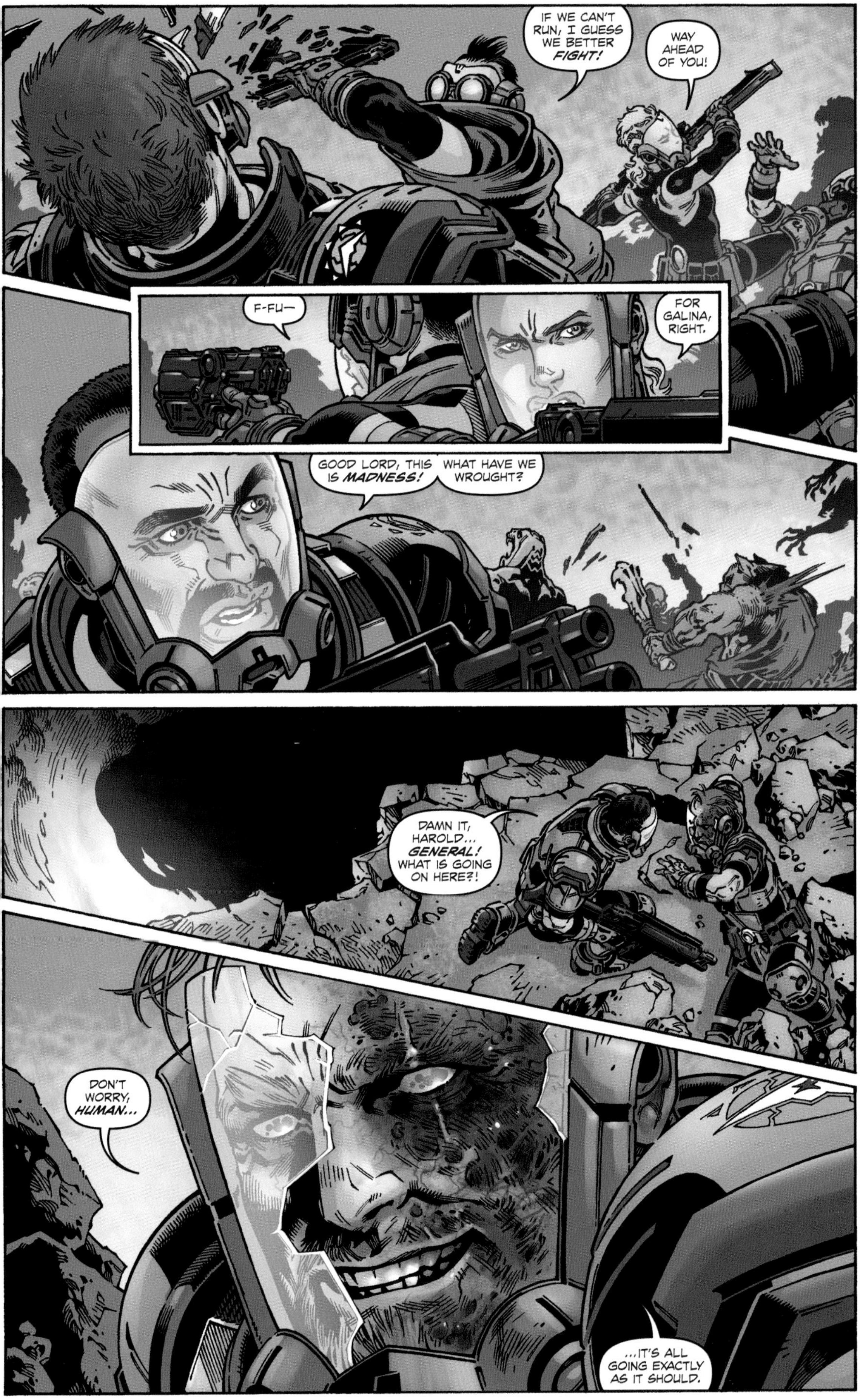
IF WE CAN'T RUN, I GUESS WE BETTER FIGHT!
WAY AHEAD OF YOU!
F-FU—
FOR GALINA, RIGHT.
GOOD LORD, THIS IS MADNESS!
WHAT HAVE WE WROUGHT?
DAMN IT, HAROLD... GENERAL! WHAT IS GOING ON HERE?!
DON'T WORRY, HUMAN...
...IT'S ALL GOING EXACTLY AS IT SHOULD.

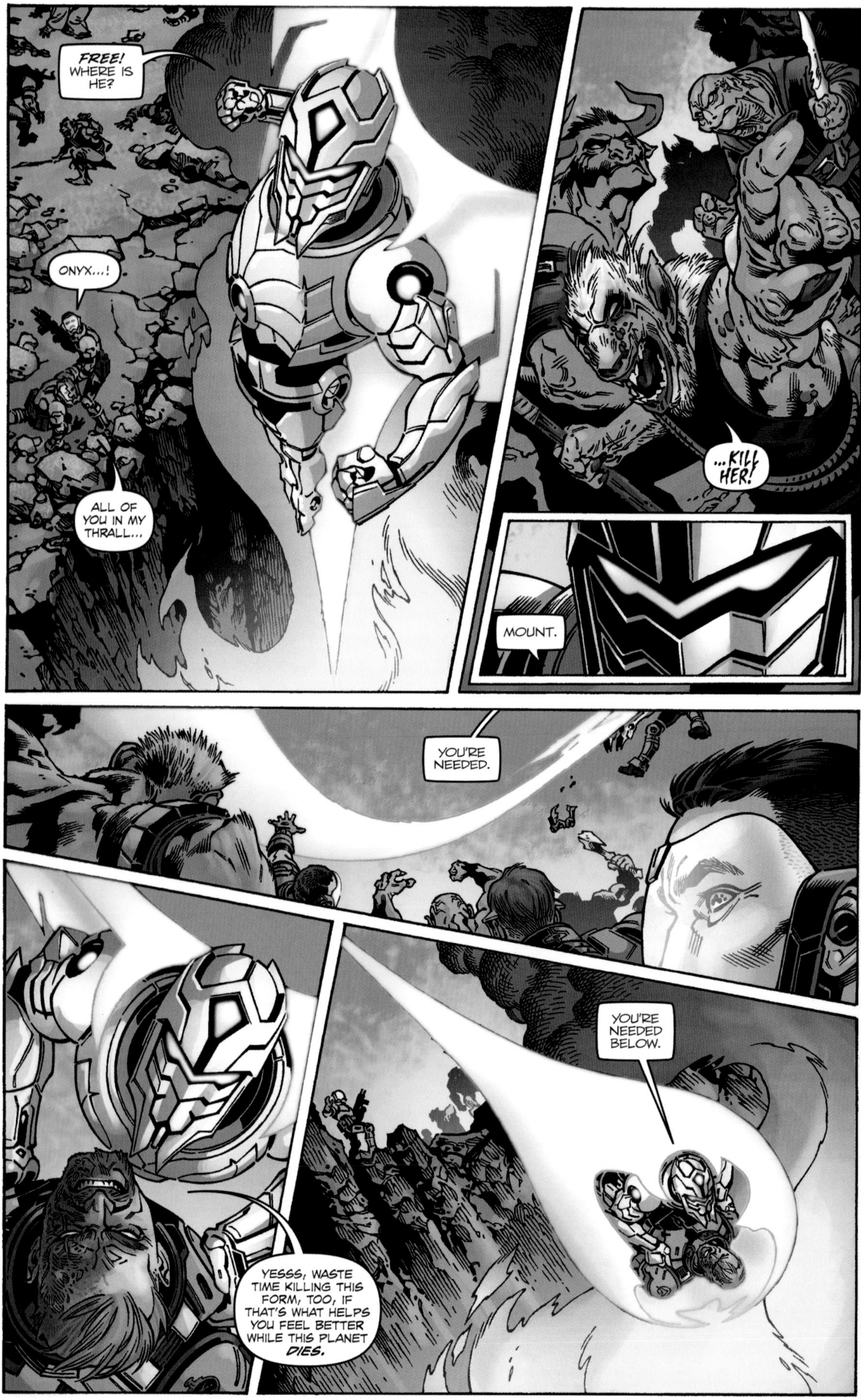
FREE! WHERE IS HE?
ONYX...!
ALL OF YOU IN MY THRALL...
...KILL HER!
MOUNT.
YOU'RE NEEDED.
YESSS, WASTE TIME KILLING THIS FORM, TOO, IF THAT'S WHAT HELPS YOU FEEL BETTER WHILE THIS PLANET DIES.
YOU'RE NEEDED BELOW.

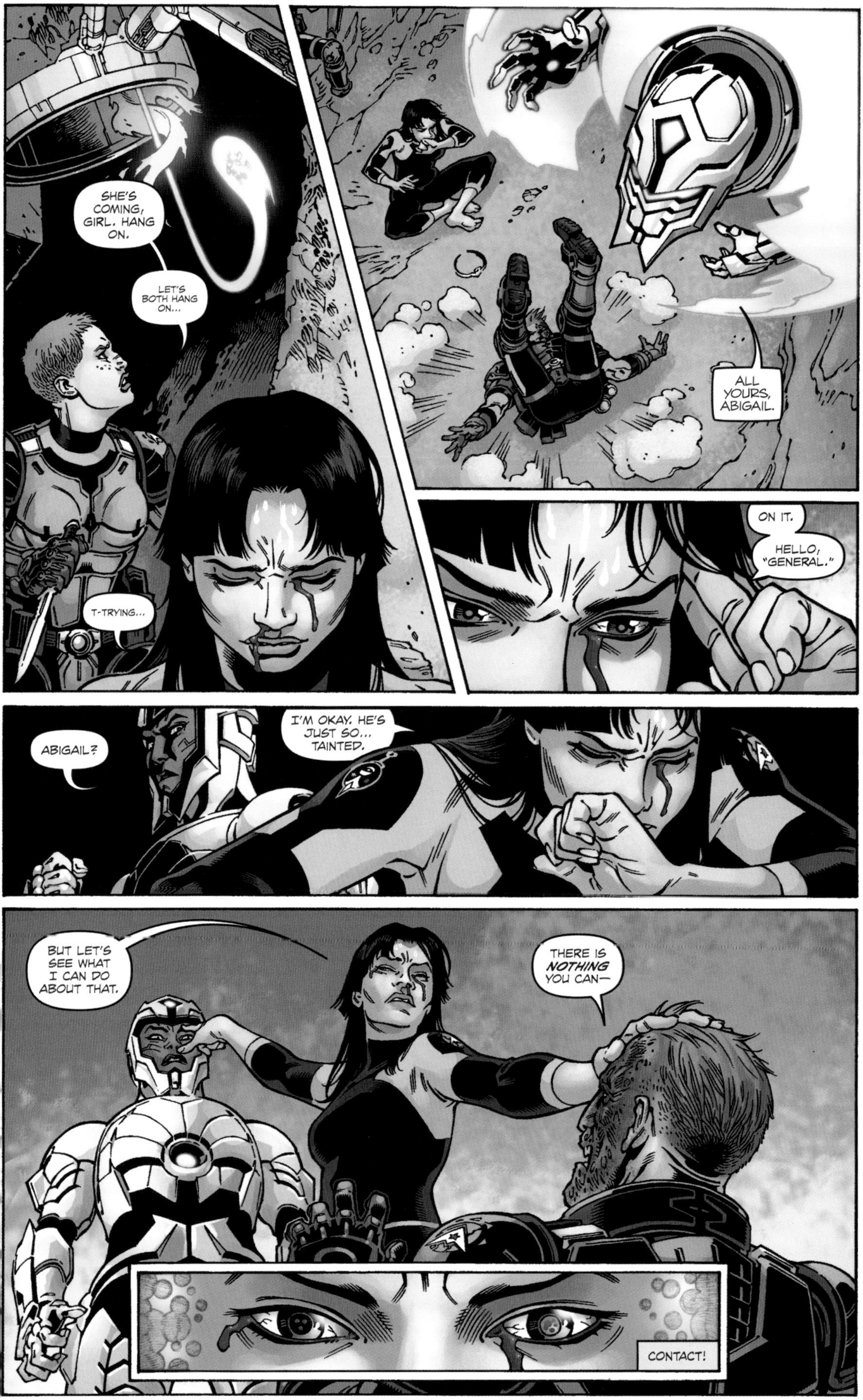
SHE'S COMING, GIRL. HANG ON.
LET'S BOTH HANG ON...
T-TRYING...
ALL YOURS, ABIGAIL.
ON IT.
HELLO, "GENERAL."
ABIGAIL?
I'M OKAY. HE'S JUST SO... TAINTED.
BUT LET'S SEE WHAT I CAN DO ABOUT THAT.
THERE IS *NOTHING* YOU CAN—
CONTACT!

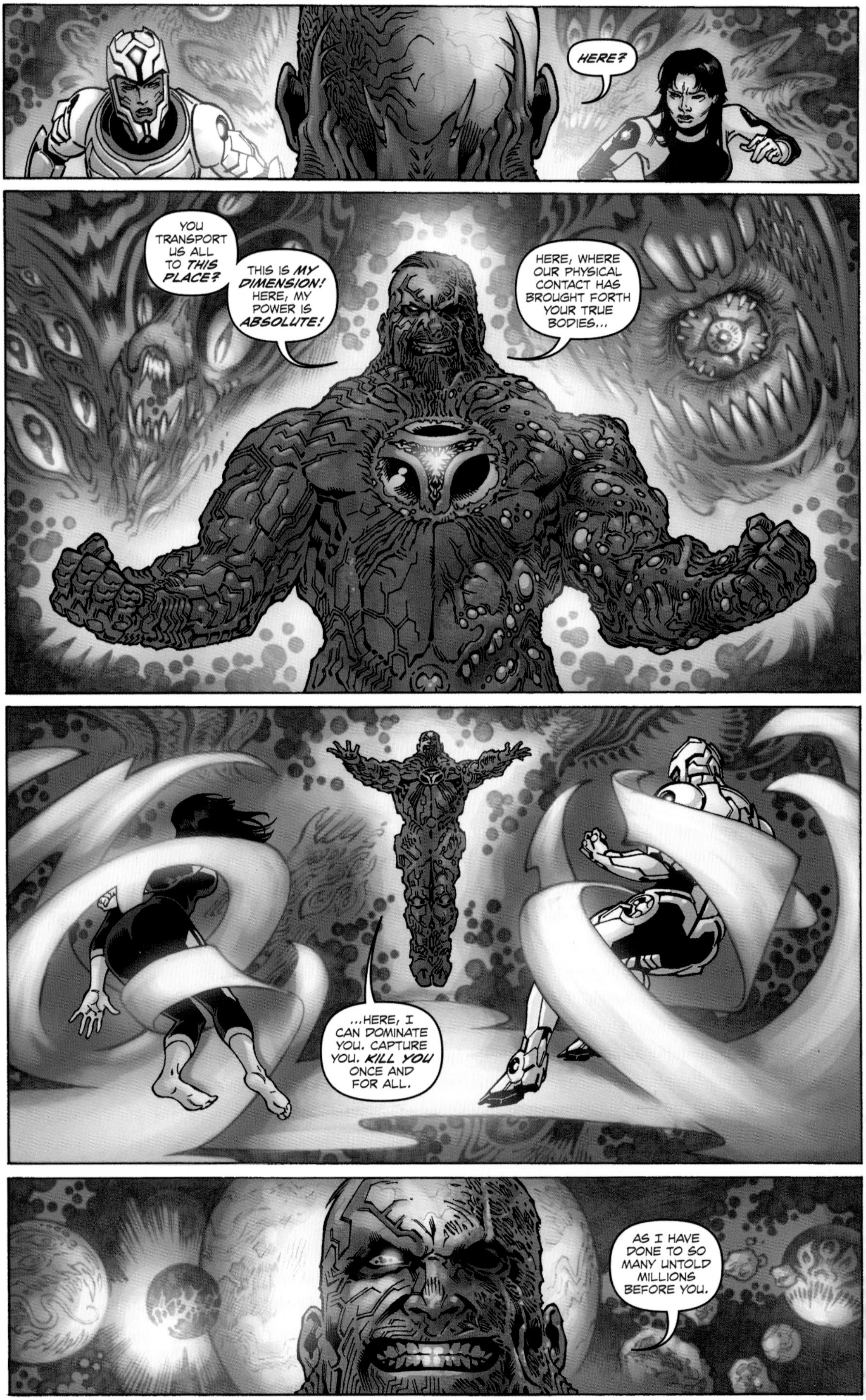
HERE?
YOU TRANSPORT US ALL TO THIS PLACE?
THIS IS MY DIMENSION! HERE, MY POWER IS ABSOLUTE!
HERE, WHERE OUR PHYSICAL CONTACT HAS BROUGHT FORTH YOUR TRUE BODIES...
...HERE, I CAN DOMINATE YOU. CAPTURE YOU. KILL YOU ONCE AND FOR ALL.
AS I HAVE DONE TO SO MANY UNTOLD MILLIONS BEFORE YOU.

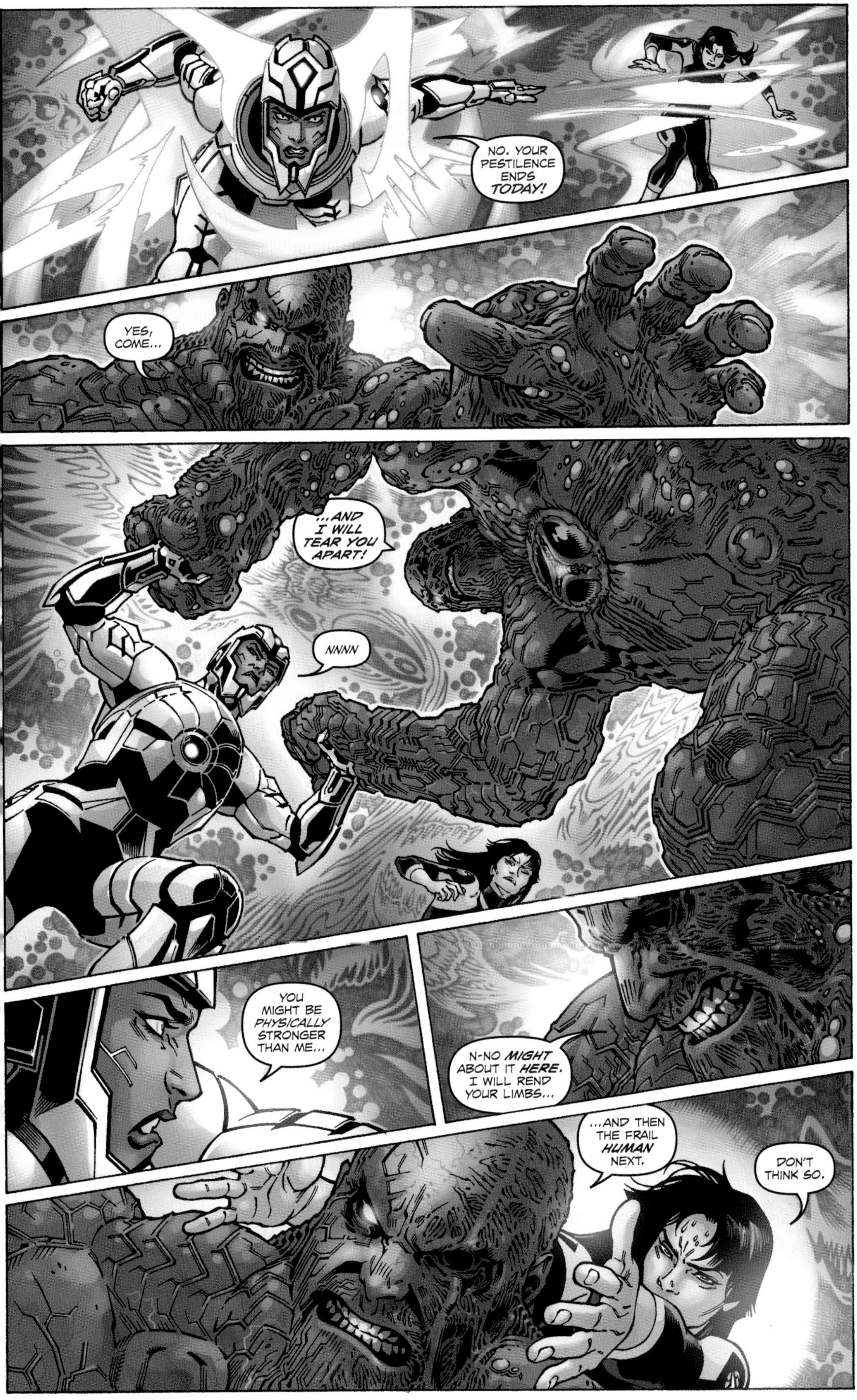
NO. YOUR PESTILENCE ENDS *TODAY!*
YES, COME...
...AND I WILL TEAR YOU APART!
NNNN
YOU MIGHT BE *PHYSICALLY* STRONGER THAN ME...
N-NO *MIGHT* ABOUT IT *HERE.* I WILL REND YOUR LIMBS...
...AND THEN THE FRAIL *HUMAN* NEXT.
DON'T THINK SO.

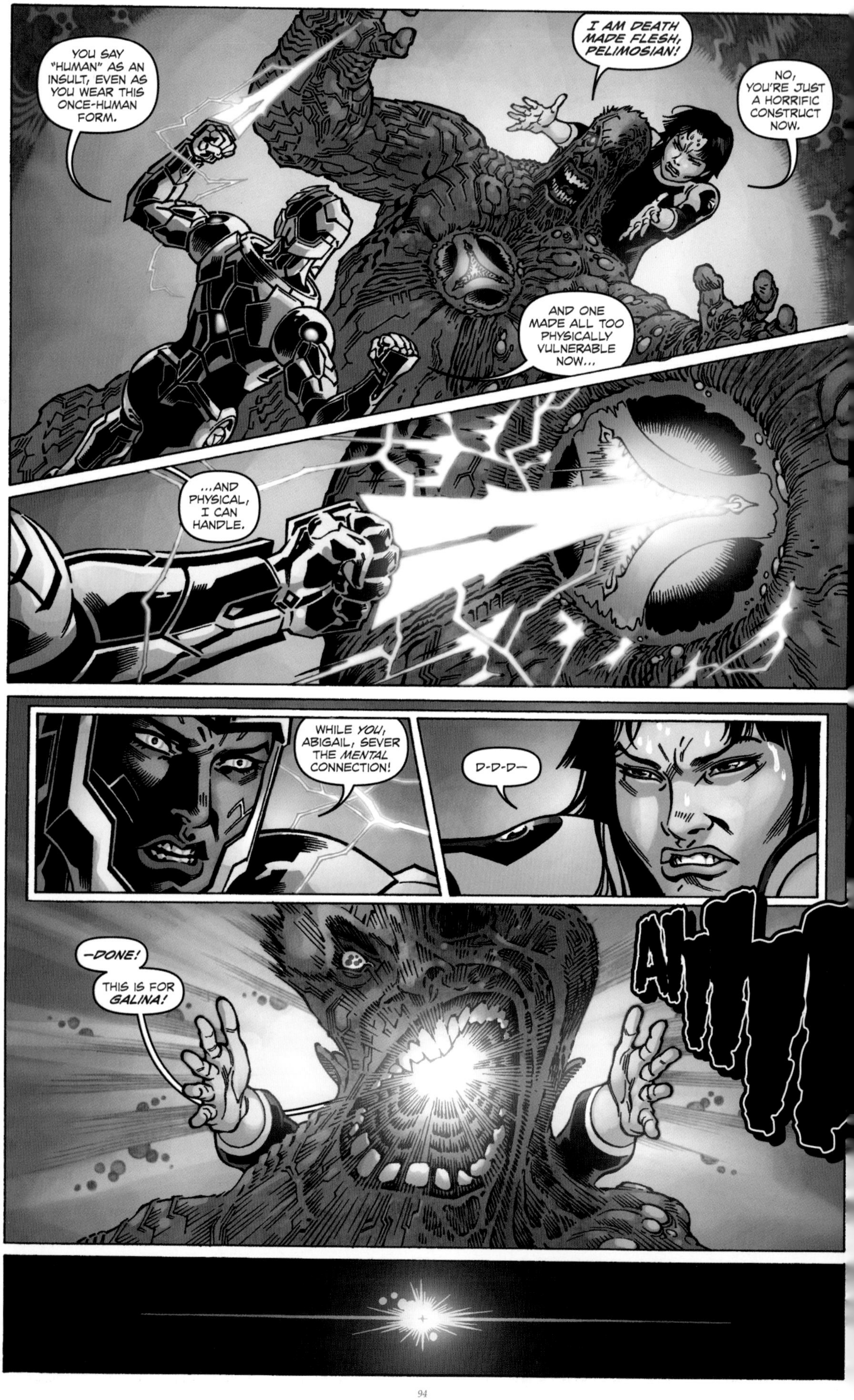
YOU SAY "HUMAN" AS AN INSULT, EVEN AS YOU WEAR THIS ONCE-HUMAN FORM.
I AM DEATH MADE FLESH, PELIMOSIAN!
NO, YOU'RE JUST A HORRIFIC CONSTRUCT NOW.
AND ONE MADE ALL TOO PHYSICALLY VULNERABLE NOW...
...AND PHYSICAL, I CAN HANDLE.
WHILE YOU, ABIGAIL, SEVER THE MENTAL CONNECTION!
D-D-D—
—DONE!
THIS IS FOR GALINA!

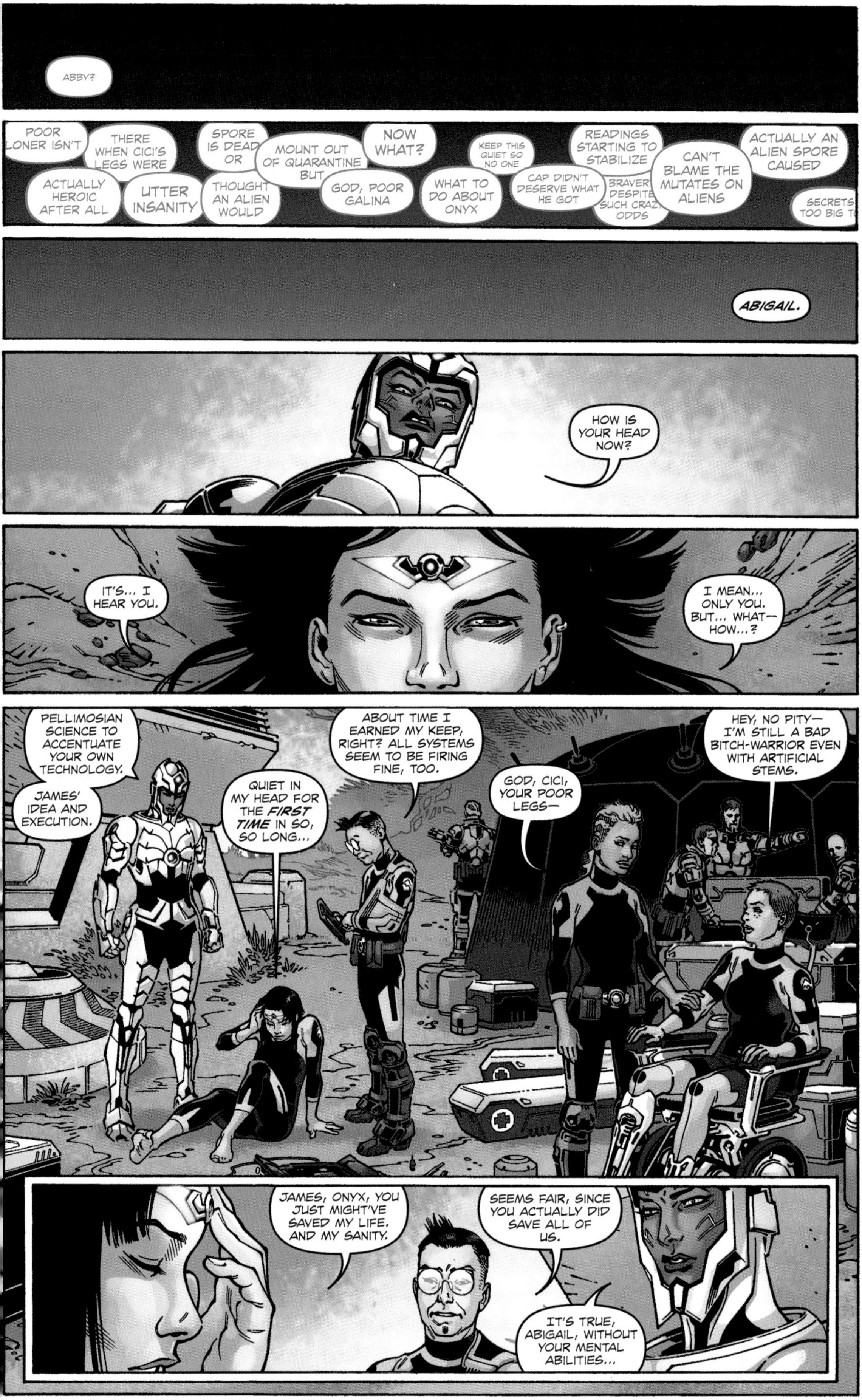

ABBY?
POOR LONER ISN'T
THERE WHEN CICI'S LEGS WERE
ACTUALLY HEROIC AFTER ALL
UTTER INSANITY
SPORE IS DEAD OR
THOUGHT AN ALIEN WOULD
MOUNT OUT OF QUARANTINE BUT
NOW WHAT?
GOD, POOR GALINA
KEEP THIS QUIET SO NO ONE
WHAT TO DO ABOUT ONYX
CAP DIDN'T DESERVE WHAT HE GOT
READINGS STARTING TO STABILIZE
BRAVER DESPITE SUCH CRAZ ODDS
CAN'T BLAME THE MUTATES ON ALIENS
ACTUALLY AN ALIEN SPORE CAUSED
SECRETS TOO BIG T
ABIGAIL.
HOW IS YOUR HEAD NOW?
IT'S... I HEAR YOU.
I MEAN... ONLY YOU. BUT... WHAT— HOW...?
PELLIMOSIAN SCIENCE TO ACCENTUATE YOUR OWN TECHNOLOGY.
JAMES' IDEA AND EXECUTION.
QUIET IN MY HEAD FOR THE FIRST TIME IN SO, SO LONG...
ABOUT TIME I EARNED MY KEEP, RIGHT? ALL SYSTEMS SEEM TO BE FIRING FINE, TOO.
GOD, CICI, YOUR POOR LEGS—
HEY, NO PITY— I'M STILL A BAD BITCH-WARRIOR EVEN WITH ARTIFICIAL STEMS.
JAMES, ONYX, YOU JUST MIGHT'VE SAVED MY LIFE. AND MY SANITY.
SEEMS FAIR, SINCE YOU ACTUALLY DID SAVE ALL OF US.
IT'S TRUE, ABIGAIL, WITHOUT YOUR MENTAL ABILITIES...

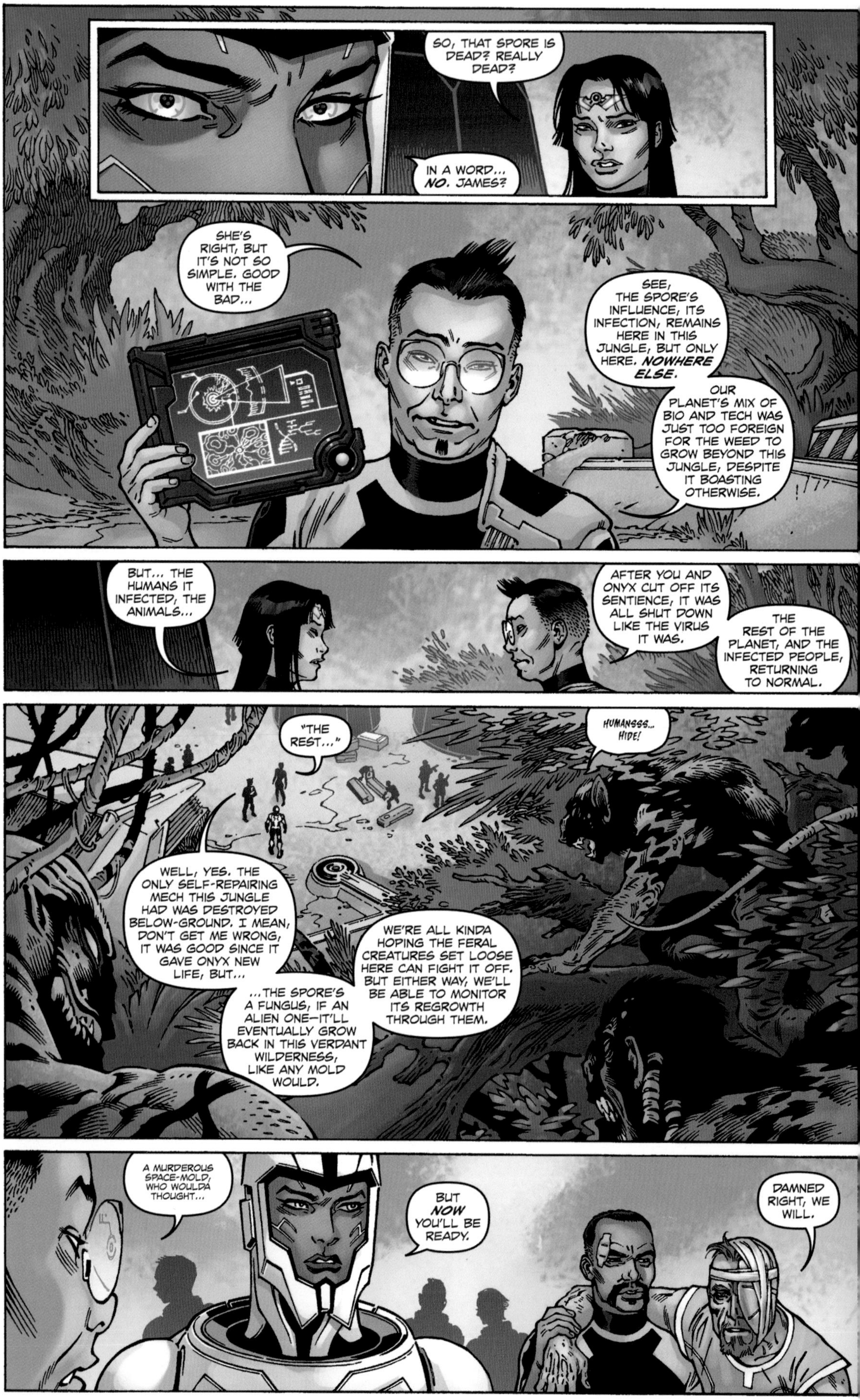
SO, THAT SPORE IS DEAD? REALLY DEAD?
IN A WORD... NO. JAMES?
SHE'S RIGHT, BUT IT'S NOT SO SIMPLE. GOOD WITH THE BAD...
SEE, THE SPORE'S INFLUENCE, ITS INFECTION, REMAINS HERE IN THIS JUNGLE, BUT ONLY HERE. NOWHERE ELSE.
OUR PLANET'S MIX OF BIO AND TECH WAS JUST TOO FOREIGN FOR THE WEED TO GROW BEYOND THIS JUNGLE, DESPITE IT BOASTING OTHERWISE.
BUT... THE HUMANS IT INFECTED, THE ANIMALS...
AFTER YOU AND ONYX CUT OFF ITS SENTIENCE, IT WAS ALL SHUT DOWN LIKE THE VIRUS IT WAS.
THE REST OF THE PLANET, AND THE INFECTED PEOPLE, RETURNING TO NORMAL.
"THE REST..."
HUMANSSS... HIDE!
WELL, YES. THE ONLY SELF-REPAIRING MECH THIS JUNGLE HAD WAS DESTROYED BELOW-GROUND. I MEAN, DON'T GET ME WRONG, IT WAS GOOD SINCE IT GAVE ONYX NEW LIFE, BUT...
...THE SPORE'S A FUNGUS, IF AN ALIEN ONE—IT'LL EVENTUALLY GROW BACK IN THIS VERDANT WILDERNESS, LIKE ANY MOLD WOULD.
WE'RE ALL KINDA HOPING THE FERAL CREATURES SET LOOSE HERE CAN FIGHT IT OFF. BUT EITHER WAY, WE'LL BE ABLE TO MONITOR ITS REGROWTH THROUGH THEM.
A MURDEROUS SPACE-MOLD, WHO WOULDA THOUGHT...
BUT NOW YOU'LL BE READY.
DAMNED RIGHT, WE WILL.

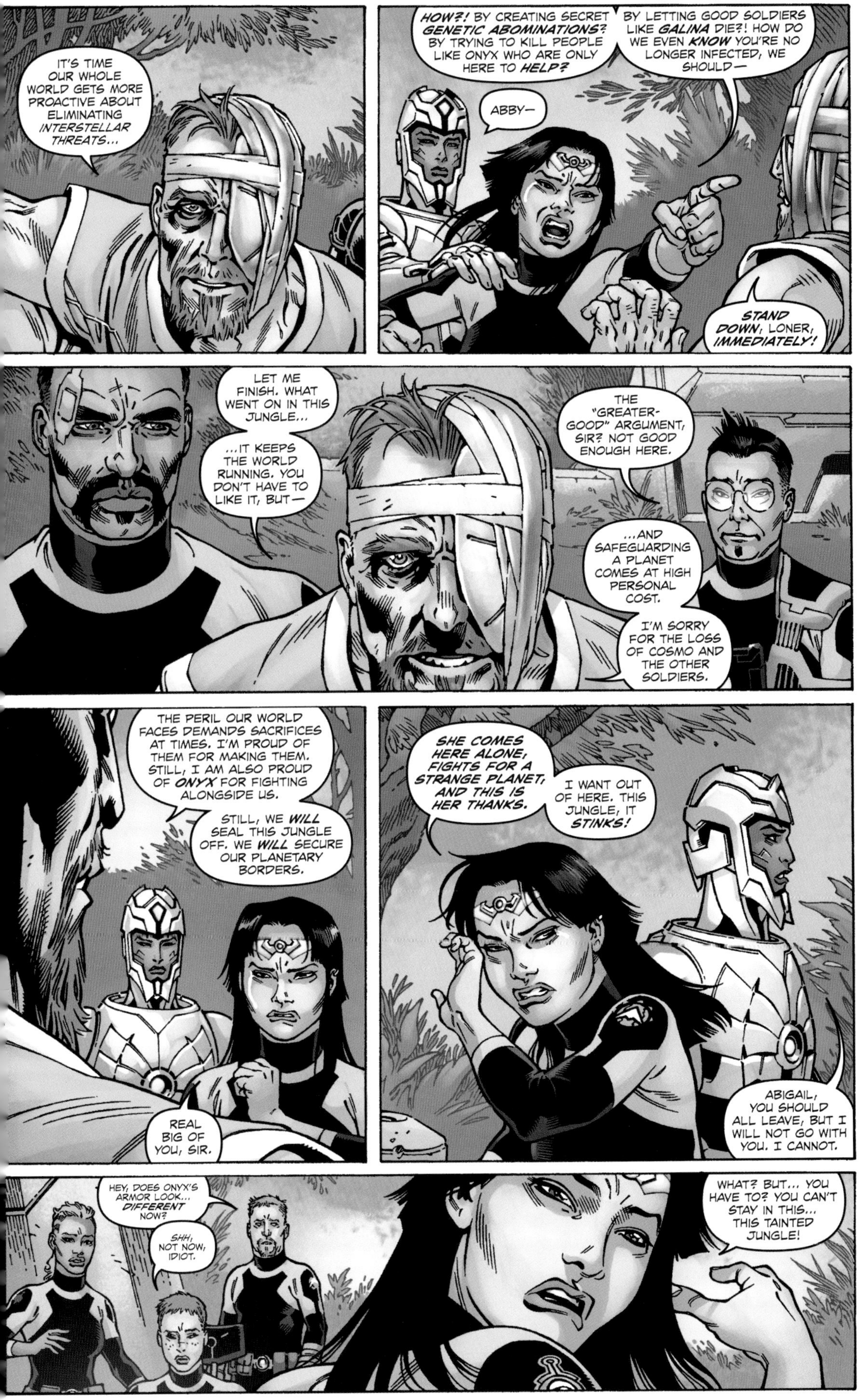
IT'S TIME OUR WHOLE WORLD GETS MORE PROACTIVE ABOUT ELIMINATING INTERSTELLAR THREATS...
HOW?! BY CREATING SECRET GENETIC ABOMINATIONS? BY TRYING TO KILL PEOPLE LIKE ONYX WHO ARE ONLY HERE TO HELP?
BY LETTING GOOD SOLDIERS LIKE GALINA DIE?! HOW DO WE EVEN KNOW YOU'RE NO LONGER INFECTED, WE SHOULD—
ABBY—
STAND DOWN, LONER, IMMEDIATELY!
LET ME FINISH. WHAT WENT ON IN THIS JUNGLE...
...IT KEEPS THE WORLD RUNNING. YOU DON'T HAVE TO LIKE IT, BUT—
THE "GREATER-GOOD" ARGUMENT, SIR? NOT GOOD ENOUGH HERE.
...AND SAFEGUARDING A PLANET COMES AT HIGH PERSONAL COST.
I'M SORRY FOR THE LOSS OF COSMO AND THE OTHER SOLDIERS.
THE PERIL OUR WORLD FACES DEMANDS SACRIFICES AT TIMES. I'M PROUD OF THEM FOR MAKING THEM. STILL, I AM ALSO PROUD OF ONYX FOR FIGHTING ALONGSIDE US.
STILL, WE WILL SEAL THIS JUNGLE OFF. WE WILL SECURE OUR PLANETARY BORDERS.
REAL BIG OF YOU, SIR.
SHE COMES HERE ALONE, FIGHTS FOR A STRANGE PLANET, AND THIS IS HER THANKS.
I WANT OUT OF HERE. THIS JUNGLE, IT STINKS!
ABIGAIL, YOU SHOULD ALL LEAVE, BUT I WILL NOT GO WITH YOU. I CANNOT.
HEY, DOES ONYX'S ARMOR LOOK... DIFFERENT NOW?
SHH, NOT NOW, IDIOT.
WHAT? BUT... YOU HAVE TO? YOU CAN'T STAY IN THIS... THIS TAINTED JUNGLE!

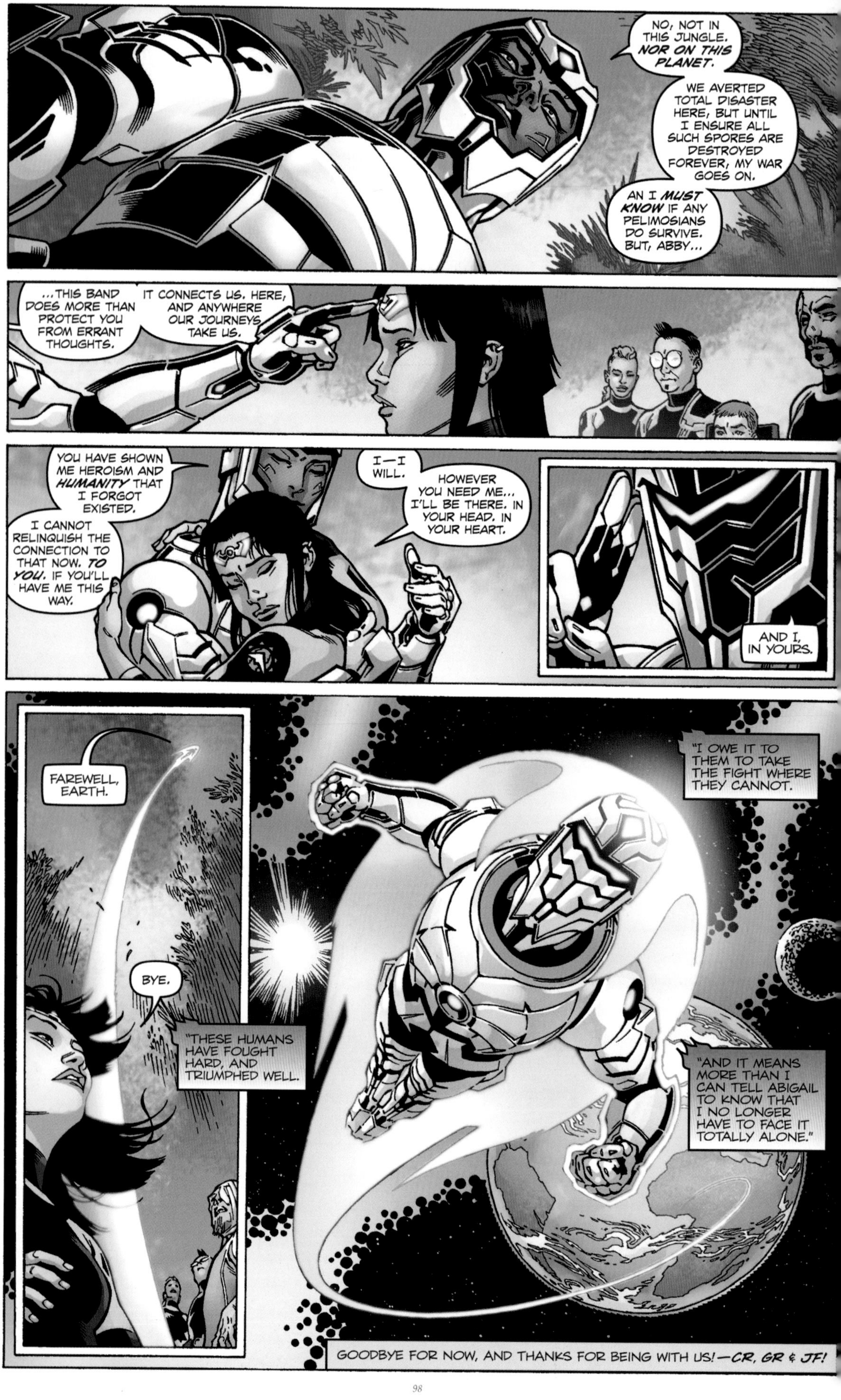
NO, NOT IN THIS JUNGLE. NOR ON THIS PLANET.
WE AVERTED TOTAL DISASTER HERE, BUT UNTIL I ENSURE ALL SUCH SPORES ARE DESTROYED FOREVER, MY WAR GOES ON.
AN I MUST KNOW IF ANY PELIMOSIANS DO SURVIVE. BUT, ABBY...
...THIS BAND DOES MORE THAN PROTECT YOU FROM ERRANT THOUGHTS.
IT CONNECTS US. HERE, AND ANYWHERE OUR JOURNEYS TAKE US.
YOU HAVE SHOWN ME HEROISM AND HUMANITY THAT I FORGOT EXISTED.
I CANNOT RELINQUISH THE CONNECTION TO THAT NOW. TO YOU. IF YOU'LL HAVE ME THIS WAY.
I—I WILL.
HOWEVER YOU NEED ME... I'LL BE THERE. IN YOUR HEAD. IN YOUR HEART.
AND I, IN YOURS.
FAREWELL, EARTH.
BYE.
"THESE HUMANS HAVE FOUGHT HARD, AND TRIUMPHED WELL.
"I OWE IT TO THEM TO TAKE THE FIGHT WHERE THEY CANNOT.
"AND IT MEANS MORE THAN I CAN TELL ABIGAIL TO KNOW THAT I NO LONGER HAVE TO FACE IT TOTALLY ALONE."
GOODBYE FOR NOW, AND THANKS FOR BEING WITH US! —CR, GR & JF!

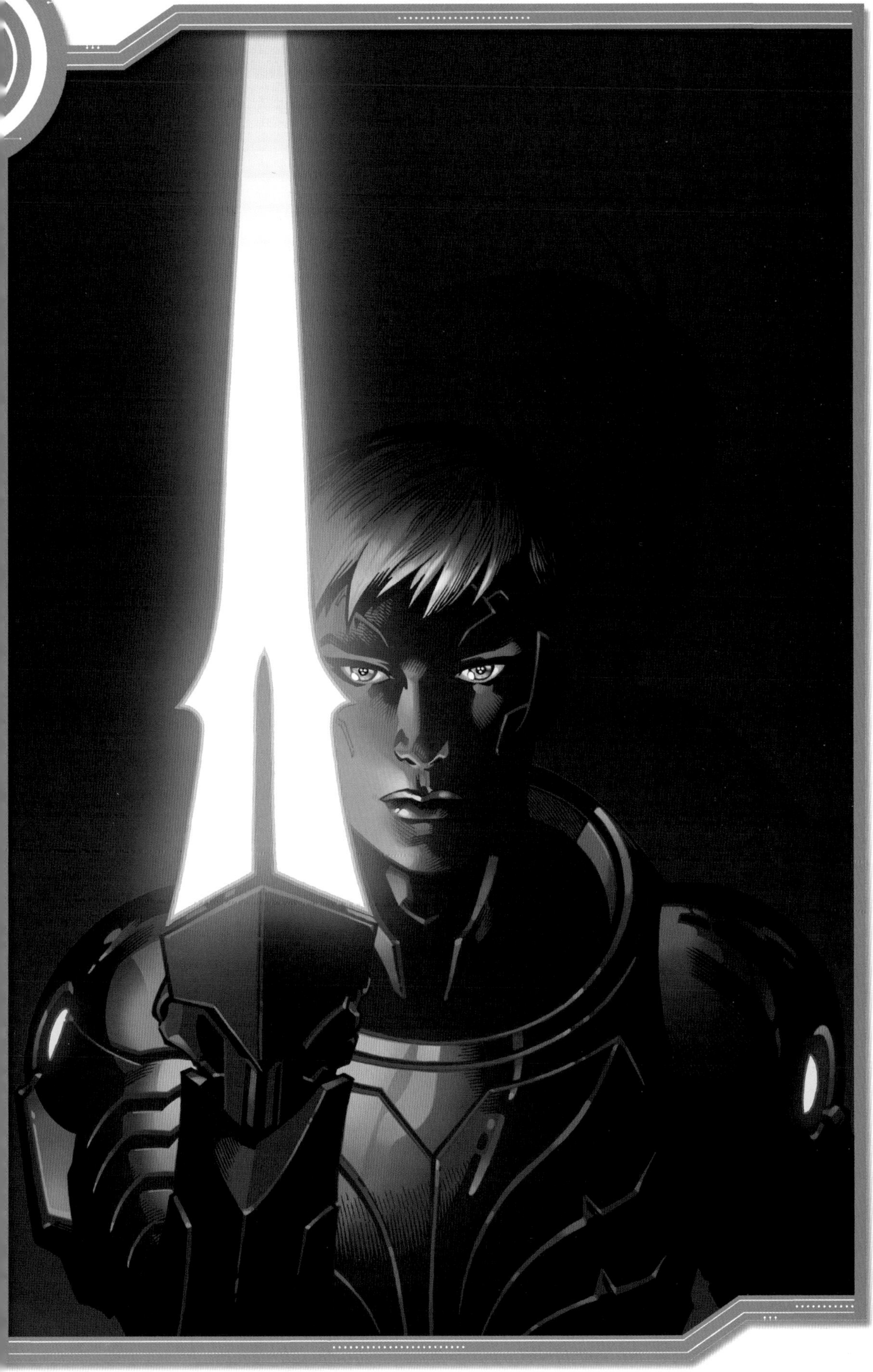

Art by GABRIEL RODRIGUEZ

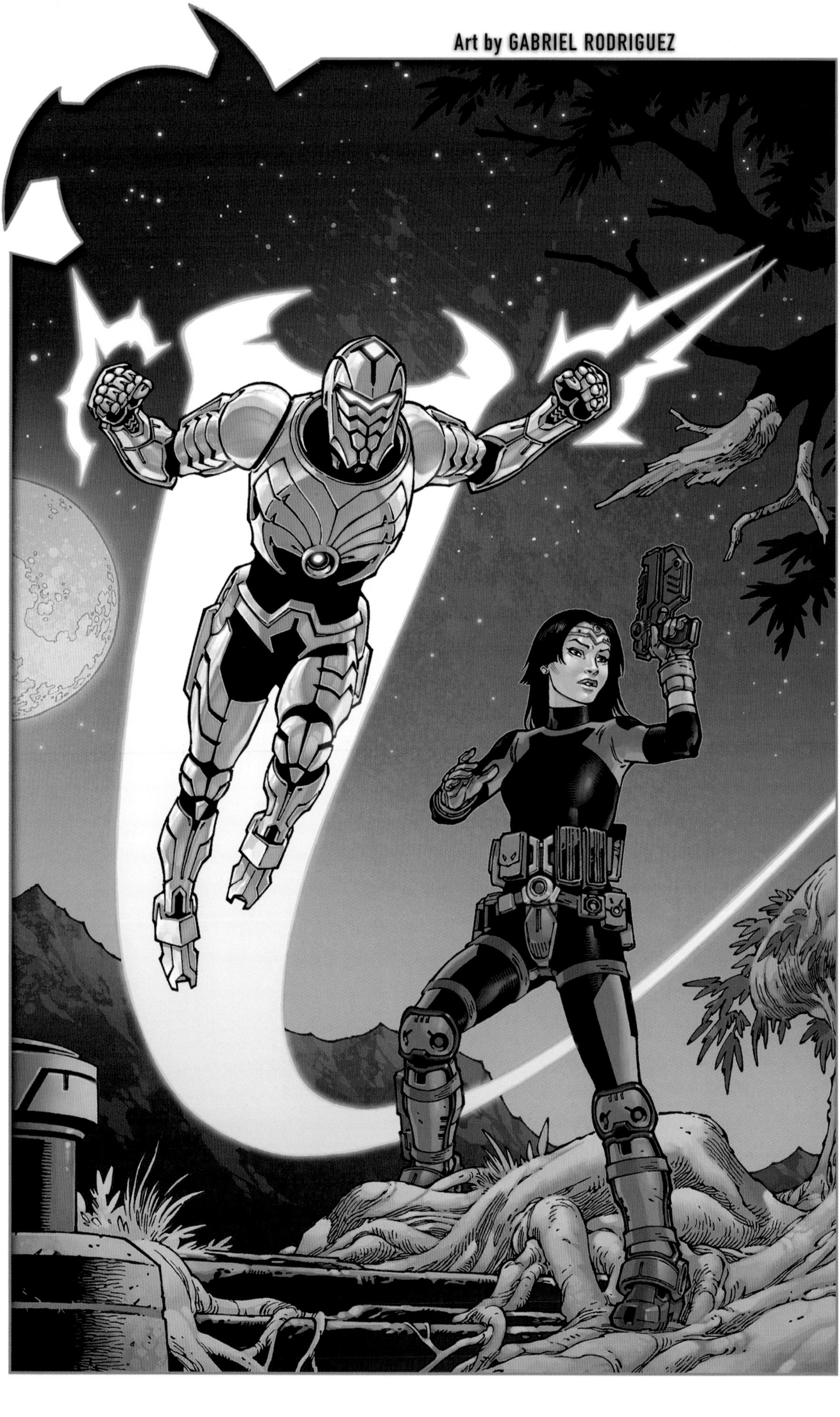

Art by SAL BUSCEMA, Colors by DIEGO RODRIGUEZ

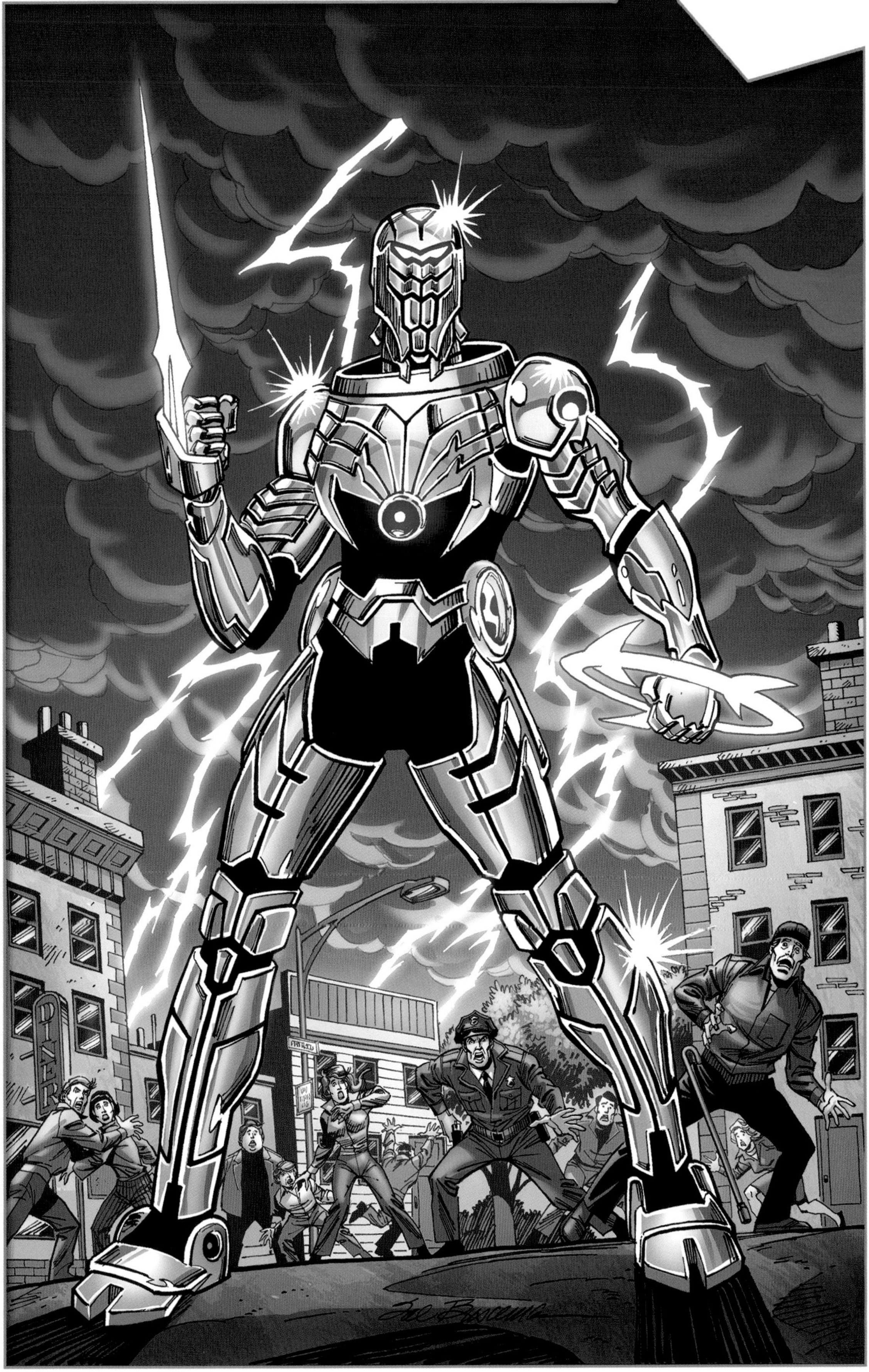
DINER

Art by JAMIE TYNDALL, Colors by ULA MOS

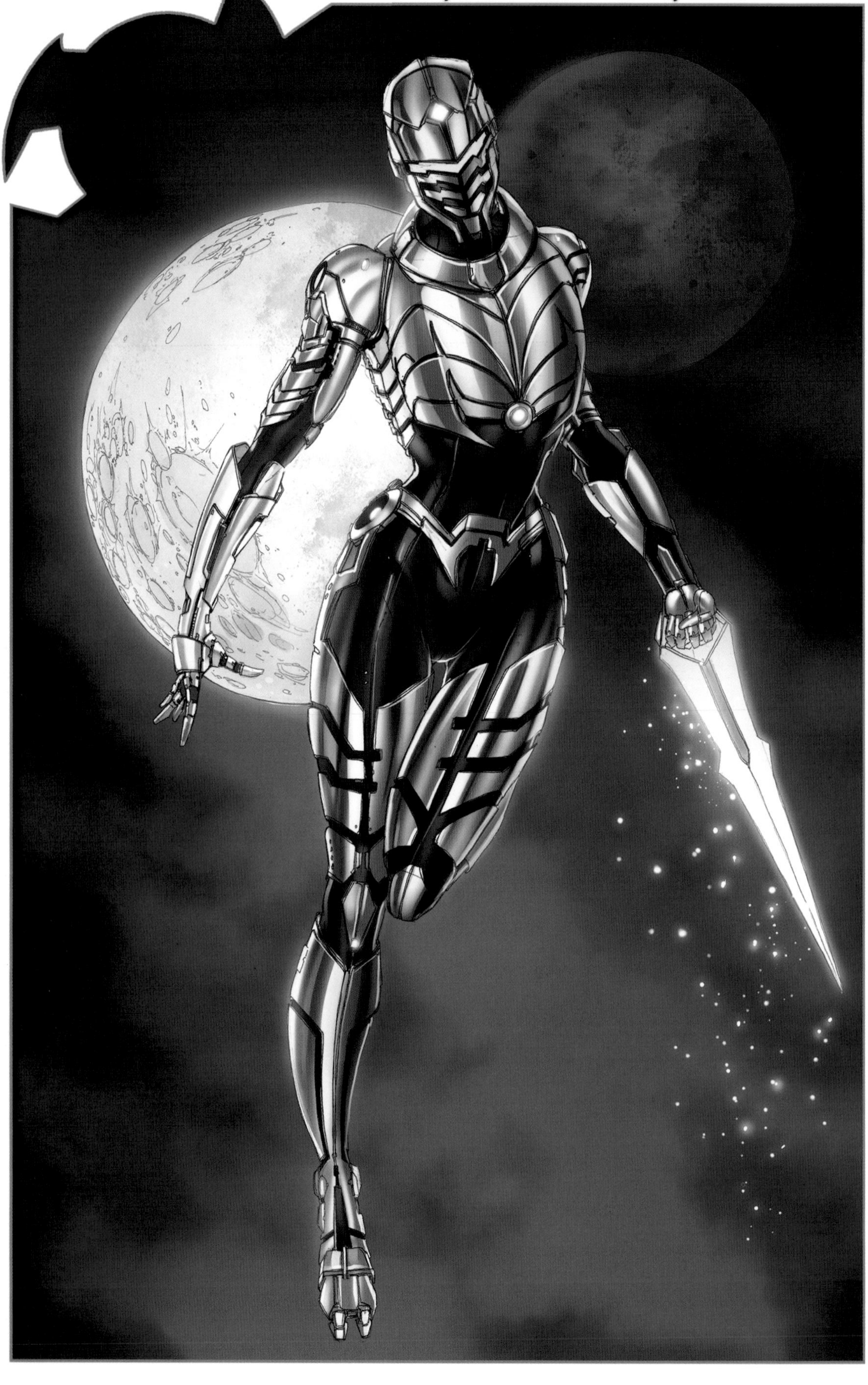

Art by ALAN ROBINSON, Colors by DIEGO RODRIGUEZ

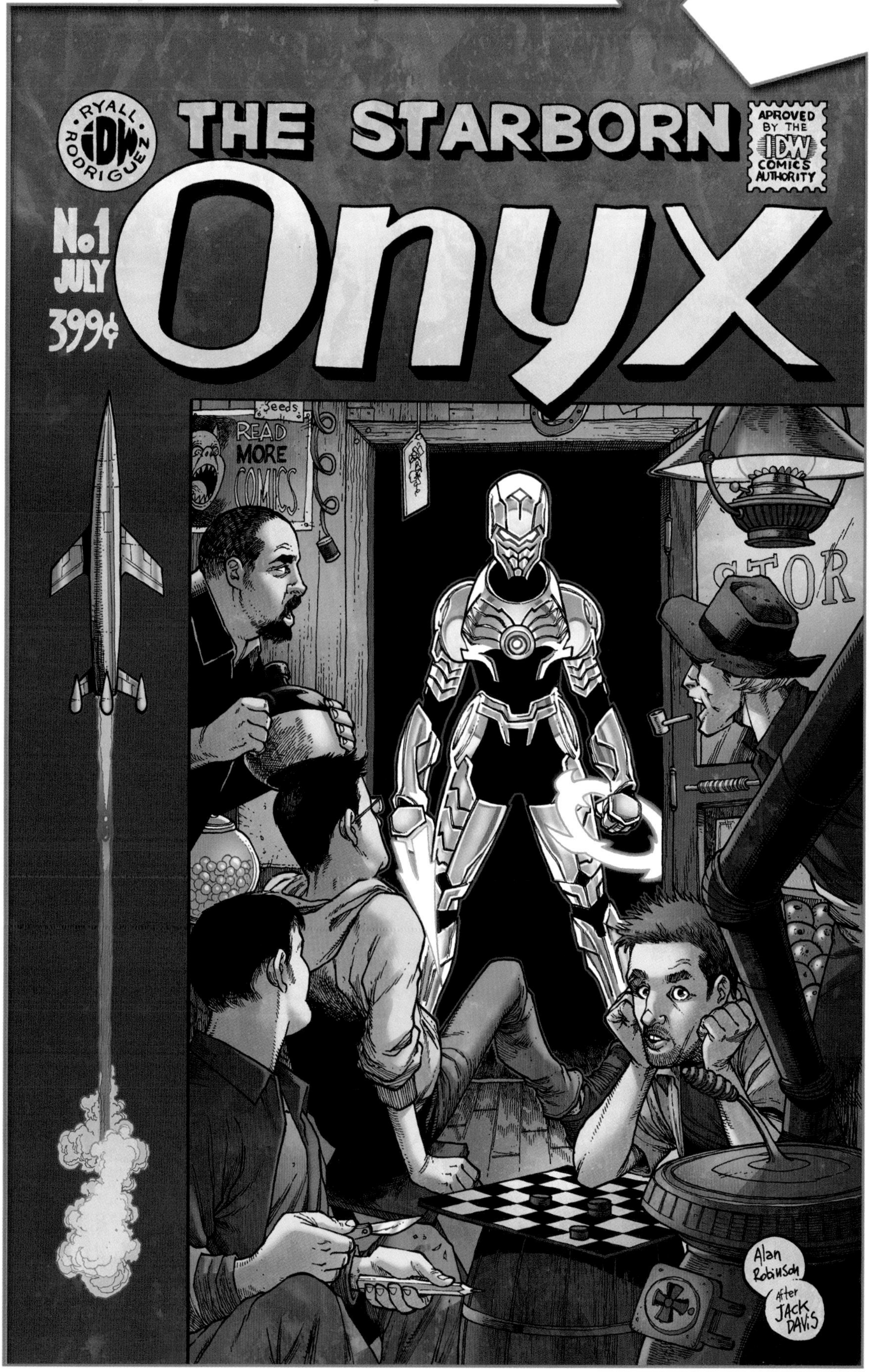

RYALL IDW RODRIGUEZ
THE STARBORN
APROVED BY THE IDW COMICS AUTHORITY
No.1
JULY
399¢
Onyx
Seeds
READ MORE COMICS
STOR
Alan Robinson After JACK DAVIS

Art by ASHLEY WOOD

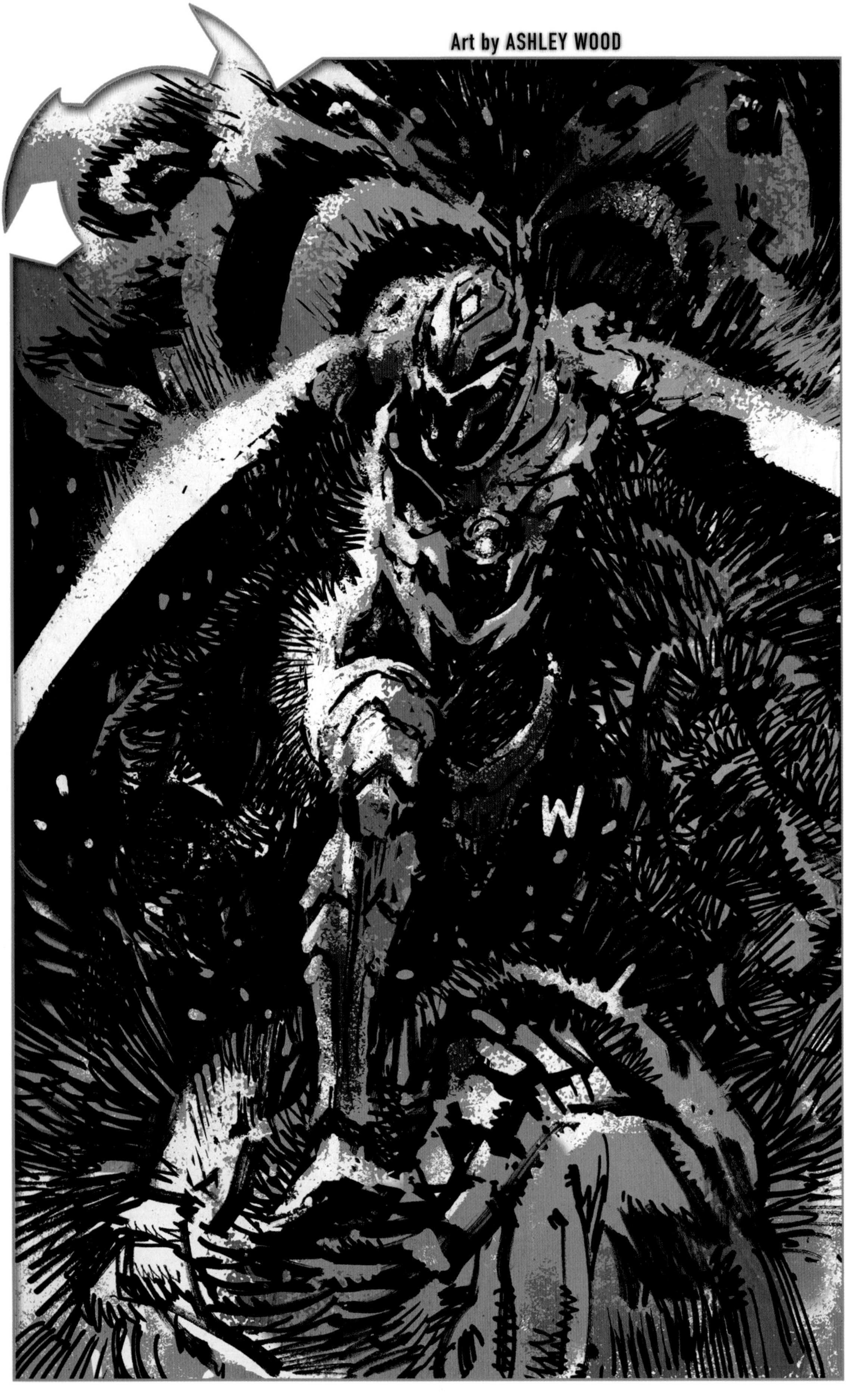

Art by CHARLES PAUL WILSON III

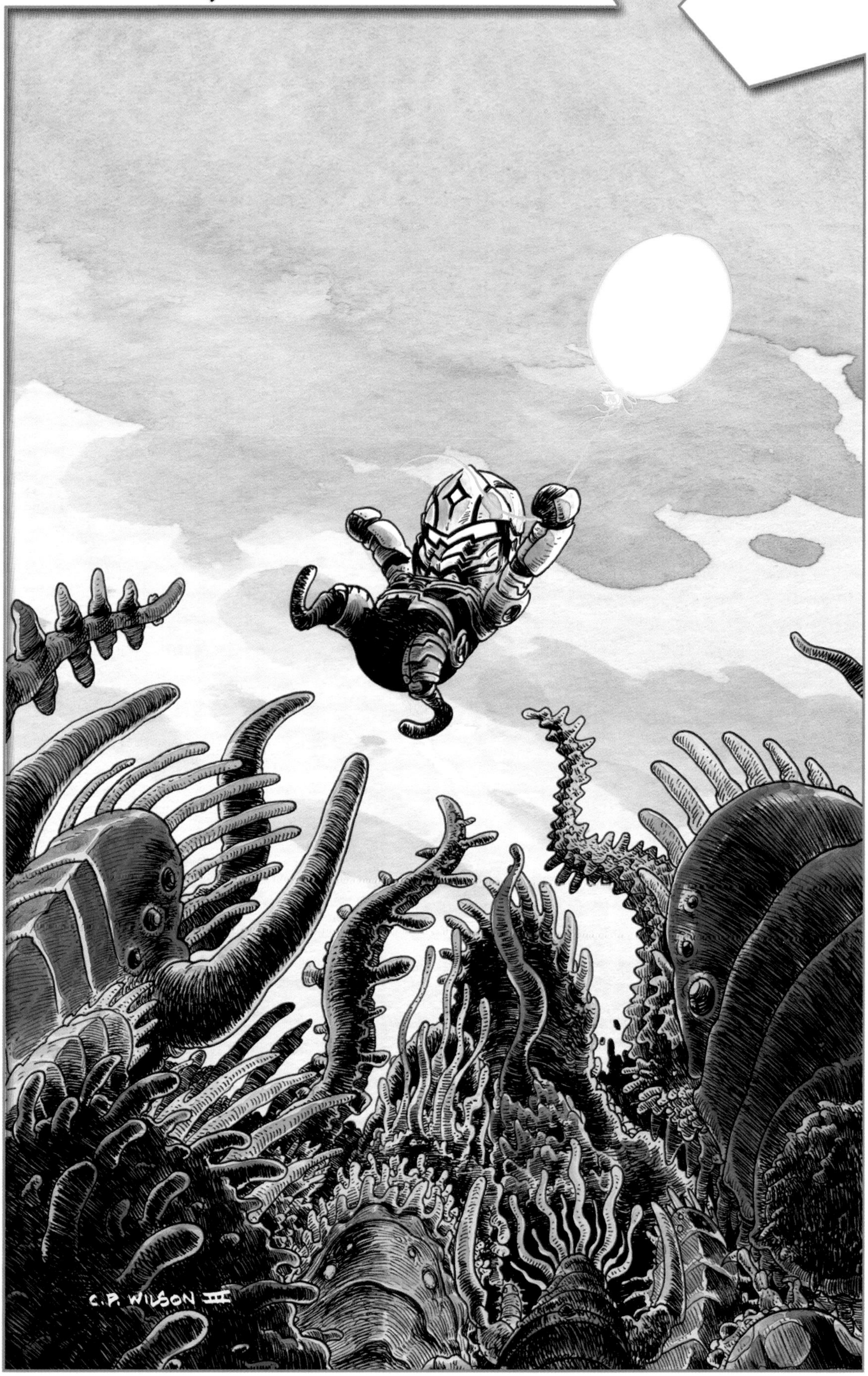
C.P. WILSON III

Art by JEFFREY VEREGGE

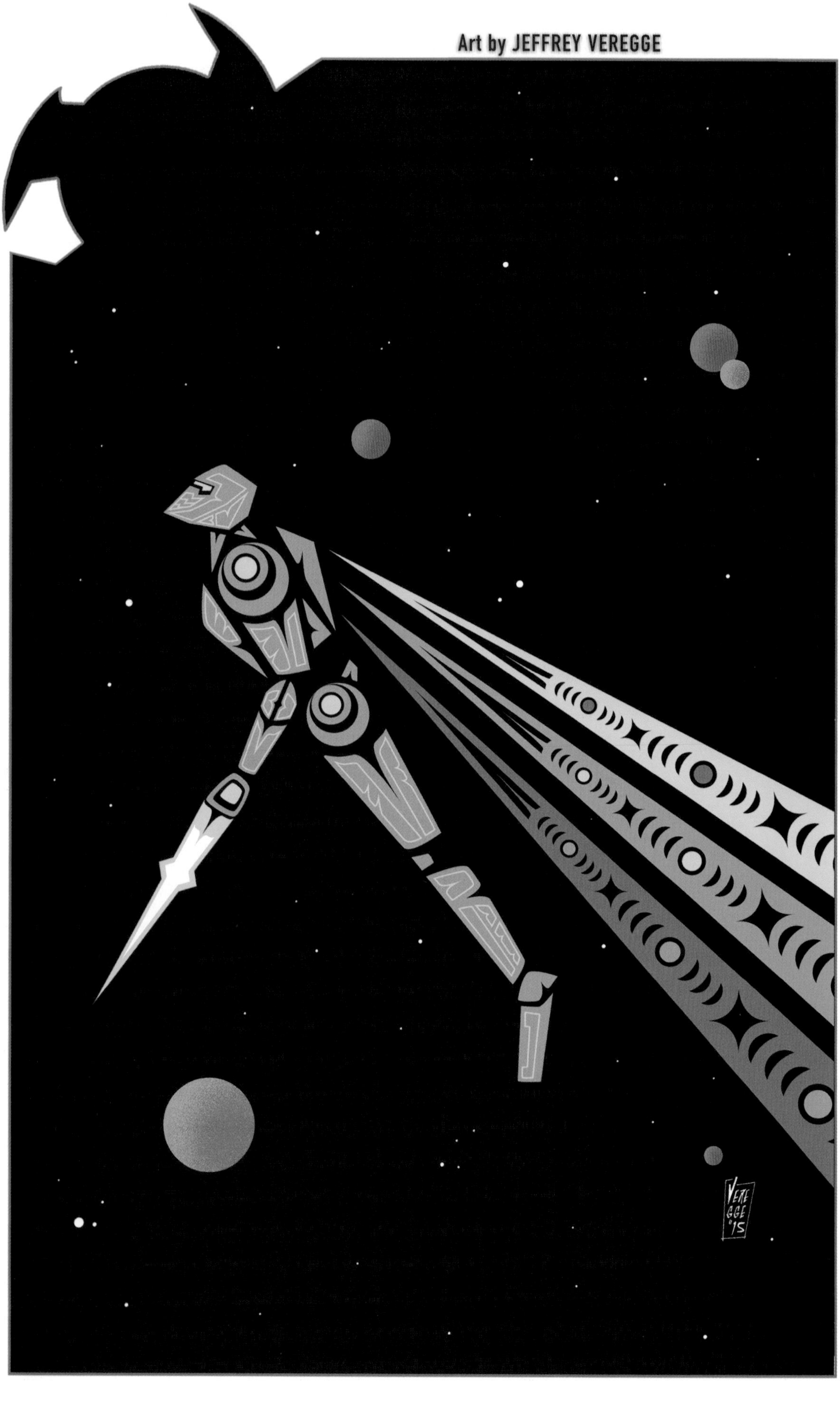
VEREGGE '15

Art by PAUL HANLEY

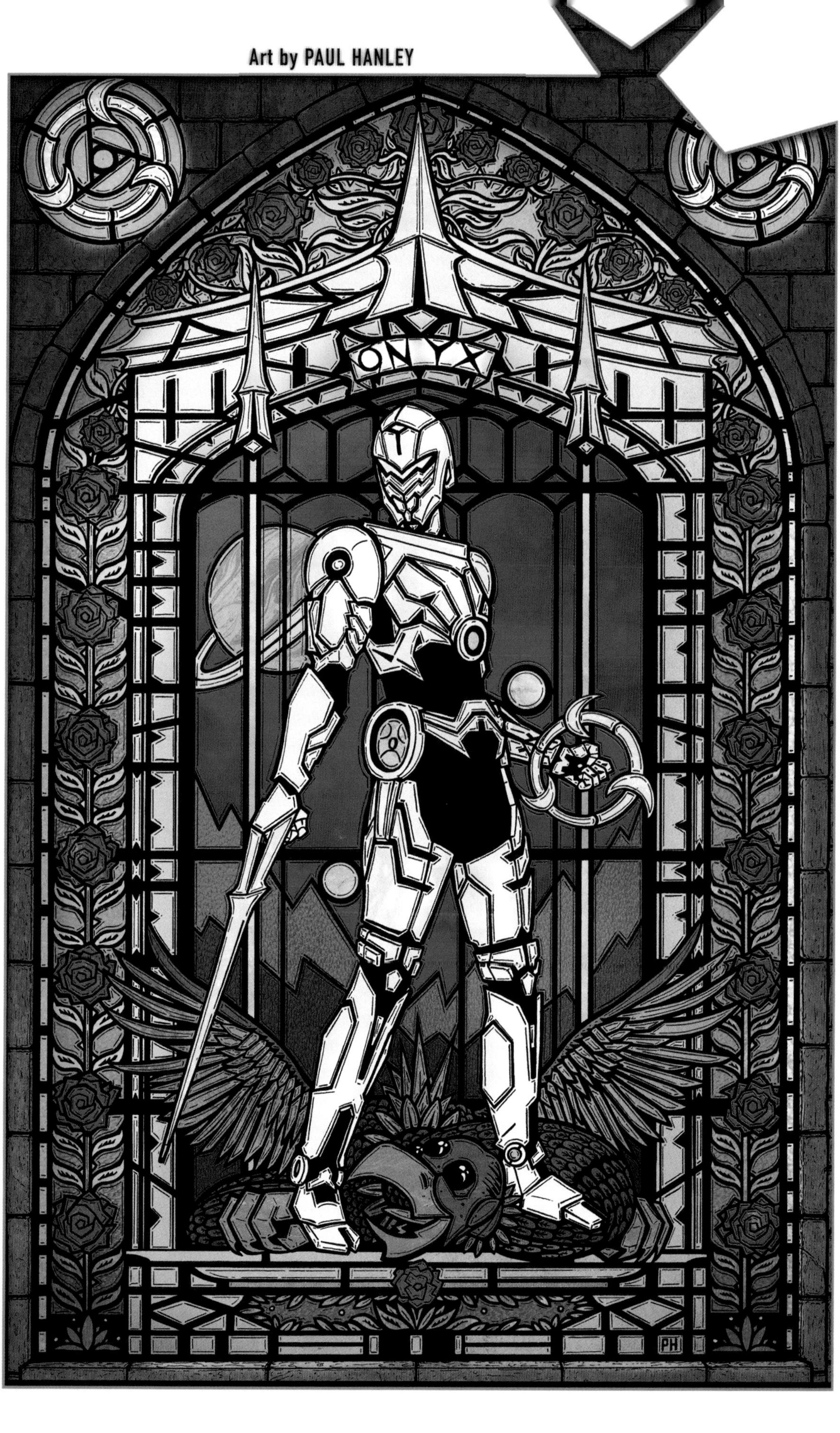
ONYX
PH

Art by JEFFREY VEREGGE

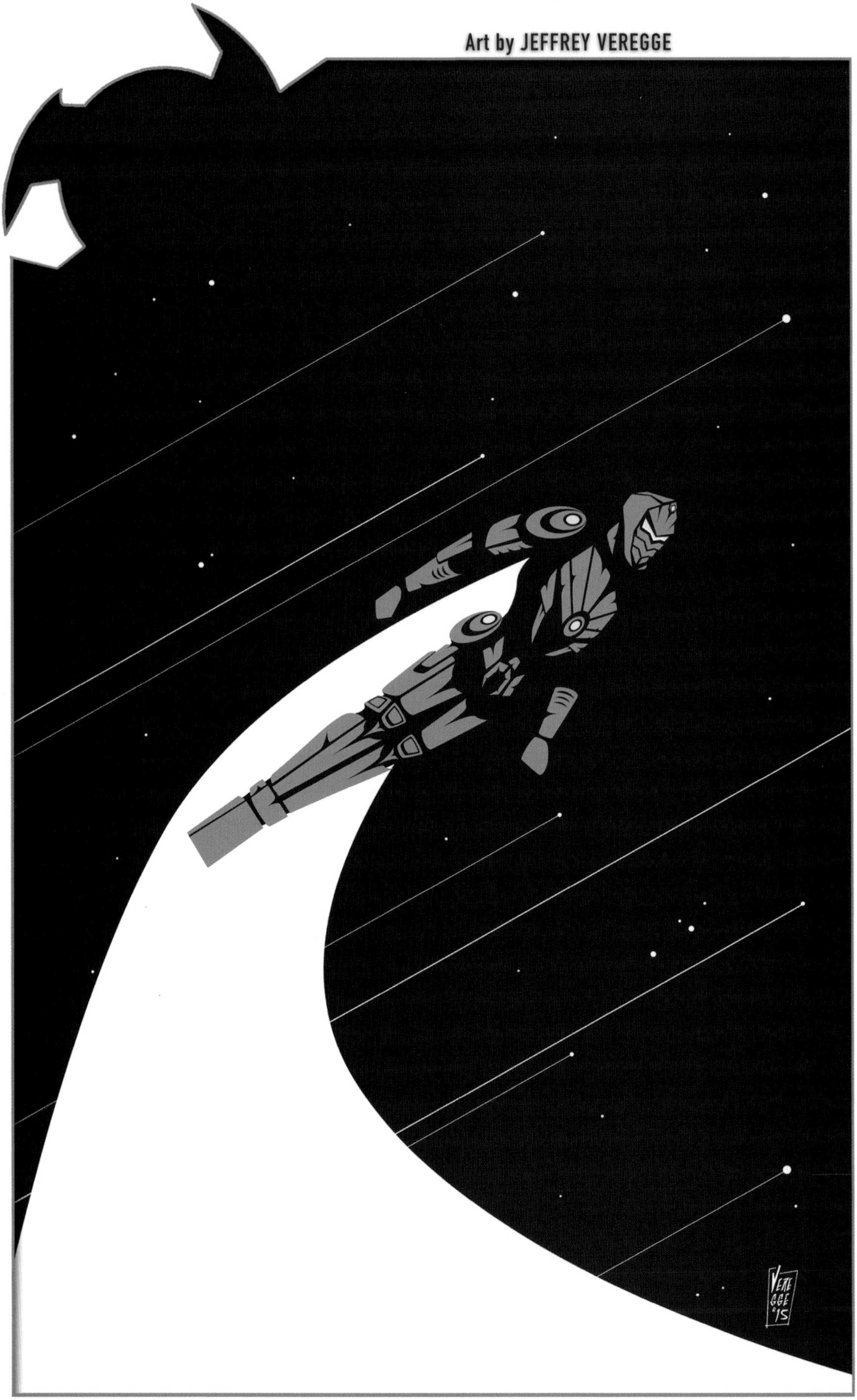
VEREGGE '15

MARK TORRES

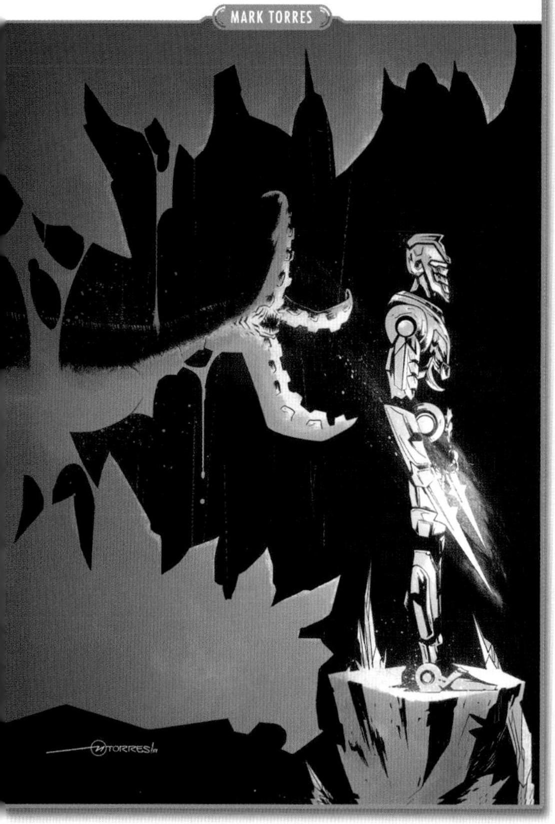

CHARLES PAUL WILSON III

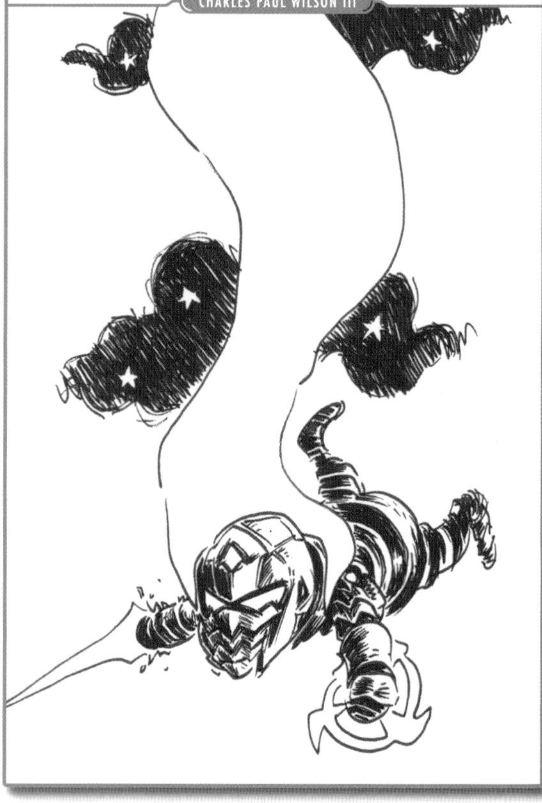

JOSH BURCHAM

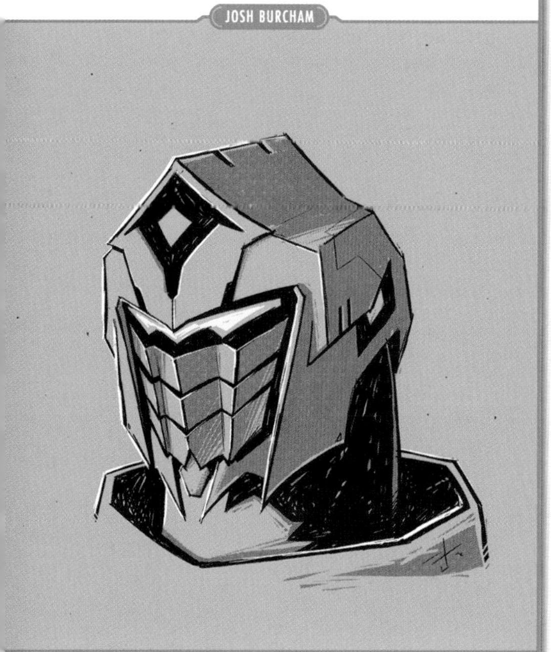

Twitter: @jcburcham

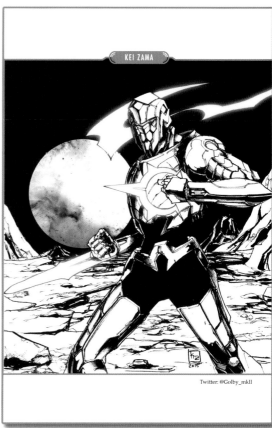

KEI ZAMA

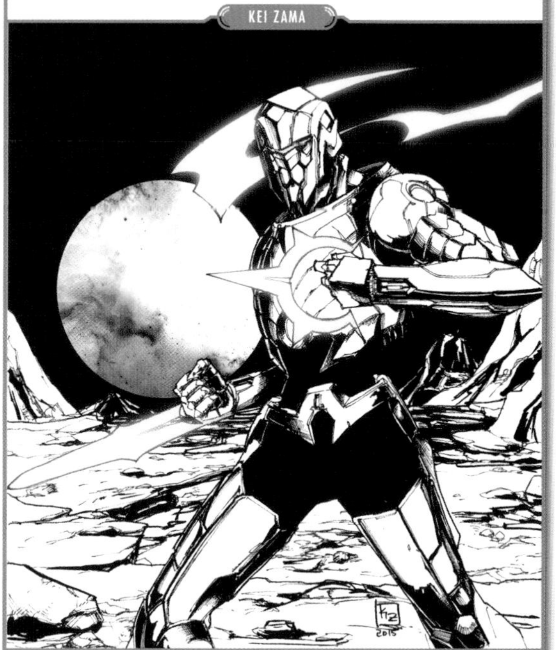

Twitter: @Golby_mkII

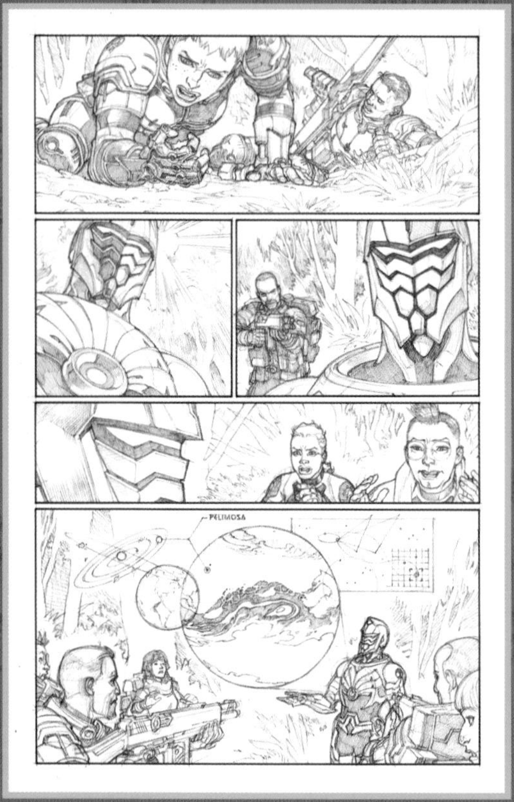
PELIMOSA

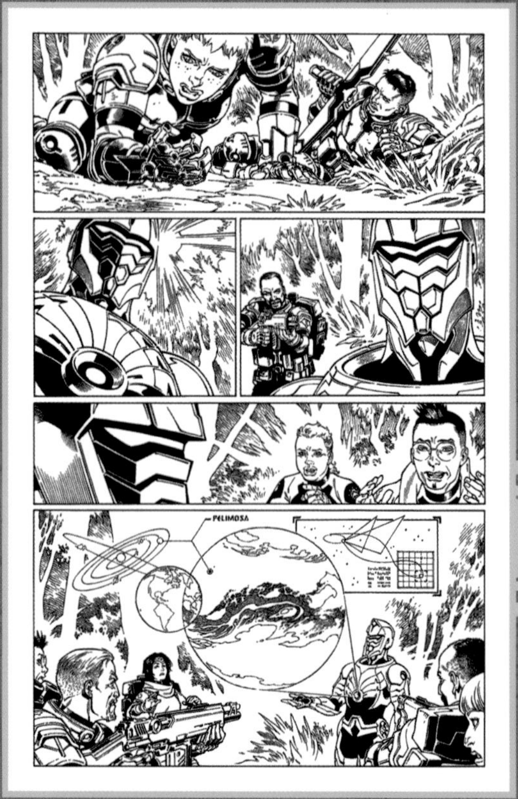
PELIMOSA

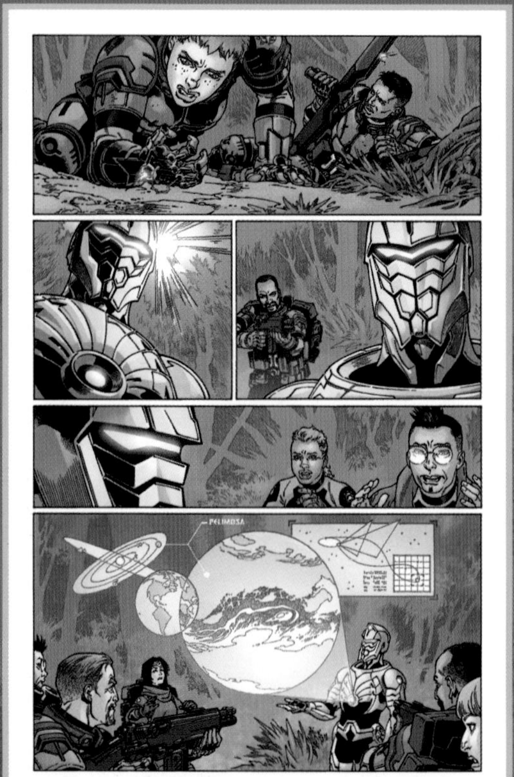
PELIMOSA

When drawing a comic book, the key challenge is to be able to construct a believable reality, and present it in a way that carries the story properly. In this book, the first time for me working in a science-fiction/adventure story, I faced several new challenges: designing futuristic military suits, dealing with scenes with LOTS of characters, creating alien armor and alien planets, while trying to keep storytelling easy to follow and "choreographing" the action scenes properly.

I'm aware that despite my efforts to keep them as simple as possible, the characters were going to be heavily detailed and complex in shape (damn Onyx's helmet geometry!!), so it was a creative decision to work most of the backgrounds and scene stages in a mostly abstract approach, hinting at details and mixing shapes and depth through texture work and shading. It was key to take this path to know that Jay Fotos would be coloring the book, as I knew his painter-like approach to coloring would fit very well with it. You can also notice in the pages how his approach to different kinds of lighting enrich the graphic language of every scene.

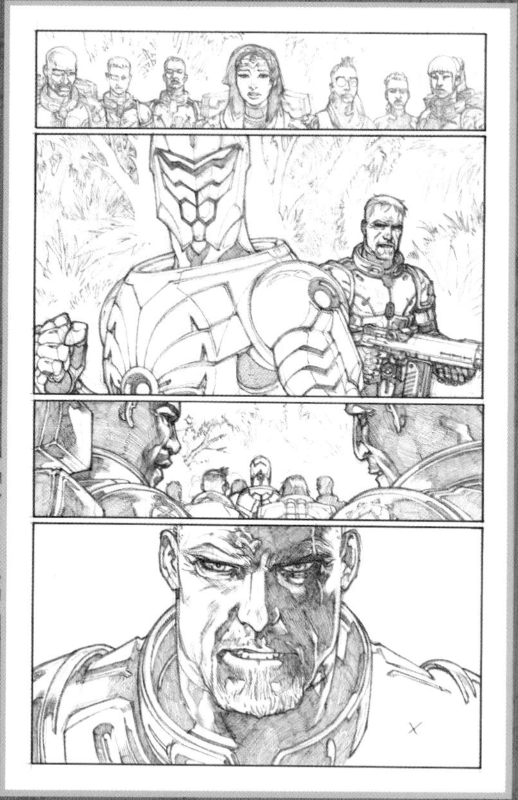

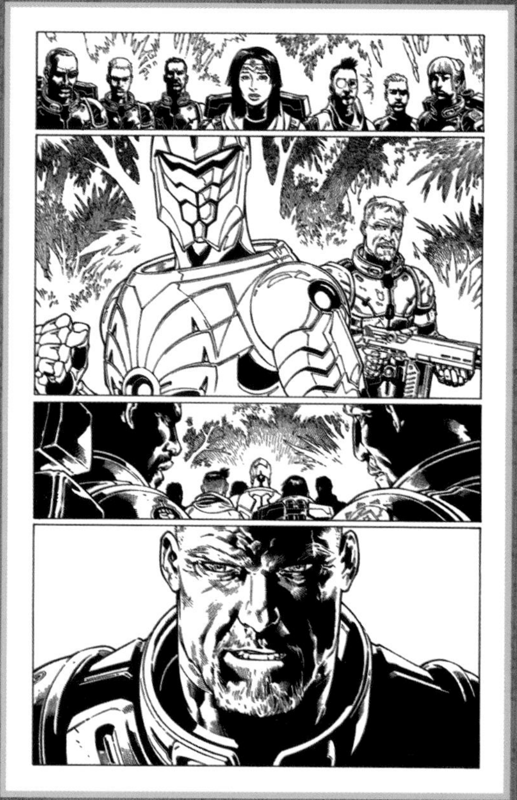

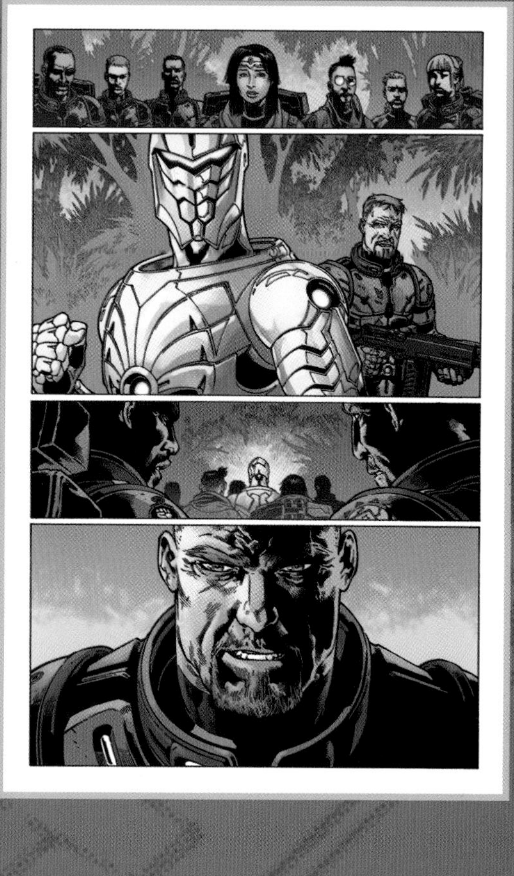

When you have several characters dressed in the same outfit constantly interacting, it's very important to be able to give them distinctive looks that might help the reader easily follow them through the story, even when they appear in small size in certain panels. That should rely on certain distinctive design details, obviously, but also in keeping a consistent size correlation, or even distinctive body languages for different characters. So when understanding your characters as deeply as possible helps you drive the story, you and your creative partners must keep thinking about them in every possible detail, way beyond what you'll need written in the script.

Another thing that was new for me in this book was to try a more "realistic" approach to the characters' portrayal, and with a more extreme use of shading and textures in their graphic depiction. In my mind, my personal goal would be to make the pages work successfully in black and white, but giving Jay comfortable room to add his color magic. That's when his sense of mood and drama add additional layers to the storytelling, helping build more solid characters and a more appealing story.

Hope you'll enjoy it, we're having a blast making this book. Welcome to the world of *Onyx*.

–*GR*

Chris Ryall has been the Chief Creative Officer/Editor-in-Chief of IDW Publishing since 2004. Along the way, he's won a couple Best Editor awards and also been nominated for "Best Short Story" Eisner alongside artist/frequent collaborator Ashley Wood.

Onyx is the first series Ryall and artist Gabriel Rodriguez have created together, but they have previously collaborated many times, notably on the 12-issue adaptation of *Clive Barker's The Great and Secret Show*, *George Romero's Land of the Dead*, and *Beowulf*. Ryall also edited the entire run of the **Joe Hill/Gabriel Rodriguez** series, *Locke & Key*.

Ryall has also co-created the series *Zombies vs Robots* (with artist **Ashley Wood**); *Groom Lake* (with artist **Ben Templesmith**); *The Colonized* (with artist **Drew Moss**); and *The Hollows* (with **Sam Kieth**). Other series he's written include *The Transformers*, *Doomed*, *Weekly World News*, *Dirk Gently's Holistic Detective Agency*, *String-Divers*, and many others. He and *Onyx* colorist **Jay Fotos** collaborated on the "Neanderthal" one-shot for Fotos' Frazetta Comics line. Ryall spends his spare free seconds of the day on Twitter at @chris_ryall.

Gabriel Rodriguez is a Chilean comic books artist, and co-creator (with writer **Joe Hill**) of IDW's award-winning graphic novel series *Locke & Key*.

In addition to work with **Eric Shanower** on the multiple Eisner Award-nomiated *Little Nemo: Return to Slumberland*, some of Gabriel's other collaborations with IDW, spanning over a decade, include IDW's first licensed comic series, *CSI*; *Clive Barker's The Great and Secret Show*, *Beowulf*, *George Romero's Land of the Dead*, and comic-book covers for *Transformers*, IDW's crossover event *Infestation*, *Star Trek*, *Angel*, *Astro Boy*, *Joe Hill's WRA1TH*, *Edward Scissorhands*, *TMNT*, and others. Rodriguez also contributed the cover art to Ryall and co-writer **Scott Tipton**'s prose book about comics, *Comic Books 101*, for IMPACT Publishing.

Rodriguez has also illustrated for card games, advertising, magazines, and books. He currently lives in Santiago, Chile, with his family, but you can also find him on Twitter @GR_comics.

Jay Fotos has worked on hundreds of projects for more than a decade. To name just a few for IDW: *Godzilla*, *Transformers*, *Clive Barker's The Great and Secret Show*, *Teenage Mutant Ninja Turtles*, *Judge Dredd*, *30 Days of Night*, and the #1 New York Times Best Seller *Locke & Key*. For other publishers, Jay has worked on *Spawn*, co-created '*68*, and spearheaded the Frazetta Comics line, including *Frank Frazetta's Death Dealer* and numerous other Frazetta Comics.

Fotos has colored hundreds of Rodriguez's pages, including *Clive Barker's The Great and Secret Show*, *George Romero's Land of the Dead*, *Beowulf*, *Clive Barker's Seduth*, the entirety of *Locke & Key* and now *Onyx*.

Fotos lives in Arizona with a wife and numerous zombies of his own creation.